# THE ALL-MOUNTAIN SKIER
## SECOND EDITION

BEN FERGUSON IN SURFER BOWL, MT. BACHELOR

# THE ALL-MOUNTAIN SKIER
## SECOND EDITION
### THE WAY TO EXPERT SKIING

**R. Mark Elling**

Illustrations by Brian Elling
Photographs by Kirk DeVoll

**Ragged Mountain Press / McGraw-Hill**

*Camden, Maine* | *New York* | *Chicago* | *San Francisco* | *Lisbon* | *London* | *Madrid* | *Mexico City*
*Milan* | *New Delhi* | *San Juan* | *Seoul* | *Singapore* | *Sydney* | *Toronto*

*The McGraw·Hill Companies*

DOC 10 9 8 7 6 5 4 3 2 1

LIBRARY OF CONGRESS CATALOGING-IN-PUBLICATION DATA
Elling, R. Mark.
 The all-mountain skier : the way to expert skiing / R. Mark Elling ;
illustrations by Brian Elling.—2nd ed.
    p.     cm.
Includes index.
 ISBN 0-07-140841-X
 1. Skis and skiing. I. Title.
 GV854 .E48 2003
 796.93′5—dc21                              2002006994

Questions regarding the content of this book should be addressed to
Ragged Mountain Press
P.O. Box 220
Camden, ME 04843
www.raggedmountainpress.com

Questions regarding the ordering of this book should be addressed to
The McGraw-Hill Companies
Customer Service Department
P.O. Box 547
Blacklick, OH 43004
Retail customers: 1-800-262-4729
Bookstores: 1-800-722-4726

*This book is dedicated to the many skiers*
*who have given me something to think and write about,*
*and to the excellent few like Neal Scholey,*
*Rick "Oz" Oswald, and Erik Korman,*
*who remind me to shut up and ski.*

GREG RUBIN ABOVE THE NORTHWEST EXPRESS LIFT, MT. BACHELOR

# Contents

# Preface to the Second Edition

There is no time better than now to become an expert skier. Recent changes in ski equipment technology have given skiers the edge in their quest to become the athletes on snow they've always hoped to become—if they know how to tap this new resource. The advantage is out there for the taking.

Getting the skills can be the easy part, if you have a guide for how to develop and apply them. The real trick to breaking through to expert skiing is learning how to maximize the advantages available to you through equipment. Getting the right gear and knowing how to adjust it to suit your body is a huge part of breaking into high performance skiing, and *The All-Mountain Skier: The Way to Expert Skiing* is your ultimate guidebook.

This second edition is entirely revised and expanded to address the new equipment and the changes it brings to skiing technique. While this book is a helpful guide to skiers no matter what they slide on, it provides a comprehensive resource for skiers interested in staying at the forefront of our sport.

The expert skier has the skills, the new tools, and an all-mountain playground for testing them.

*The All-Mountain Skier* gives you what you need to know to take you where you want to go.

# Acknowledgments

*I would like to thank Rossignol for its ongoing support and special assistance with this project.*

*Thanks also to Mt. Bachelor Ski Resort of Bend, Oregon, for providing the perfect proving grounds for research into carving, powder, crud, moguls, steeps, and trees.*

Additional gratitude goes to Mt. Bachelor Ski and Sport for tolerating my continual gear experimentation, to Black Diamond Equipment for their interest in this book, and to Smith Sport Optics.

Special thanks also go to the staff of the Green Mountain Orthotic Lab at Stratton Mountain, Vermont, and to the instructors of Masterfit University, for their technical assistance with the Boots and Alignment chapters.

# PART I

# Introduction

Sports are more than games or pastimes. They give us the means to reformat our existence, if only briefly, into intensely focused events. Sports provide a window to our athletic and adventurous selves, which might otherwise be lost amid the mundane crush of work.

In some sports, the goal is to compete and destroy an opponent's strategy. Some sports focus on teamwork, with each player performing a specific role. But in others, the goal is individual performance, and the players focus internally, charting their progress not by wins or group performance but by their own set of mental expectations.

This is the world of the recreational skier.

There is a reason why millions of people strap sticks to their feet and slide down snow-covered hills. Skiing is a method of self-discovery. Skiers test themselves, and in the process they find both challenges and tranquillity. The sport has its own kind of magic. But the magic that skiers search for isn't found at the end of a run or at the end of the day but in the midst of things—during the process of skiing farther or faster or smoother.

With enough time, skiing and its movements and rhythms become a kind of dance, a form of expression. Just as an artist paints with an unlimited choice of colors, a complete skier works toward the goal of performance using a wide foundation of skills. Like the artist's work, the skier's quest for personal breakthrough can be ongoing. Many skiers are thirsty for new information and experiences, and the world of skiing is made rich by athletes who don't mind if their search for excellence borders on being a fanatical quest.

*The All-Mountain Skier* is written for intermediate to expert skiers who want to continually push their limits: to ski stronger, ski longer, and ski varied terrain and steepness with the grace and power of an elite athlete. This book is for skiers who have reached a plateau in their skiing ability, for athletes who want to break the barriers that have slowed their progress, and for skiers interested in further exploring their athletic potential.

The primary strength of this book is its flexibility. It is a guide for intermediate skiers who want to catapult their skills into the realm of the expert, and the pages ahead lead intermediate skiers through a progressive self-instruction program. This book is also a reference text for advanced to expert skiers who want to test their limits and improve their skiing performance. This book speaks to athletes who are ready to learn and who enjoy the process as much as the product.

This book was born from my own experience. I am an avid skier who loves everything about the sport. But I am particularly encouraged by the way my skiing has improved over the years. I am addicted to skiing runs that challenge me, and I'm hooked on seeing if my body will do what my brain tells it to do. Every season I seek the joy that the inclined environment gives me once it is covered with snow.

I began as a recreational skier twenty-five years ago. In order to support my skiing habit, I became a full-time ski instruction professional. After several years as a professional instructor and later as an assistant director and trainer for a ski school, I became a full-time researcher of

A kind of dance—and sometimes it's deep. NEAL SCHOLEY AT MOUNT BAILEY SNOWCAT SKIING

how to improve someone's skiing. I looked not only at my students' skiing, but also at my own skiing ability and the abilities of other instructors. I became both an experimenter and a guinea pig, and my goal was twofold: to find the most effective ways to teach and learn in the sport and to make ski instruction simple, cohesive, and entirely practical.

Writing nonfiction and technical articles for skiing publications made it clear to me that there was a need for a comprehensive, self-teaching guide for intermediate and advanced skiers.

There are many skiers with untapped athletic potential who either don't wish to take lessons or don't believe there is any route for improving their skiing. Spending several years guiding in the backcountry, testing ski products for magazines, and working in a ski shop provided an alternative perspective that helped me identify what it was that most decent skiers were looking for in their search for improvement.

In *The All-Mountain Skier* I have compiled a guidebook so well grounded in simplicity that skiing skills that once seemed complicated may now seem easy. I have also gone beyond the typical learn-to-ski themes by exploring the subtle elements involved in teaching oneself to become an expert skier. This book helps you take your skill development into your own hands and lets you enjoy the experience of charting your own growth within the sport—at your own pace, on your own time.

*The All-Mountain Skier* gathers information included in the philosophies of the Professional Ski Instructors of America (PSIA), the United States Skiing Coaches Association (USSCA), and from the technical staffs of both the Green Mountain Orthotic Lab at Stratton Mountain, Vermont, and Masterfit University. I have also utilized technical input from alpine racers, freestyle competitors, and other instructors. I have relied on feedback from students and the skiing public and on my own experience as an improving skier and ski industry professional.

The best way to learn from this book is to read it from start to finish, because the skills taught build upon themselves through the course of reading. However, you don't have to start at the beginning if you feel you would benefit from the shotgun scatter approach of reading and practicing a section here or a section there.

The next section in the book is called Creating a Toolbox. I strongly suggest that you read and practice the skills taught there; they form the framework that supports later, more advanced sections on equipment and the nuances of technique.

*Note: All sections are written under the assumption that the reader is an intermediate skier who has progressed beyond the wedge turn, or snowplow, and is making at least rudimentary parallel turns.*

While *The All-Mountain Skier* is designed to lead skiers to their expert skiing goals using modern gear, the skills information is pertinent no matter what kind of skis they ride on, for the core elements of good skiing remain fundamentally the same. However, new information specific to new ski, boot, binding, and alignment technologies is provided in the section You *Can* Blame It on Your Gear! Sometimes, and this revised edition has been entirely rewritten with new ski equipment in mind.

For each skill taught in this book, I provide a series of exercises you can use in your process of self-instruction. These on-snow methods of practice are very important, because nobody becomes a better athlete simply by thinking about it.

Pay close attention to the book's illustrations and the movement-specific captions. They provide a visual image of what the text explains.

I have also included a troubleshooting system to refer you to other skills that bear directly upon improving the task at hand. Use the reference guides in the troubleshooting sections as a way to teach yourself how all the skills of skiing play off one another.

Expert skiers know the truth: all skiing is fundamentally the same, but certain skills are used more heavily at some times than at others. Advanced skiing is a blending game, and one that many skiers assume is a product of experience alone. In fact, the subtle blend of skills so often attributed to experience *can* be taught, but not in a traditional way. As you begin to understand that skiing is a web of skills that interrelate according to greatly varying conditions, you will begin to learn the subtle art of skill blending used in effective, all-terrain skiing.

The mystique of skiing may reside in the process of learning, but as skiers, we still want to perform. That finished product of the polished athlete—the dance of skiing—is a result born from both body and mind. There is an entire mental game of tactics and methods for skiing, which I will discuss later in this book. But the physical skills of skiing come first, and this is where our journey will begin.

They have a saying at my home ski area of Mt. Bachelor in Oregon: "Shut up and ski." So it's time to stop talking about skiing and begin. Start your process of skiing self-discovery and become the athlete you've always wanted to be. But keep in mind that throughout your journey, *fun* is the goal. If skiing stops being fun, then it's hardly skiing at all.

Enjoy.

# PART II
# Creating a Toolbox

What does a toolbox have to do with skiing? Does the idea of a skiing toolbox take away the sport's artistry and change it into an activity akin to auto mechanics? To answer these questions, we need to look at how we acquire skills.

We learn new motor skills in much the same way as we acquire language. When we first learn to speak our native language, we listen to its sounds for a year or so and practice simple words until we formulate a vocabulary and understand usage.

If you consider any skill that you do proficiently, you likely remember your first crude attempts at performing that skill. Whether you were learning to throw a ball or solve linear equations, your first attempts were probably less than stellar. But the end result was probably not your primary focus during those initial attempts. Maybe your goal was simply to learn how to hold the ball or write out the problem. Somebody probably helped you master the small attainable steps because they knew the final result would simply be the sum of those small steps.

We learn by attacking chunks of a skill, by breaking an entire feat down into manageable components. This allows us to have small successes along the way and forestalls the frustration that comes from attempting to perform a complex skill before we are ready. This is the best way to improve our skiing—piece by piece, in a series of small successes that help us build fundamental skills.

Hence, the *toolbox* is the label I've given to a skier's repertoire of fundamental skills. The implication of the word *tool* is that a skier's skills are useful implements in getting the job of skiing done. The word also implies that skiing skills are both versatile and job-specific—you might need a certain skill for a certain type of skiing, or you might be able to get by with any one of several tools. In *The All-Mountain Skier*, I've identified the elemental building blocks of expert skiing. Some may sound familiar, others less so, but all are crucial tools in attaining high-end skiing goals. The skills of stance, steering, outside ski dominance, footwork blend, edging, pressure control, body mass movement, turn size and shape, and using your poles make up the expert skier's toolbox. This may sound like a lot, but you're probably already proficient with many of them.

## A NOTE ON TEACHING YOURSELF SOMETHING NEW

Throughout this book, self-teaching exercises are suggested so you can practice your skills. While it is important to try the drills, it is even more important to try them in an effective way.

Learning research has shown that people learn most quickly if they remain in their comfort zone—the state in which a person is not intimidated by the environment or the task. A person's comfort zone is a sort of neutral territory from which the person ventures out.

One way to reduce feelings of frustration and intimidation when learning a new skill is to learn while maintaining your comfort zone. Guidelines for maintaining your comfort zone while you learn new skiing skills follow.

1. Choose unintimidating terrain when practicing drills. A drill's focus is based on the skill, not on how steep a slope you can perform it on.
2. Work on your skills when you feel adequately prepared. Unfamiliar movements and drills can become difficult, even dangerous, when an athlete is fatigued, hungry, or cold.
3. Make new movements feel like your own by trying to blend them into your own skiing style. The tools in this book may feel strange at first, but they should rapidly begin to strengthen your skiing.
4. Choose times for playing with the new ideas presented in this book, but give yourself some time off too. Don't forget that skiing is fun—no matter how well or how poorly you think you're doing.
5. Realize that your skiing partner may not care how he or she skis, much less how you do, so don't force your newfound skills and drills upon those who aren't interested. It's a surefire way to trash their comfort zone and start a fight.

It's hard to learn when you focus on your grade. Lighten up and give it a shot.
BEN FERGUSON (FOREGROUND) AND SETH WARNER (AIR) ON THE EAST SIDE, MT. BACHELOR

# Stance

Stance, or how you stand on your skis, is either the most common focus of ski lessons or the most commonly forgotten one. How skiers stand on their feet and skis is so fundamental that people tend to view stance either as a cure-all or as something too basic for further refinement. Neither philosophy is entirely accurate.

Stance involves balance, which is not simply the ability to balance on one foot or jump into the air and land gracefully. A skier's balanced stance is an ever-changing position. When you are skiing—sliding along, changing direction, changing turn size and shape, speeding up or slowing down—you must continually make subtle changes to maintain your balance and stance.

What is a proper stance? Let's start with what it's not. It's not contrived or fashionable, it's not inefficient, and it's not hard to do. The problem with stance is that, over the years, certain ways to stand on skis have evolved—either out of a fad or because certain equipment required a particular stance modification.

The concept of stance continues to evolve. Today, ideas about stance tend toward simplification, and stance is driven by function and nothing else. A functional stance is strong and energy-efficient.

Racers, instructors, and expert skiers have found a simple answer: *tall* is the key word. A tall stance accomplishes three basic things.

First, a tall stance prevents the muscle fatigue that results from a crouched, defensive stance. If you've ever done a wall-sit (an exercise in which you sit against a wall as though there were a chair supporting you), you know that before too long your quadriceps are screaming for mercy. Too many skiers believe this muscle pain is the result of not skiing enough and being out of shape. But, beyond minor fatigue, muscle burn during skiing is typically a product of adopting an overly crouched stance. Stand up!

In addition to reducing muscle fatigue, you gain strength by elongating your skeletal frame into a tall, self-supporting structure. Instructors call this "having your bones stacked up." In this position, the basic support for all movements comes from your bones rather than your muscles. This increases strength and reduces fatigue. For the same reason, we stand with almost straight legs rather than severely bent ones when we are doing anything nonathletic: a tall skiing stance modifies what we have naturally discovered outside of the world of sport.

Finally, when you assume a tall stance you put your body into a ready position with legs slightly bent and muscles relaxed. This position allows for quick muscle reaction and maximum range of motion. The crouched position loads up leg muscles, prohibiting quickness and strength, and reduces the range of motion skiers need for absorption in variable terrain.

Stance width is not determined by what is or isn't cool. Rather, it should be determined by your anatomy. There should be some space between the knees and boots—enough so each leg can work independently of the other but not so much that

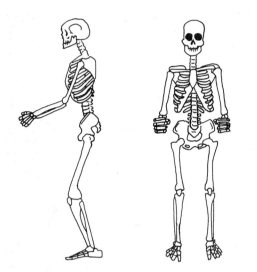

A tall, relaxed stance utilizes skeletal strength and reduces fatigue.

either ski becomes difficult to control. A hair less than shoulder width is a fair guide for stance width. You may also vary the width of your stance in order to allow for better performance in varying terrain. I will discuss this later in the book.

One of the biggest changes in skiing over the years has been the idea of centering your stance fore and aft along the ski. With older skis, it was necessary to drive your knees forward to pressure the front of the ski and initiate a turn. Today's skis are designed to turn more easily, and it's not necessary to continually drive your shins into the tongues of your boots.

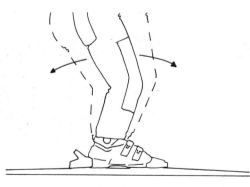

Extreme fore-aft stance adjustments are not necessary.

When you assume a centered stance, you do not rely on the back of the boots to hold yourself up. In theory, you should be able to ski in a pair of tennis shoes clicked into your bindings (don't try this!), and thereby eliminate the front and back of the boot. Expert skiers use their boots laterally (except when making minor pressure control adjustments). When you stand on the arch and ball of the foot, rather than rely on the front or back of the ski boot, you exert pressure over the entire ski. With this stance, you utilize the entire ski's design instead of maximizing use of only the front and rear sections.

Many instructors focus too much on exact hand placement, overlooking other, more important aspects of balance and stance. Still, hand and arm placement are important. Keep them out front. Most coaches and instructors insist your hands remain out in front of your body, and a few simple concepts help to understand why. For one, keeping your arms and hands away from your torso or hips will help you achieve good poling action. A hands-forward position will also prevent you from developing some bad habits.

Leaning back is the body position that causes more trouble for skiers than any other. You may be leaning back for a number of reasons: fear, loose boots, weak muscles (which cause you to rely on your boots), or simply because you do not know any better. There are some other reasons why skiers lean back as well; be sure to read Fore-Aft Alignment in the section You *Can* Blame It on Your Gear! Sometimes.

Expert skiers continually strive to avoid leaning back. You may hear racers and mogul competitors say, "I got back." They lost. If you keep your hands in a forward position, your body tends to stay forward. This is not a physical law, but it is a tactic of stance that works.

Stance is a dynamic element in skiing. Skiers are always changing their stance to adapt to turns, speed, and snow conditions. The functional stance we have discussed here is most effective if you understand that the position represents a neutral position—a home base—you

Learning to keep hands forward now will translate into balanced performance later.

ERIK KORMAN ENTERING THE BOWL, MT. BACHELOR

can return to when the forces that may have altered your stance abate. Strive to maintain a functional stance, or return to it as often as possible. But remember that stance is active, not static.

*You can feel*
### A TALL, BALANCED, EFFICIENT STANCE

1. The pressure exerted on the bottoms of your feet is concentrated around the center of your arch, with some pressure migrating to the ball of the foot. Noticeable pressure on your heel or calf is a sign that your fore-aft position is not centered.
2. Your overall body is slightly flexed. While your stance is tall, your legs are not locked in a straight position. One way to achieve a slightly flexed stance is to ski down a beginner run, stand normally, and hop very gently. This slight hopping (don't leave the ground) will elongate your stance and encourage an athletic, flexed position. Practice hopping while maintaining centered foot pressure inside your boots.

*You can see*
### A FUNCTIONAL STANCE

1. Look at your shadow when the sun is directly at your back to see if there is space showing between your boots, knees, and lower thighs. Try to stand tall enough so that this space is created.
2. Using your peripheral vision, you should see your hands to your sides and out in front of your hips. If your hands are not visible, they have dropped toward your hips, which can mean you are assuming a leaned-back stance.

## OTHER DRILLS

The following are other drills that will help you achieve a functional stance.

### Parameter Skiing

In this drill, you make turns at a comfortable speed while modifying the extremes of your stance. Make several turns while leaning as far forward as possible, as far back as possible, as tall as possible, as short as possible, as stiff as possible, as loose as possible, etc. This exaggeration drill should help you identify the happy medium—the sweet spot—in your stance. These stance extremes will feel awkward and tiring, and the feel of your functional stance will become clear to you.

### No-Poles Skiing

No-poles skiing can cause more problems in your skiing than it solves if a no-poles drill makes it difficult to ski. However, skiing without poles can be an excellent stance and balance drill simply because it forces you to feel abnormal, which in turn forces you to focus on making changes in stance that will increase your efficiency. Try the drills in this section with and without poles.

### Loose-Boots Skiing

This drill can be potentially dangerous, so be careful. Loosen the upper buckles and power straps of your boots and leave the lower buckles tight. This reduces your boots' fore-aft support but allows you to maintain foot control. Make turns of different sizes on smooth and gentle terrain. Feel how you are utilizing the movements of your foot to control the ski, rather than driving with your shin or levering on the back of your boot with your calf. Feel your fore-aft position and stand tall. You probably are well centered.

### Tall, Centered Wedge Turns

Wedge turns may have the stigma of being turns that only beginners and ski instructors do. But the wedge turn is an excellent drill. It allows you to focus on a particular skill or maneuver while your speed control and turning is taken care of by the wedge. Make wedge turns on gentle terrain and focus on standing tall and being centered over your skis.

## TROUBLESHOOTING STANCE

Achieving a functional stance can be a major accomplishment for some skiers. Our anatomical shapes and ski equipment determine how easy or difficult a functional stance will be.

For example, being bowlegged or knock-kneed can cause problems with stance width. How much forward lean our boots are set at can also play a major role. (I discuss these factors in the chapters on boots and alignment in the section You *Can* Blame It on Your Gear! Sometimes.)

However, not all stance problems are due to equipment and body shape or alignment. A poor stance is often the result of using ineffective movements to make turns. For example, if a skier is forcing the start or finish of a turn, he may be assuming an ineffective stance as a result. His stance may be too low, leaned back, or marked by being bent at the waist. This skier has learned a less efficient way to stand on his skis, and he needs to relearn a proper stance; first he may need to work through the other tools in this section to smooth out his movements.

One final factor that can affect stance is fear. Whether you are afraid of falling, skiing too fast, or losing control, fear can force you out of a functional stance. Skiers tend to lean toward the hill (uphill) when they are intimidated and want to escape the vast unknown down below. As you will learn later, leaning into the hill causes problems for everybody.

If fear is affecting your stance, you need to get off the challenging slope and ski on less intimidating terrain where you can make effective movements and tune in to your functional stance.

# 2

# Steering

Steering is one of the methods you can use to make your skis turn. Because the word *steering* implies turning, you might think this is the only way to turn. Don't be fooled: steering is simply one way of turning.

Steering skills are some of the most subtle, often never learned, yet most useful skills an expert skier can master. Learning to master this tool will help smooth out your turns on groomed terrain and improve your perfor-

Steering skills are most noticeable in the inside ski, which is guided along to match the arc of the outside ski. ETHAN DEVOLL ON CLIFFHANGER, MT. BACHELOR

mance in varying snow conditions. Steering is also a fundamental skill in achieving the quiet upper body so often billed as a trait of the expert skier.

To understand steering, pick up a pencil or pen and lay it on a flat surface. Grasp the middle of the writing instrument with your thumb and forefinger, as if you were going to lift it. Don't pick it up. Just hold it on the surface and twist it back and forth, imitating a plane's propeller that can't decide which way to turn. If your pencil was your ski and your fingers were your boots, you would have been steering like mad.

Steering is the muscular guidance of your skis to the left and to the right via the use of your ski boots. To picture steering, imagine yourself riding a chairlift with your skis on. Pretend you are making turns by simply twisting your feet to the left and to the right. Your skis are turning, and the turning force comes from the lower leg area below your knees and above your ankles and feet. You can also do this at home. Sit in a chair and twist your feet to the left and right. Notice the way your foot rotates on an axis near its arch. Also note that there is no rotation of your thigh because your legs are bent in a sitting position. Notice that the foot's range of rotation is limited.

We call this foot steering. This is the most basic form of steering, and it is a serious fine-tuning tool for expert skiers. Because the muscles in the lower leg used for foot steering are relatively weak and your foot's range of rotation is limited, foot steering is used for making minor direction adjustments of the ski. Foot steering is not an adequate tool for making larger, more powerful movements.

Take the exercise to the next level. Extend both legs out in front of the chair so your legs are straight and your toes (or ski tips) are pointing skyward. Twist your feet (or skis) to the left and right. Two things have changed: your entire leg is rotating now, all the way into the hip socket, and your overall range of motion has increased. This is called leg steering, which is more effective and powerful than foot steering.

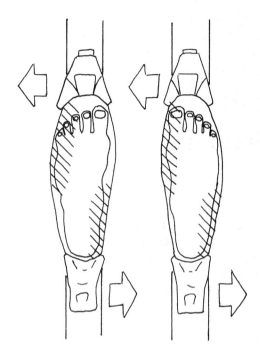

Cross-hatching indicates areas of foot pressure during a turn to the left.

In leg steering, you are using stronger muscles in your upper leg (primarily your quadriceps) and you have a greater range of motion. Leg steering is one of the primary tools used in all turn initiation and a major skill used when skiing bumps, powder, crud, and steeps.

Steering can be used alone to make effortless turns, and many nonaggressive skiers utilize this tool to make graceful, skidded turns on groomed terrain.

Expert skiers use steering as a way to guide their skis through a turn, and even though newer shaped skis reduce the need to actively twist the ski, experts utilize steering as a subtle movement that helps keep a ski on track. Steering also minimizes the need to use your upper body in awkward swinging or twisting movements throughout a turn.

Visualize a skier making a steered turn on smooth, intermediate terrain. The skier's stance would be upright and would not change dra-

Foot and leg steering is a critical skill for high-performance bump skiing. CHRIS SMITH ON BOOMERANG, MT. BACHELOR

matically. This stance pattern relates to what is going on at the level of the skis. The skis remain fairly flat against the snow in a steered turn, and the master of a steered turn has learned how to maintain a flat ski in order to maximize the use of steering.

Again, less accomplished skiers might use steering to make nonathletic, skidded turns. The expert skier, however, will utilize steering most at the moment when the ski becomes flat. This flattening happens all the time between turns, when the skier goes from one set of edges to the next. We are jumping ahead to the subject of edging, but the two tools are so interconnected that some explanation is needed here.

In any turn, you use your edges. In a turn to the left, you engage your left edges. During a turn to the right, you use the edges to the right sides of your skis. Between turns those edges are changing. In this transition from one set of edges to the other, there is a brief moment when the skis sit flat on the snow.

Steering is what I consider the most important tool for initiating turns. Skis flatten at the time of turn initiation, and at that moment they can be easily steered. Expert skiers capitalize on this moment and steer their skis gently toward the new turn when the skis become flat. But steering must go hand in hand with the ability to let your skis flatten, which is in itself another tool.

Many instructors will comment that new shaped skis engage turns so readily that steering is no longer important, but I disagree. Steering has indeed become a less dominant skill because of newer skis, but having this tool at your disposal will do more to save a poorly executed turn than any other.

Without the ability to steer, skiers have a difficult time starting turns—especially when the terrain is steep or the snow is thick or bumpy. Have you ever completed a turn on intimidating terrain and next found yourself locked into a traverse, heading to the far side of the run and unable to get the next turn started? Or have you started a turn in that situation, only to have your outside ski wander off in the wrong direction? If so, steering may be the tool you need.

*You can feel*
**PROPER STEERING**

1. When starting a turn on gentle terrain, you should feel some twisting tension in your leg muscles, mainly in the quadriceps and calves (the same kind of tension you felt when you twisted your outstretched legs in your chair). Your skis may feel slippery, or squirrelly, while they are being steered.

2. When making steered turns, especially when initiating turns, you should feel the big toe of your outside foot against the side of the boot while the little toe of the inside foot is pressed against the side of its boot. This pressure is the result of the leg and foot twisting against the boot, which in turn twists your ski.

 *You can see*
**PROPER STEERING**

1. You can tell if your skis are steering by looking down at the tips of your skis while skiing on gentle terrain (where it would not be dangerous to watch your skis!). During a turn, look to see if your ski is twisting across the snow, smearing over it the same way a knife spreads butter on a piece of bread. You may see your inside ski's tip pulling away from the other ski because it is being steered in that direction. This is a sign you are steering well.

2. Make medium-sized turns and look down at your chest, hips, and arms. Focus on steering your turns and see if your chest, hips, and arms are turning in the direction of the turns. If you are steering correctly with your leg and foot, you should be able to turn and keep your upper body still and facing straight down the hill.

## OTHER DRILLS

The following are other drills that will help enhance your steering skills.

### Boot Skiing

This drill is effective but funny looking. Leave your skis behind and hike partway up a hill with firmly packed snow. Try skiing straight down the slope in your boots. Digging the tips

of your boots into the snow will send you over the top. Once you can slide safely in a straight line, try to make some gentle turns by steering your boots. There should be no "butt wiggle" movements here. Make symmetrical tracks down the hill and then copy them on successive runs. This drill is effective because it reduces the resistance you often feel with your skis on.

### Swivel Sideslips

Knowing how to sideslip well is a prerequisite for this drill. (You may want to read the chapter on edging before attempting this drill.) In a fast sideslip on smooth, firm snow of moderate pitch, make 180-degree turns without deviating from an imaginary corridor running straight down the slope. Performing this drill successfully requires a lot of steering and a well-developed ability to maintain a flat ski. If you are traveling outside your imaginary corridor, you are most likely using too much edge (review the chapter on edging, primarily the section on edge release). For an advanced version of this drill, try the Swivel Sideslip while maintaining a quiet upper body where hips, shoulders, and hands face straight downhill, as shown in the illustration next page.

### Marking-Time Turns

Just as if you were marching in place in a parade, ski on moderate terrain and make turns while marching your feet up and down a few inches. Keep turning while you are marching. You will notice that each time you pick up a ski, you are steering it either to the left or the right before setting it down. Focus on the time when the ski is off the snow, guiding it with the foot and leg toward the direction of your turn. This drill enhances steering by momentarily reducing all friction on your ski. More advanced skiers should progressively reduce the height of each step until both skis stay on the snow while your steering continues.

Precise movements of edge release allow you to steer your skis through a turn without deviating from a straight corridor along the fall line.

### Staircases or Garlands

This drill emphasizes the role of steering in initiating turns. Ski across the hill in a traverse. Then start a turn by steering both feet toward the fall line, or toward the bottom of the hill. Don't finish the turn. Instead, steer your feet back across the hill and into another traverse. Repeat this movement. You will travel from one side of the run to the other in a cascading traverse that will leave tracks shaped like a staircase.

### Jump Turns

The jump turn is an effective steering drill for advanced skiers and a useful tool in extreme terrain. On steep terrain, stand with your skis across the hill, or perpendicular to the fall line. In one swift movement, jump into the air and steer your skis into a 180-degree, airborne turn. You should land facing the opposite direction. It is easier to do this if you allow yourself to travel down the hill while you are in the air. This gives you more time to complete the turn. Try to keep your hips and upper body facing down the hill and twist only your legs and feet. Complete a sequence of five to ten turns, or as many as you can complete in a row.

### Twisters

The twister is an aerial trick that also serves as an excellent drill for leg steering with expert skiers. Catch air off a familiar jump without exceeding your ability. While maintaining a straight, tall body position in the air, twist both your legs 90 degrees so your skis are traveling sideways through the air. Return to your original position and land. (Be sure your skis are pointing straight ahead before you land!) Keep

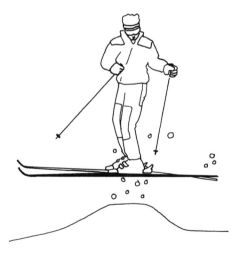

Elongated legs enhance the steering movements of a twister.

Steering is the skill used to guide the skis toward the next turn during the rebound that comes from dynamic skiing. MARK ELLING ON THE SNOW BRIDGE, MT. BACHELOR

your upper body facing straight ahead while you are twisting. This is much easier to do than you might think! Focus on how this movement utilizes steering.

## TROUBLESHOOTING STEERING

The primary problem intermediate, advanced, and even expert skiers have with steering is that early in their ski careers they never learned this tool for making turns. Instead, they relied primarily on edging and pressuring. Many skiers might consequently feel that steering is a nonathletic tool that lacks power and is for beginners.

For skiers who have never truly steered their legs and feet, the benefits of steering will come only when they blend steering skills with the tools they already know. These kinds of skiers should read the Footwork Blend chapter and the section Getting Tough: Advanced Situations, both of which cover steering's role in skiing powder, crud, and bumps.

Some skiers may still have difficulty with steering. This could be attributed to two main reasons: improper boot fit or poor alignment.

Sloppy boot fit will prevent leg- and foot-steering movements from being transmitted to your skis. Your foot may be steering well, but it may be twisting inside an oversize boot. A small amount of play in your boots can affect your ability to steer. If you fall into this category, read the chapter on boots in You *Can* Blame It on Your Gear! Sometimes.

Alignment is discussed thoroughly in a later chapter. Briefly, alignment is the way a skier's body—primarily the feet, ankles, lower legs, and knees—line up. Proper alignment produces a biomechanically sound structure where no undue stress is placed on any of these body parts. The word *alignment* also describes the art of correcting poor body alignment or adapting one's equipment.

Skiers who experience difficulties with steering because their skis' edges dig in too often (which prevents the ski from becoming flat so it can be steered) should first read the chapter on edging and note the drills for releasing edges. If you still experience problems with flattening your skis and steering, you may have alignment problems. Read the alignment chapter carefully.

Finally, if you are still unable to accomplish steering, and you are confident your equipment is not holding you back and you can flatten your skis, read about counter-rotation in the Getting Techno section. Counter-rotation is the relationship between a skier's upper and lower body. Effective counter-rotation will enhance several fundamental skills, including steering.

# Outside Ski Dominance

Outside ski dominance puts power in your skiing. You may already know this tool on a basic level. Outside ski dominance occurs when you feel yourself pushing on one ski more than the other during a turn.

Although outside ski dominance is the tool of choice for the majority of skiers, and the skill that is most commonly taught by inexperienced instructors, it is still commonly misused. Skiers typically use too little or too much outside ski dominance.

Understanding why outside ski dominance occurs will help you understand how and when to use it. Remember: this discussion of outside ski dominance assumes you are at least an intermediate-level skier, capable of making some sort of parallel turn and using your edges from turn to turn.

Now, shift gears and imagine that you are driving your car down a twisting road. A pile of letters, a pair of sunglasses, or some other items are on your dashboard. Because you are traveling fast and your dashboard is a slick surface, the things on your dashboard are not going to stay in place. Your letters or sunglasses will slide from one side of the dashboard to the other as you change directions and turn. Specifically, the things on the dashboard will slide to the outside of the turn.

The same principle applies in skiing. Your skis want to zip straight down the hill at lightning speed. As the skier atop those skis, however, you usually don't want to travel that way,

so you turn back and forth to control your speed as you descend the hill. Each time you make a turn using your ski edges, you are deviating from the straight-down route your mass would like to take, and friction between your edges and the snow results. Just like the car's tires that squeal in high-speed turns, your edges make various scraping noises. While this friction is occurring at the level of the car tire or ski, things are also moving around above: The pile of letters slides to the outside of the turn; a skier's body also wants to move to the outside of the turn.

If you didn't do anything to resist that force, you would fall across your skis and land downhill on your face. As skiers, we have figured out

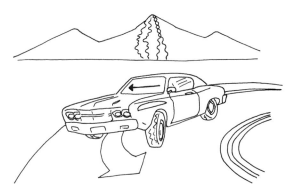

Car passengers feel some of the same forces that skiers do during turns. The car's contents will shift toward the outside of the turn.

how to deal with that force: we balance against it to find a state of equilibrium from turn to turn. Still, this force does change a few things, one of which is how we distribute pressure from foot to foot, from ski to ski. The force that builds in a turn wants to pull you toward the outside of the turn, which means that your outside foot and ski bear most of the load.

This comes down to the feeling that, during a turn, the outside foot is pushing harder than the inside foot against the snow. This may be a passive sensation, where the snow seems to push harder against your outside foot, or it can be an active sensation, where you push against that outside ski. Either way, this is one of the laws of skiing: the outside foot will bear more force.

Now that you better understand the physics of outside ski dominance, it will be easier to see why this tool is the powerhouse of skiing. First, more pressure exerted on the outside ski creates a more stable turn. Friction builds along the edge of the outside ski, and a noticeable buildup of force results.

This increased pressure on the *inside* edge of the outside ski functions the same way as snow chains on a car tire. Without chains, the tire might slide out, but the chains bite into the road. A ski edge works the same way—the edge bites into the snow. When increased pressure builds under the outside ski, the ski edge digs deeper into the snow. When an edge's bite is increased, the ski becomes more stable and tracks along its designated course without slipping or washing out.

With outside ski dominance, the skis do the work while you are turning. All skis are designed with sidecut, and now shaped skis have more of it. You may think of sidecut as the marketing mumbo-jumbo you hear from salespeople at a ski shop, but in fact it is one of the major reasons we are able to ski.

*Sidecut* is the arc shape built into every ski. It is easily detected by looking down the length of the ski from tip to tail. The hourglass shape you see—a fatter tip and tail and a narrow waist—is the sidecut, or arc, of the ski. This shape determines, to a large extent, the size of turn a ski will make. Think of a ski's sidecut as one portion of a large circle that happens to be on the edge of a ski. When this ski's edge is on the snow and allowed to slide, it will follow the circle's outline.

Note the arc built into the edge of the ski. This is a ski's shape or *sidecut.*

This skier is pulled to the outside, and she compensates by balancing against the outside ski.

But a ski also has *camber*, which is like the curve in an archer's bow. Camber gives a ski energy and bounce, but it also makes it tougher for a skier to simply lay a ski on its edge and let it ride the natural curve of the sidecut. This is because the ski's camber doesn't want to flatten out completely; you have to push on the ski to squash the camber out and achieve edge contact with the snow. Once you do that, however, the ski's sidecut is yours to manipulate, and turns become easier because the ski is doing much of the work for you.

Outside ski dominance enables you to de-camber your outside ski and drive your ski's edge into the snow so you can use the ski's side-cut to make the turn easier. The force that builds on the outside ski and your ability to push back against that force are the elements you need to utilize a ski's sidecut.

A purely carved turn without any skidding is a product of sidecut. Skiers who carve are riding the arc shape that is built into their skis; they do not leave skidded tracks but rather leave singular, well-defined lines in the snow.

It is difficult to quantify how much outside ski dominance should be used, because it is a matter of feel. Too little outside ski dominance means the ski is not being driven into the snow, making it feel unstable, unathletic, and squirrelly. Too much outside ski dominance can "lock you up" on your legs, impeding your fluidity and performance on varying snow conditions. Use the following kinesthetic and visual cues, as well as the related drills, to develop an adequate degree of outside ski dominance. Also pay close attention to the next chapter, The Footwork Blend.

The arched, or bowlike, shape of the ski is its *camber*.

## *You can feel*
## OUTSIDE SKI DOMINANCE

1. You're using outside ski dominance when you feel increased pressure along your outside foot. If you are feeling a natural buildup of pressure in the turn and not forcing things, you should feel the majority of this pressure along the inside edge of your foot—from the big toe to the inside of your arch and, to some degree, on the inside edge of your heel.

2. Another sign that you're using outside ski dominance is when you feel as if you're on a stair-motion exercise machine with pedals that move only a few inches during a series of turns. The pedaling should feel rhythmic, smooth, and slow, and you should feel as if you are pushing down on pedals. (Lifting your skis off the snow is not desirable here.) There is only one pedal push per turn: the left foot for the right turn; the right foot for the left turn.

*You can see*
**OUTSIDE SKI DOMINANCE**

Look at the tracks your skis have left in the snow. You can tell if you are beginning to engage your outside ski's edge and starting to carve, or if you are simply skidding. Look for sharper lines where the outside ski traveled. You should be able to tell the difference between the inside ski's track and the outside ski's track. The inside ski's track should be wider, and the snow will look smeared.

## OTHER DRILLS

Following are other drills that will strengthen outside ski dominance.

### Flying Wedges

Ski in a straight line down the hill in a narrow wedge. Stand tall and allow yourself to build up speed. In a wedge, your skis are already on edge and partially steering (toward each other). Therefore, all you have to do to make an outside ski-dominant turn is begin pushing on one ski with the arch and ball of one foot. Maintain a wedge throughout a series of turns so you can focus on being outside ski dominant. Vary your speed and turning radius and note how the degree of outside ski dominance varies with these changes.

### Kick-Starters

While making turns of varying sizes, try picking up and setting down your inside ski, lifting it no more than about 6 inches off the snow. When you change directions or start a new turn, begin picking up the new inside ski. The inside ski should always be moving, as though you were kick-starting a motorcycle. This drill forces the

outside ski to bear the entire amount of force during the turn, but only in small portions since the inside ski is set down on the snow over and over again to enhance your balance and sense of safety.

### Outside Ski Skiing

This drill is an extension of Kick-Starters. Lift your inside ski and keep it raised off the snow for the entire duration of a turn. When you start a new turn, set the ski down and lift the new inside ski off the snow. This drill accomplishes the same thing as the Kick-Starters drill, but it creates extreme outside ski dominance and enhances balance.

### 1,000 Steps

This drill can enhance several different tools —depending on the skill focus you use. To

Amplifying a natural movement pattern, the 1,000 Steps drill allows you to free the inside ski for steering and weight the outside ski. Holding the inside ski off the snow requires proper body position.

Even in soft snow where more equal weighting of both feet is desired, the outside ski remains dominant. Here you can see the outside ski is driven deeper. LIZ ELLING AT MOUNT BAILEY SNOWCAT SKIING; PHOTO BY R. MARK ELLING FOR KIRK DEVOLL PHOTOGRAPHY

strengthen your outside ski-dominance skills, begin making large-radius turns on gentle terrain where you have a lot of room. As you turn, begin by taking a step with your inside ski away from the outside ski. Follow it with a step with the outside ski and repeat. You will feel as if you are sidestepping toward the center of the turn while you are skiing. Do this throughout an entire turn to one direction and then start a new turn and continue taking steps. You should feel the pressure increase over your outside ski as you step away from it. Try increasing this outside ski dominance by taking larger steps, pushing away from the outside ski, and lengthening that outside leg.

## TROUBLESHOOTING OUTSIDE SKI DOMINANCE

If you are having difficulty achieving an outside ski-dominant turn, you may simply be judging yourself too harshly. Making a turn in which both skis are weighted equally is very difficult to do, and only a little more pressure on the outside ski versus the inside ski makes for an outside ski-dominant turn.

However, it is possible to overweight the inside ski during a turn. This can result in losing control over the outside ski. This is usually a product of leaning into the turn, which puts your center of balance in a nonfunctional position. If this seems to be happening, jump ahead to the chapter on edging and also check the hip angulation and counter-rotation sections in Getting Techno.

While leaning onto the inside ski is most commonly the problem for skiers who have trouble increasing their outside ski dominance, some skiers simply don't apply enough pressure to decamber their ski and bring the ski's edge into firm contact with the snow. Due to gravity and inertia, centrifugal force builds up in a turn and will aid you in pressuring the outside ski, but you still need to do some work. This generally means learning how to increase pressure on the ski by extending the outside leg and retracting the inside leg. These tactics are explained in the chapter on pressure control, which comes later in the Toolbox section.

It may not be your fault if you can't fully decamber your ski. The ski itself may be too stiff to be adequately bent. This situation dooms you from the start, because expert skiing is based on the ability to bend your skis. If this problem sounds familiar, see the information on ski length and stiffness in You *Can* Blame It on Your Gear! Sometimes.

# The Footwork Blend

Skiing sometimes seems foreign to a beginner, even if she has a strong sports background. Primarily, this is because she may have played high school or college softball, volleyball, and golf but may not have played much soccer. In fact, *most* American sports are hand-eye coordinated sports, but skiing—like soccer—is a foot-eye coordinated sport. People may believe hands are important in skiing, but most performance problems involving a skier's hands and poles ultimately stem from a skill weakness at the level of the skier's feet.

You have already explored two of the most fundamental and useful tools in skiing: steering and outside ski dominance. Many skiers tend to prefer one or the other of these tools when developing their own toolbox. But it is important to understand that these tools work together. An expert skier's ability to blend these tools together serves as a foundation for unlocking peak performance in varying snow conditions.

When you work on your steering, it may become apparent that your skis don't work in perfect unison. It might seem that the inside ski steers well but the outside ski is locked up and does not want to twist in the direction of the turn.

The outside ski bears the main load during a turn, and it drives the edge of the ski deeper into the snow and makes the turn powerful and stable. At the same time, this edge bite makes it more difficult to guide the ski across the snow in a steering movement than when the ski was flat on its base. The inside ski may feel light and easy to steer, and for good reason—the inside ski is pressured less than the outside ski under most circumstances, which translates into less edge pressure, or edge bite, on the inside ski. This allows the inside ski to be steered more effectively. Remember that steering is easiest to do when a ski is flat, as it is between turns. But steering can be used when the ski is on edge, too.

During a turn, the outside foot is standing on the outside ski and driving its edge into the snow to carve a stable turn. The inside ski is also performing an important duty: steering. You now have the footwork blend: a different athletic job description for each foot.

The expert skier will take advantage of the lighter feel of the inside ski and steer the inside ski along the same arc that the outside ski is following. This combination of outside ski dominance and inside ski steering results in a powerful and graceful turn. The inside ski does not interfere with the movements of the outside ski; it actually helps you create a strong and balanced stance as you steer on the snow, rather than "tagging along" next to the outside ski or hovering in the air off the snow.

There isn't always such an obvious division between the roles of outside and inside skis. For example, the outside ski can be steered at the same time it is under pressure. This is a fine-tuning skill that helps you keep your outside ski from "tracking away" and heading out on a tangent. Also, the inside ski does not always have a light feel. In some situations—such as in bumps, crud, or powder—the inside ski plays a role similar to that of the weighted outside ski. In these conditions, you may utilize more of the inside ski's design when making turns rather than simply steering this ski.

Newer, shaped skis have changed the nature of the footwork blend as well. Because it doesn't take as much force to engage a shaped ski and begin carving, skiers can carve with the inside ski as well as the outside ski. This doesn't mean that the inside ski isn't steered along the inside path of the turn, but there's no reason the outside edge of the inside ski can't do a little carving too.

The ability to blend the two tools of outside ski dominance and steering between the outside and inside skis will begin to turn an intermedi-

ate skier into an advanced skier. This blending is what it takes to ski tough and intimidating terrain.

 *You can feel*
**THE FOOTWORK BLEND
AT WORK**

1. Tune into the direction of force at work with your feet. In a typical turn on groomed snow, your outside foot is primarily working in a downward direction, pressing the ski's inside edge into the snow. You will feel this force center around your foot's arch. On the same turn, your inside foot is working in a horizontal plane, twisting in the direction of the turn, or across. You will feel this force

Though the outside ski bears most of the load, the inside ski is guided onto its outside edge and may engage a carved turn as well. CHRIS SMITH BELOW COW'S FACE, MT. BACHELOR

In many situations, the outside ski functions differently than the inside ski. On firm snow, the outside ski is pressured in a downward fashion while the inside ski is guided onto its outside edge, where it can carve along the arc of the turn.

center around the outside edge of that foot where it is pressing against the boot and steering it.

2. Play with blending outside ski dominance and steering on one ski at a time when making turns. This movement feels similar to crushing out someone's smoldering cigarette or squashing a cockroach: push down and twist.

*You can see*
## THE FOOTWORK BLEND AT WORK

1. As you turn, look down at your ski tips and watch the way they move through the turn in relation to each other. Both skis are edged

during the turn, and you feel as though you are outside ski dominant. Look to see if the inside ski's tip pulls away from the outside ski's tip. This is a good visual indication that the inside ski is being steered in the direction of the turn while the outside ski remains dominant.

2. Sit in a swiveling office chair and place both feet flat on the floor in front of you. Watch what happens to your feet when you push off of one of them in order to turn your chair to the left or to the right. Note how the pushing foot's arch presses against the floor while the other foot rolls onto its outside edge and begins to twist away from the pushing foot in the direction of the chair's turn. This is exactly how the footwork blend works.

## OTHER DRILLS

Below are other drills that can help you refine your footwork blend.

### 1,000 Steps, Part II

Perform this drill as described on pages 22 and 24. However, rather than focusing on the outside ski, pay attention to the *inside* ski. As you take that step with the inside ski toward the center of the turn, feel how you are steering that ski while it is off the snow. Now feel the way the outside ski is being pushed against at exactly the same time that the inside ski is being steered. This is an exaggerated blend of outside ski dominance and inside ski steering.

### Tip Tow Turns

This drill requires a little imagination. Pretend that your ski tips are connected by an invisible rope exactly the length that usually exists between your ski tips when you are skiing. As you turn, imagine that you are starting the turn with the inside ski by steering it away from the outside ski. The inside ski's tip will tow the other ski into the turn because of the invisible rope. As the outside ski is towed into the new turn, you will feel it become outside ski dominant while the inside ski continues to steer. For more practice, try to stretch the rope by aggressively steering the inside ski. You will see the imaginary rope stretch when the inside ski's tip pulls away from the outside ski's tip.

### Tip-Lead Turns

You may have already noticed that the inside ski's tip runs a little farther ahead of the outside ski's tip during a turn. You can enhance your footwork blend skills by increasing the amount of inside ski tip-lead. This forces the outside ski to bear more weight, freeing the inside ski to be steered. You will notice that pushing the inside ski slightly ahead will also help engage its outside edge, allowing the inside ski to begin to carve inside the arc of the outside ski.

### Bellows Turns

This is a fairly advanced drill that involves coordination and balance. As you make turns on moderate, well-groomed terrain, lift the tail of the inside ski about one foot off the snow and allow the tip of that ski to glide along the snow's surface. The trick is to steer the inside ski's tip onto its outside edge, as if the entire ski were on the snow. Make turns by lifting the tail, guiding the tip onto its outside edge so that it can run along the same arc as the outside ski, and then setting the tail back onto the snow before starting a new turn. This up-and-down tail movement looks like the movement of a bellows from the side. This drill enhances outside ski dominance because the inside ski is lifted. It also improves inside ski guidance because it takes a major steering move to guide the inside ski onto its outside edge when the tail is lifted.

### TROUBLESHOOTING THE FOOTWORK BLEND

It is rare that a skier has difficulty becoming outside ski dominant after some instruction. But it is common for a skier to have trouble steering the inside ski. I have talked about steering the inside ski when it is off the snow, flat, or on its outside edge. Many skiers, however, cannot get the inside ski off its inside edge and instead remain positioned the way they would be in a wedge turn.

The inability to flatten the inside ski and guide it onto its outside edge can stem from alignment problems. These skiers may have to pick up their inside ski during a turn in order to steer it though the turn. They can't perform this move with the ski on the snow because the ski's inside edge continues to grab the snow.

By lifting this ski into the air, the skier can then steer it. But this move forces the skier to assume an off-balance position, and this can result in an awkward turn or even a crash. This inside ski lift will become more pronounced as the terrain becomes more intimidating.

If you experience this problem, read the chapters on alignment and edging. More information on advanced applications of the footwork blend can be found in the chapters on skiing powder and crud in Getting Tough: Advanced Situations.

# 5

# Edging: Getting on Them, Getting off Them

Apart from the contributions world-class skiers have made to the sport, equipment development has been largely responsible for the evolutionary leaps skiing has made over the years. Along with releasable bindings, plastic ski boots, and laminate ski design, metal edges made skiing a different sport.

We may take our metal edges for granted. Many skiers get away with inefficient edging movements simply because technologically advanced skis can pick up the slack.

The tool of edging has not changed as dramatically as the edge itself. Edging as a tool has been reduced to its most basic and functional form. The mastery of this simple tool will lend power to your turns and enable you to slip from turn to turn in effortless transitions. However, misuse of edging can be your worst enemy.

As you now know, the tools of skiing interrelate, and each tool enhances the others if used properly. Edging affects your ability to steer and become outside ski dominant. When edging is used improperly, it can prevent you from performing some of the most basic movements in skiing.

To better understand how edging works, lay a ski on your living room floor. Take your empty ski boot and click it into your ski's binding. Find something you can use as a lever: a baseball bat, a golf club, or a long stick. Insert one end of the lever into the boot and push the lever down to the boot's footbed. Grab the top of your lever and move it forward and backward, then side to

side. Watch what happens to the ski. When you move the lever toward the tip or tail of the ski, the lever meets resistance from the tongue and back of the boot but the ski itself does not move much. When you move the lever from side to side, the ski easily tips over onto its edge without much resistance at all.

*Edging* is your ability to put your ski on edge or take an edged ski and lay it flat on the snow. Termed a different way, edging is the ability to increase or decrease the angle created between the bottom of the ski and the snow. In effective edging, you make these adjustments with the least amount of wasted effort.

The edging tool is simple. Many skiers make edging more complicated by trying to understand it in combination with other skills, without learning first the basic movements of edging by itself. Skiers also forget that edging is not just about *increasing* a ski's edge; it is also about *decreasing*, or releasing, an edge.

In the living room floor and lever demonstration, the most efficient edging movements were produced when the lever arm was moved to the left and right, without pressing against the front or the back of the boot; this shows that lateral movements of ski boots make for functional edging. Although your legs are different than a baseball bat or golf club, they are levers. In fact, a leg is better than a bat or a club because it is not totally stiff; leg joints play a major role in edging. Your ankles, knees, and hips contribute to edging by making the adjustments that force

Movements of edge engagement can get extreme, but being able to release the edges and flatten the ski is just as important. MARK ELLING IN SURFER BOWL, MT. BACHELOR

your boots to the left or right. But each joint functions differently, and each plays its own role in edging.

The ankle is a relatively weak joint. For this reason, ski boots are made of stiff plastics and have a high cuff to lend support to your ankle. Modern boots do not completely immobilize your ankle's movements, and your ankle's range of motion, while limited, can create noticeable differences in performance. All your joints are connected in edging movements, but ankles make minor, fine-tuned adjustments to your edges during a turn. The correct ankle adjustments can transform a turn from average to perfect.

The knee is not extremely strong and is not protected by a stiff plastic boot. As a result, the knee is the undisputed weak link in a skier's frame. Many intermediate and advanced skiers overuse and improperly use their knees because their learning techniques are outdated and they lack knowledge about edging.

Edging movements should be efficient and can be effortless. CRAIG MACDONALD AT MONTANA SNOWBOWL; PHOTO BY R. MARK ELLING FOR KIRK DEVOLL PHOTOGRAPHY

The knee does not function the same way the ankle does. Like the hip, the ankle has movement in every direction, so it can change the edge angle of a ski. But the knee is a hinge joint; it won't bend sideways, which is what it would need to do to make edging adjustments. By becoming knock-kneed or bowlegged, you can bend your knee and roll your foot in or out to edge your ski. But notice what is happening to the kneecap: it points in and out, which means that the leg is being rotated, or steered slightly, and then bent at the knee.

This knee movement can affect edging and pressure-control movements, but it does not produce a major edge adjustment. Using your knees to make large edging movements is problematic. It causes stress on the knee, because the joint is twisted and torqued. Until I learned a more effective way to edge my skis, my knees ached after a hard day of skiing. I thought my knees were shot, but I changed my edging methods and my knee pain went away.

Elvis was right—the hip is cool. The hip is also strong. This joint links two massive structures: the bone in your thigh (the femur) and the pelvis. The hip is a ball-and-socket joint, allowing the femur to move fore and aft, laterally, and rotationally. This range of motion, combined with the size of the bone structure, enables the hip to serve as a fulcrum to your leg, which in turn acts as a lever, during a turn.

When you edge your feet in street shoes, your hips will help by sliding to the left or right. This lateral gliding of the hip is smooth and energy-efficient. Edge your feet and make your body position tall and relaxed (as discussed in the chapter on stance). Trying to make edging movements like this using only your knees requires bent legs, thus tiring your legs. Expert skiers move their hips laterally to make major edge adjustments. Then, they fine-tune that edge with the knee and ankle.

Many accomplished skiers practice only half this tool. Remember, as stated in the chapter title, edging is all about getting on them and getting off them, or increasing and decreasing the

The majority of edging movements should be made with the hip and modified with smaller movements of the knees and ankles.

sits on its inside edge, and this edged position becomes the status quo until you learn how to make parallel turns. You may ski around in some form of wedge with your inside edges engaged for years and never know there is another set of edges or such a thing as a flat ski. It is natural for skiers to have difficulty learning how to disengage the inside edge, flatten the ski, and engage the outside edge.

You increase your edge to control a turn once it's started and to carve through a turn as described in the chapter on carving. An increased edge lends power and stability to a turn by enhancing the skis' bite on the snow. Increasing the edge angle during a turn involves more of the ski's sidecut, letting the ski do much of the work and making the turn more efficient. Increasing the edge angle of a ski during a turn, combined with increased pressure, will produce a stronger, more athletic turn. However, muscling the turn in this way comes after the turn is already started. If you muscle, or force, turn initiation, you produce erratic and ineffective movements.

edge angle. Getting on your edges is easy. It's one of the first things you learn when you make a wedge for the first time on flat terrain. Each ski

Two different turns, two different styles. Both skiers make the major edging movement with their hips and keep their upper bodies upright and balanced. LEFT: KAREY SCHOLEY BREAKIN' THE LAW ON THE EAST SIDE, MT. BACHELOR. RIGHT: ERIK KORMAN ON LEE WAY, MT. BACHELOR

Starting turns requires the finesse of releasing your edge.

Releasing your edge means reducing the edge angle of your ski. As a beginner, you learned that skiing was about placing your skis on their inside edges and keeping them there. You tended to push against one inside edge for one turn, then push against the other inside edge for the next turn, and continue this pattern with each turn. This practice may have served you well in the beginning when you used a wedge, and even as you did parallel turns on firm, groomed snow. But this inside-edge-to-inside-edge pattern is a major stumbling block for the skier who ventures into bumps, crud, powder, and steeps, where transitions between turns are key. You will struggle with starting smooth turns in these environments if you do not master edge release.

Edge release often works in combination with steering. Steering is most effective when your ski is flat on the snow. This flattening of your ski, which happens between turns, is made possible by edge release. Flattening your skis after a turn is what makes the start of your next turn look smooth. Releasing your edge makes steering easier, and steering your skis into a new turn is one key to effective turn initiation.

A skier who cannot release his edges after a turn will be forced to do something to make the transition from one set of edges to the other to make the next turn. Some skiers do this by stepping from one ski to the next rather than allowing their skis to roll from one set of edges to the other. This step movement produces an awkward, halting style; this movement may work on firm snow but it fails in softer snow because the step places all the pressure on one ski, and the ski drives down into the snow where it usually trips up the skier.

Many skiers have difficulty with edge release. But it is extremely easy to do once you understand how it works. Edge release is the opposite of increasing your edge. If you can increase your edge with your ankle, knee, or hip, you can also *release* your edge using these joints. Making an edge-release movement mainly with the hip and fine-tuning it with the knee and ankle is the most effective method. To release your edges at the end of a turn, simply shift your hips across your skis, rolling the skis off their edges to make them momentarily flat; now you can steer them for a split second, aiding their entry into the next turn where you guide them onto the other set of edges. (For a more detailed discussion of the specific movements and timing of edge release, read the chapter on body mass movement.)

Releasing your edges to start a new turn allows you to keep both skis on the snow rather than stepping to the new ski. Maintaining snow contact with both skis is a fundamental requirement for skiing well in variable snow conditions. Learning to release your edges will improve every turn you make, no matter what terrain you are on. Your turns will begin to flow from one to the next without difficult transitions.

*You can feel*
**A MASTERY OF EDGING**

1. Experiment with making edge adjustments with the ankle, knee, and hip. Feel the way your foot's arch is flattened and pressed against the floor of your boot when you increase the ski's edge using your ankle. Then feel the way your arch lifts away from the floor of the boot when you release that edge with your ankle. Try to increase and decrease your edging using your knees only. Feel the way you must twist your knees in the direction of the turn to increase your edge. Feel the smooth glide of your hips from side to side as you increase and decrease your edging. This shifting laterally at the hips feels something like slow dancing.

2. Notice how the feel of your ski changes as you modify your edge angle. When you increase your edge, feel how your ski wants to

track (or follow one arcing path). Also notice how stable your ski feels, as though it were doing the work for you. Your ski can feel uncontrollable if you give it too much edge and cause it to travel according to its own design. As you release your edges and flatten your skis, feel the way the skis become slippery, even unpredictable. Try to maximize this floating feeling. Let the skis hover and slide without using any edging. Try to guide them while they feel this way and steer them in the direction you want.

*You can see*
**PROPER USE OF EDGING**

1. Watch your shadow as you ski away from the sun. Make turns and notice how your shadow grows taller as you release your edges between turns and grows smaller during the turn as you increase the amount of edge you use. This happens because as you move your hips laterally to increase your edge, you are basically folding your body sideways and making it smaller. When you release your edges to start a new turn, there isn't a need to fold your body at the hips and you return momentarily to a tall, neutral stance.

2. Make a run on groomed snow under a chairlift and focus on engaging and releasing your edges smoothly from turn to turn. Then get on the lift and look at your tracks below. See if you can tell where in the turn you were using the most edge and where you were using the least. Pretend you made the tracks on a clock's face: generally, you should see the most edging appear as deep marks in the snow near 3:00 and 9:00. The least edging should appear between turns, leaving marks of little depth near 12:00 and 6:00.

a. Skier begins pressing the new outside ski, exiting the turn;

b. skier's frame elongates at turn initiation, guiding skis muscularly through transition;

c. edges engaged through body mass movement;

d. knees fine-tune edge angle;

e. edges released through lateral body mass movement.

Basic edging movements are subtle. Note how the skier's frame elongates as he passes between turns. This enhances the skier's movement sideways, or across his skis. His center of mass controls the major edging, and his knees and ankles help with minor adjustments.

## OTHER DRILLS

Here are some other drills that will help improve your edging skills.

### Sideslips

Sideslips, one of the most basic drills in the ski instructor's bag of tricks, are invaluable to skiers who want to refine their edging skills. Primarily an edge-release drill, sideslips can also help you improve your edge-increase skills. Find moderate to steep terrain with groomed or smooth snow. Stand sideways on the hill in a place where you are not at risk of being hit by skiers. While you stand still on the trail, notice that you are not sliding down the hill because you are using your edges. Now try to let your skis slip sideways down the hill by decreasing your edging. Try doing this with your ankles, then knees, then hips. Fine-tune your amount of edging so you glide smoothly straight down the hill with your skis constantly pointing toward the side of the run.

### Wing-Dips

This drill combines edge release with steering to smooth out turn initiation. Begin with a straight sideslip as described above, then add foot and leg steering without swinging your upper body. Continue slipping down the hill, but steer your ski tips downhill and then uphill—as if your skis were the wing of a plane dipping left and right.

### Sideslip Staircases

In this drill, make the same movements you make in Wing-Dips, but concentrate on steering your ski tips almost completely downhill and then back across the hill. Sideslip through these partial turns in a controlled skid. Carry these half turns across the slope to the right side, then back to the left. You will leave tracks that look like a staircase. Try to do the steering with your feet and legs, not your upper body.

### Railroad Turns

This is an excellent edging drill you can use while cruising along a cat track or a long road where speed control is not a problem. Start by standing tall and skiing straight with your skis riding flat on the snow. Try to edge both skis (using left edges or right edges) dramatically by moving your hips laterally. Keep your balance evenly centered over both skis. If you are edging enough, your skis will carve clean arcs along a radius determined by your skis' sidecut. After one turn, shift your hips laterally to the other direction and carve another long, drawn-out turn. You will leave carved parallel tracks that look like railroad tracks. This drill emphasizes hip movement in edging, and it demonstrates edging's role in carving turns and utilizing a ski's sidecut.

### Edging Extremes

Edging is one of those tools that is easy to learn but more difficult to apply in the proper amounts. Using the right amount of edge throughout a turn is something that comes with time and a keen body awareness. However, you can learn to acquire this kind of judgment by exploring the parameters of edging. Try using as much and as little edge as possible during turns. If you use too much edge, your ski will stop turning and track away. If you use too little edge, you might slip or skid during the turn. Also try to turn using only your ankles to adjust your edges, and then try to use only your hips to edge.

## TROUBLESHOOTING EDGING

Skiers commonly have problems when it comes to fine-tuning their edging skills. Difficulties can arise when you are learning to use your hips to make edging movements. If you feel overly stiff or locked-up, read the chapter Body Mass Movement in the Creating a Toolbox section and then read about counter-rotation, hip angulation, and pelvic tilt in Getting Techno.

If you have tried the drills in this section and still have trouble, your problems could be equipment related. A ski in need of a tune can make it almost impossible for you to release your edges. This is caused by a ski that is edge-high, which means that the base of the ski has shrunk below the level of the edges, and the edges dig down into the snow like runners on a sled. Skis like this feel hard to place on edge and hard to release. Skiers with this problem should read the information on ski tuning in You *Can* Blame It on Your Gear! Sometimes.

Another common edge-release problem associated with equipment has to do with alignment. It is rare that a skier buys a pair of ski boots off the rack, puts them on, steps into a pair of skis, and rides a flat ski whenever he wants to. Without needed adjustment to his equipment's alignment systems, a skier will ride on his inside or outside edges, even if he thinks his skis are flat. The skier who rides on his inside edges will have a hard time releasing them, and a release move must be extremely exaggerated to achieve a flat ski. The skier who rides on his outside edges will find that it is difficult to get enough edge during a turn, and he may skid and feel out of control during turns. Skiers with these symptoms should look at the alignment chapter in You *Can* Blame It on Your Gear! Sometimes.

# Pressure Control

The sense of feel is important in all kinds of performance. Take automotive performance, for example. A lot of time and money is spent on researching ways to control a car's feel on the road. Most of the effort is spent on the suspension systems: springs, shocks, independent suspension, fixed-axle suspension, swing arms, torsion bars. These systems affect the car's feel and the way it rides and handles. An expert skier is like a well-suspended car: one of her tools is her suspension system, and this suspension system is called pressure control.

Before you begin to feel pressure control, it helps to know what you are feeling for. There are only a few things you can do with the pressure your skis exert on the snow. First and most fundamentally, you can transfer pressure, or weight, from one ski to the other. And you can regulate the degree to which you transfer that weight.

You've already felt this in becoming outside ski dominant, when you pushed harder against one ski than the other. That was lateral pressure control, or lateral weight transfer, which is something like a heartbeat in skiing: it happens to some degree every time you make a turn. Lateral pressure control can make turning quicker and easier.

Stand on the floor with your feet spread shoulder width apart. Keep your body tall and center your hips between your feet. Push down on the floor with your right foot. Which way did your hips move? Either you shifted your hips

over your right foot, in order to apply weight to that foot, or you pushed against your foot and shifted your hips to the left, away from that push. Which hip movement felt more like skiing?

As you push against your outside ski in a turn, forces build that try to tip you over. But you resist this force by moving your hips toward the center of the turn to find a balanced position. I will talk more about hip movement later. For now, it is important to feel how hip movement starts at your feet as one foot pushes down and your hips shift away from your foot.

Try this standing drill a few more times. Push down on one foot and watch your hips shift away from that foot, but now focus on the feel of the movement that increases pressure on your foot. It may help if you try feeling what your nonpushing leg is doing. It is bending slightly. The pushing leg gets longer and extends in a type of leg press against the floor, and your other leg retracts by bending a bit and getting shorter. This long-leg/short-leg phenomenon is easy both to see and feel if you do the drill and lean against a wall in order to push against the outside foot.

I discussed how important outside ski dominance is to powerful skiing. Now you understand how to exert pressure on that ski. It's important to feel how your pushing leg extends to a not-quite-locked position, just like a cyclist's leg at the bottom of a pedal stroke. Your muscle is most powerful at this position, and your leg is almost straight—a position that also allows the leg's skeletal structure to bear some of the force that builds in the turn. Maintaining a tall stance is one way to ensure you will apply pressure to your skis with effective long-leg extension.

The second component of strong pressure control is the ability to use the long-leg/short-leg skills (or extension and flexion) in order to increase or decrease pressure on your skis during a turn. The mechanics of this move are very basic: When you extend your leg, pressure goes up; when you bend your leg, pressure goes down. Imagine that you are standing on a bathroom scale and you suddenly bend both legs. At that moment you feel as if you are riding a descending elevator and the scale briefly reads a lighter weight, which means there is less pressure under your feet. From your squatting position, extend your legs quickly. As you push against the scale, it reads a heavier weight, which means pressure was increased.

Being able to decrease or increase the pressure on your skis helps you enhance both steering and edging during a turn to make a powerful turn more efficient. Remember that steering is a muscular guiding of your skis. When you reduce pressure on your skis, steering becomes easy. Your inside ski during a turn feels light, and this is why the inside ski is steered while the outside ski remains pressure dominant.

You can, however, make one or both your skis feel light enough to steer at any time by making a move to decrease pressure. You can feel this between turns, when your lateral weight transfer occurs as you start a new turn. Simply stop pressing on your skis for a second. Allow yourself to float momentarily and steer your skis into the new turn without pressuring the new outside ski. You will feel your skis respond to your foot and leg steering movements more quickly and with less effort.

Decreasing pressure helps you ease into a turn. Increasing pressure on a ski during a turn can enhance your equipment's potential. We know how a ski's sidecut allows a ski to follow a predetermined arc when the ski is put on its

edge. A ski is also designed with a flex pattern that allows the ski to bend under your weight. You need to make contact between your edges and the snow by flexing the ski and squashing the camber out of it. But a ski's flex can play a larger role.

Being able to bend a ski during a turn using leg flexion and extension could be one of the best things about our sport. This lower-body motion is responsible for the energy you feel from turn to turn and for your ability to vary the size of carved turns. As you increase pressure on a ski once you're in a turn, you drive the ski's edge deeper into the snow. This locks the ski into a stable arc, but it also increases the bend of the ski and allows the ski to engage an even deeper arc than the one predetermined by the ski's sidecut (see illustration, page 40).

Whether done through a slow, progressive extension of the leg during a large turn or in a more rapid, bouncing fashion made for small turns, bending the ski into a tighter arc is a versatile tool for the expert skier.

Finally, one of the most common uses of pressure control is shock absorption. Just like a car, skis are difficult to control if you can't keep them on the snow. Your ability to extend and retract your legs allows you to maintain contact between your skis and the snow. This absorptive pressure control is a valuable tool in moguls. I will discuss shock-absorbing pressure control and fore-aft pressure control further in later chapters.

*You can feel*
**PRESSURE CONTROL AT WORK**

1. Most skiers never fully utilize their pressure-control skills because they cannot feel their range of motion and, therefore, cannot maximize that range. Make a traverse on gentle terrain or ski down a road and try to extend

Being able to control pressure between the inside and outside ski is the key to versatile off-piste skiing. MARK ELLING IN THE NOTCH, MT. BACHELOR

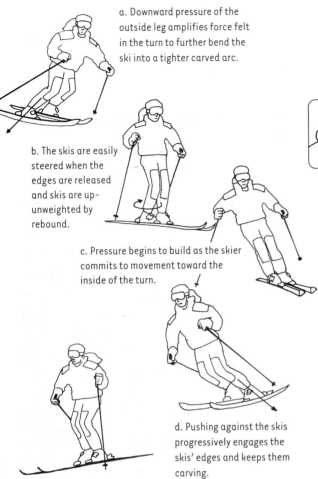

a. Downward pressure of the outside leg amplifies force felt in the turn to further bend the ski into a tighter carved arc.

b. The skis are easily steered when the edges are released and skis are up-unweighted by rebound.

c. Pressure begins to build as the skier commits to movement toward the inside of the turn.

d. Pushing against the skis progressively engages the skis' edges and keeps them carving.

e. A return to an elongated stance again up-unweights the skis and helps release the edges.

Feel the way your arch flattens and the ball of your foot spreads when you increase pressure by extending your leg. If you can't feel these sensations, your boots may be too big and could be holding back your performance.

*You can see*
## PRESSURE CONTROL

1. Make turns in new or freshly groomed snow and vary the amount of pressure you use from turn to turn. Then look at your tracks to see if you can tell where you used more or less pressure. High-pressure turns will have deep, carved tracks and may have tighter turn radius. Low-pressure turns will look less defined and shallow, possibly smeared, indicating a more steered turn.
2. Watch your shadow as you ski with the sun at your back. Look for a long-leg/short-leg pattern and try to take your shadow to the extreme—one leg totally straight and the other as bent as possible while maintaining snow contact with both skis. Then try to minimize the difference between the long and short legs.

### OTHER DRILLS

These drills will help you improve your pressure control.

### Leapers

Make medium-sized turns on moderate terrain at fairly high speed. Try to leap into the air at the start of each turn by forcefully extending both legs throughout the turn. Time this so that full extension is reached at the transition between turns, which will allow you to be airborne at the initiation of the new turn. Note how the turn

your legs as much as possible. Then retract them as much as you can. Try making these moves more rapidly and feel the way they dramatically alter the pressure on the bottoms of your feet.
2. The fit of your boots has a lot to do with how effectively you can manage the pressure exerted by your skis. Feel the way the top of your foot pulls against your boot when you decrease pressure by retracting your legs.

feels stable and powerful during extension and how you utilize steering with both legs while you are airborne. Try toning down this drill so that your skis never leave the snow.

### 1,000 Steps with Pressure Control Focus

Perform the 1,000 Steps drill as explained in the chapters on outside ski dominance and the footwork blend. This time, feel the way your ski bites and bends during the extension of the outside, long leg. Also note how the reduction of pressure on the stepping inside ski enhances its steering capability.

### Squatty Body Outriggers

Choreographing this drill can be a little tricky, but it's fun, too. Begin by skiing on gentle terrain where skiing straight down will not cause problems. (Wide roadcuts are good terrain for this.) Squat down so you are sitting on your haunches as you ski down the fall line. Balance over one ski and then begin extending the other leg; try to push it away as far as possible while maintaining your squatty stance. Notice how your long leg ski's edge angle increases as you extend it; that ski should want to carve along its sidecut arc. Allow it to carve a turn and then slowly retract that leg. Extend the other leg in similar fashion and repeat. Try exerting more and more pressure upon your extended outrigger so the ski bends and carves a tighter turn.

### Bump Field Traverses

Find a mogul-covered slope and traverse back and forth across it. Initially, try to maintain snow contact with your skis by extending and retracting your legs to absorb the bumps. Continue doing the exercise but don't allow your upper body to move. This will indicate that your legs are controlling pressure effectively. Once you've mastered this move, try it at a

higher speed. For an advanced application of this drill, try absorbing four bumps with a quiet upper body, then launch off the fifth bump and sail over a trough and land on the backside of the sixth mogul.

### TROUBLESHOOTING PRESSURE CONTROL

There is no secret to mastering effective pressure control. But this tool does depend on your ability to stay loose and use your legs in a dynamic

Here is a complete reduction of pressure on the skis.
GREG RUBIN OVER THE ROCK GARDEN, MT. BACHELOR

way. Stiff skiers aren't stiff by design: they haven't mastered other basic tools of skiing that would make turning easier and more relaxed. Many skiers also become rigid and unable to modify the pressure under their skis because they are intimidated by the terrain. You can't stay loose if you are scared stiff, so mellow out and try it again.

At a basic level, pressure-control skills are simple and generally easy to master. In advanced applications, pressure control is subtly intertwined with other skills. Functional movements of the body's center of mass stem from proper lateral weight transfers, and expert performance in challenging terrain such as bumps, crud, and powder require some adaptation of pressure-control movements. Pay attention in the following chapter to how pressure control is involved in body mass movements and watch for applications of pressure-control skills in expert terrain in Getting Tough: Advanced Situations.

# Body Mass Movement

Body mass movement is a fancy term for something that has been around since skiing began. But this is one performance tool that coaches and instructors have sorely overlooked—until recently. Now many instructors threaten to make body mass movement a cure-all and more complicated than it needs to be.

We could call body mass movement simply body movement, because that's all it really is. But the word *mass* is important. It implies efficient body movements, because the body's center of mass is doing most of the work. This is similar to the role your legs play when you lift a heavy object. We all know we should lift with our legs, not with our back, because our legs can effectively do most of the work. The body's center of mass, or the area with the highest concentration of density, is around the hip section but also includes the butt and abdomen. This area of our bodies can do most of the work in skiing—and it can do it efficiently.

This portion of your body moves in a way that either allows you to make turns easily on any terrain or prevents you from making those turns. I have worked with hundreds of students who were trying to break out of their intermediate rut and become expert skiers. More often than not, their body mass movements were what ultimately held them back. Why? Efficient body mass movement can feel counterintuitive and even scary at first, so some skiers make movements that feel safer to them. But this can result in bad habits that ultimately impede performance.

It is easy to understand what good body mass movement is, and why so many skiers have trouble with it, if you look at snowboarding. Visualize a snowboarder making smooth linked turns down a slope. What does the snowboarder do to start a new turn if both her feet are fixed to one board? Beginner snowboarders do a lot of steering, and you may see them flattening the board and swinging the tail of the board around behind them to act like a boat's rudder. Advanced riders do it differently, arcing from turn to turn without much sign of pressure changes or full-body twisting. These proficient snowboarders use a lot of body movement into the turn, or toward the center of the turn. They "lay it over" so far that their bodies sometimes brush the surface of the snow.

You could say that a snowboarder simply tips over to make a new turn. This makes sense to us as skiers when we review outside ski dominance and pressure control. Remember how your hips shifted during turns when the outside ski was pressured away from the pushing foot. Another way of describing this is that your hips, or center of mass, moved toward the center of the turn. As your skis begin to turn, friction builds under them. If you push harder still against the outside ski, that force builds further. At some point the force becomes so great you feel as if you are being pulled toward the outside of the turn and you have to do something to prevent yourself from tipping over. At that

Pay attention to how good snowboarders move their bodies far to the inside of one turn, then smoothly roll off the edge and into another turn. MATT KROVISKY ON COFFEE, MT. BACHELOR

point, you drop your body mass even farther toward the inside of the turn.

This is a moment of balance. If you don't move your body far enough to the inside, you perform an incomplete or overly skidded turn. If you move your body too far inside, you will crash on your side. If you move your body mass just the right amount to the inside, you produce a well-balanced turn. The trick in body mass movement is not to focus on finding your equilibrium, since that comes naturally. The trick that expert skiers have mastered is the ability to move their body's center of mass effectively at the point of transition between turns.

Skiers don't have trouble moving their center of mass toward the inside of a turn once that turn has been started: the movement toward the center of a turn is a defensive move, a safety move. As you move your mass toward the center of a turn, you get closer to the snow, and this feels safe.

It is the next part of the move that troubles many skiers: moving out of this position of safety and allowing yourself to tip over, like a snowboarder does, into the next turn is frightening—especially on steep terrain. It might feel like jumping out of a plane or into an abyss. Many intermediate and advanced skiers tend to hang onto the safe position and "hug" the hill, or lean uphill. Some skiers even rotate their bodies to face uphill—as if this will change the fact that they will eventually have to start a new turn.

This tendency would not be so bad if we were talking about snowboarders. Snowboarders naturally break themselves of this habit. With a snowboard, no matter what happens, the rider must make the board flat in order to steer a basic turn, and this requires her to make a body mass movement toward the abyss. But with skiers, it's tougher to break fearful body mass habits. Skiers have two planks, not one board, and they can cheat by stepping onto the new outside ski.

This produces a turn, albeit not always a pretty one. But it does the trick. A skier with this habit may never learn to embrace the abyss and trust her skills. She skis on intermediate terrain where she's comfortable, and she gets by with the step trick, or some other turn initiation crutch, on more difficult pitches.

To begin to understand and perform body mass movement, you need to tune into the forces at play during turns. These are the forces we work with and against to maintain equilibrium. The term *force* is intentionally generic because it covers a lot of physical phenomena involved in the dynamics of skiing. Inertia, friction, gravity, centripetal force, and centrifugal force affect our skiing. But in my experience, this technical jargon does little more than confuse us. All you need to know is how to manipulate these forces to your advantage—not understand how Newton would prove that they exist. So I lump all these terms together loosely with the word *force* and get more specific only when it's necessary.

One way to identify the existence of force in skiing is to listen for it. For example, when you schuss and speed down the hill in a straight line, you hear little sound coming from where your skis meet the snow. You hear wind whipping by, but little else. When you try to stop, you guide your skis into a hockey stop and hear your ski edges scrape against the snow. This sound gets progressively louder as you increase your edging, and the sound rapidly subsides after you come to a complete stop. This is an audible representation of force at work in skiing. When you ski straight down, there is no force pushing against you (as we're defining it here). But once you begin your hockey stop, force builds up progressively until you come to a stop. Then the force against you ceases.

It's important to visualize what happens to body mass during the above episode. During the schuss, you stand tall and balanced. As you begin the hockey stop, force begins building and you become more flexed in your lower body. Your legs bend to begin to compensate for the increased pressure building against your skis. As the hockey stop progresses, so do your edging movements, or the movement of your hips toward the hill. You do this both to increase your edging in order to slow down and to balance against the building force. Force will tip you over to the outside of the turn unless you move your body to balance against that force. This move involves bending of the legs

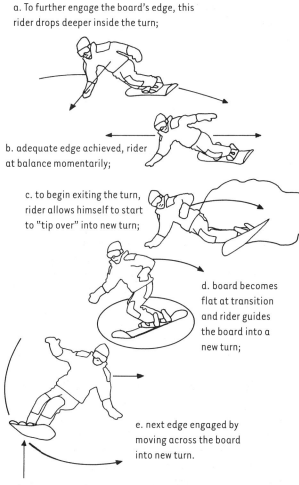

a. To further engage the board's edge, this rider drops deeper inside the turn;

b. adequate edge achieved, rider at balance momentarily;

c. to begin exiting the turn, rider allows himself to start to "tip over" into new turn;

d. board becomes flat at transition and rider guides the board into a new turn;

e. next edge engaged by moving across the board into new turn.

The snowboarder demonstrates smooth body mass movement from turn to turn. Note that movement is progressive and directly linked to edge control.

and lateral movement toward the inside of the turn.

Think of a hockey stop as a very abrupt turn. If the buildup of force during a hockey stop is rapid and extreme, then the buildup of force during a turn should be more relaxed. Turns happen smoothly and predictably—and so should the buildup of force during those turns.

It's easiest to master body mass movement by first focusing on the simple part: the bending of the legs during a turn. Think of your lower body as a human spring composed of muscle tissue, ligaments, tendons, and bones. This spring wants to remain tall and elongated in a neutral stance, but if something acts against this spring to compress it, then the spring will be compressed. However, once the force subsides, the human spring will rebound back to its original tall position.

This is what happens during every turn. Force builds against you as you turn—depending on how fast you are going, what pitch you are skiing on, and how much edge you use. As the force builds smoothly, the lower body reacts by flexing at the knees and ankles. Your upper body remains upright and unaffected. If the force continues to build, the legs continue to flex. Once the force begins to subside, the human spring begins to elongate until the force has abated and you have returned to a tall stance. At the start of the turn, a skier finds herself with her lower body extended. At the point of the greatest edge angle, she will find her lower body flexed.

The skier described above has mastered vertical body mass movement, or proper lower body flexion and extension. This is only half the battle. The vertical movements of leg flexion and extension are key to smooth skiing. They provide rhythm, smooth out transitions between turns, and enhance progressive edging and pressuring movements. But vertical movements alone are ineffective because moving one's body vertically will never induce edging, which is what it takes to move from turn to turn.

Increasing or decreasing edge angles requires lateral movement.

This brings us back to snowboarders. They move well laterally because they have to. They have only one board. Skiers must train themselves to produce rhythmic movements of flexion and extension in the lower body *and* combine those movements with lateral movements from the inside of one turn to the inside of the next.

When a skier is balancing against the greatest amount of force, she is at the deepest point of the turn and her lower body is at its most-flexed position. (Let's say she is farthest to the inside of the turn at this point.) When a skier begins moving out from the inside of this turn, moving laterally toward the next turn, she is extending her legs. When she passes the point between both turns, she is momentarily tall and elongated.

Another term commonly used among ski instructors for this movement "out of the hole" is *crossover*, as your body's mass crosses from one

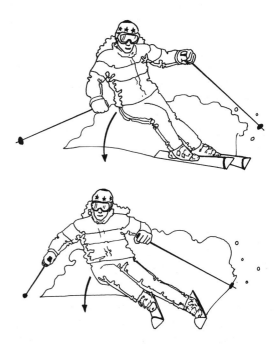

As a turn progresses toward a point of greatest edge engagement, your body mass must move farther toward the center of the turn and closer to the snow.

side of the skis to the other. This is a helpful term because it makes sense no matter where you are in relation to the slope you are skiing. Instructors often tell students to move their body mass "down the hill," but *downhill* body movement assumes that your skis are pointed across the hill at the end of the turn. However, this is not always the case, as when your body mass movement "out of the hole" and toward the next turn is toward the side of the run.

Being able to move *across* your skis is a breakthrough. What most skiers are afraid of is not going down toward the bottom of the hill, but losing control after giving up the balanced and safe position achieved by moving toward the inside of the previous turn.

Crossover—this hip movement from the inside of one turn to the inside of the next—is like a miracle drug, allowing your other skiing tools to be fully integrated into your skiing style. Without crossover, those tools are severely limited: without hip movement from one side to the other during turns, how could you change edges to turn where and how you want to? This becomes apparent any time you are perched on a steep slope and find yourself unable to start a smooth turn. Instead you hop, jump, step, or wedge your way through it. When you do make the crossover move on steep terrain (and it takes guts), your edges release, your skis steer, your new edges engage, and the turn is completed before you have time to worry.

*You can feel*
**EFFECTIVE CENTER OF MASS MOVEMENT**

1. When you start moving your body mass from turn to turn across your skis, it should feel the way a snowboarder looks: like a metronome. If you have ever ridden a bicycle at high speeds and made long, smooth turns by leaning the bike rather than by turning the

handlebars, then you know how it feels to move your center of mass properly.
2. Body mass movement *toward the inside of the turn* feels defensive, powerful, or crouched. This describes the way your body bends at the hips, knees, and ankles and bears force in a turn over the outside ski. Body mass movement across the skis *at the start of the next turn* causes a precarious, floating sensation—as if you were momentarily hanging your body out over a ledge. You must trust yourself to make this scary-feeling move; the feeling lasts only a second because your steering, pressuring, and edging skills work together to bring your skis around into the next turn.

*You can see*
**EFFECTIVE BODY MASS MOVEMENT**

Center of mass movement is best seen in other skiers. Try to find a skier that reminds you of a snowboarder. This skier enters and exits turns with smooth, uninterrupted body movement from one side of the skis to the other. Any extraneous movements, such as an overly vertical pop or jerky, swinging movements of the upper body, are indications of inefficient body mass movement. Try to mimic your role model's body mass movements.

**OTHER DRILLS**

Other drills that help you master body mass movement follow.

**Hockey Stops**

In order to understand why your body's center of mass makes a movement toward the inside of a turn, do some hockey stops. Start with gentle ones and feel how your body moves throughout the exercise. Note that your body bends at the knees and ankles slightly and your hips move toward the hill, or toward the inside of that sharp turn. Begin increasing the intensity of your hockey stops by approaching them with more speed and applying greater edge angle. Note the larger spray of snow and louder scraping sound in a more intense hockey stop. You are building more force and moving your center of mass farther to the inside of the turn.

## Free Fall

To master the crossover, the second half of body mass movement, it helps to isolate the movement without worrying about making a turn. You need to ski with a partner on moderate terrain for this drill. Pick a spot out of the way of passing skiers that has firm, smooth snow. Set your poles aside and stand with your partner, with one of you positioned downhill from the other and your skis pointing across the hill so you won't slide forward or backward. The person standing below is the catcher; the person above is the faller. The person below should ready herself by setting her edges in the snow and be prepared to catch the skier above by holding out her arms with palms out. The skier above should stand on both skis and make a crossover move so he falls across his skis and into the arms of the partner below. There are a few tricks that help ensure a positive outcome. First, the catcher should stand close so the other skier's fall is not far—maybe only a few inches at first. Second, the skier making the crossover should keep both skis planted on the snow during the move.

When the falling skier makes a committed movement across his skis, the skis automatically flatten and sideslip. It's also common to see your skis begin to point downhill, as if they are trying to enter a new turn. These results are proof that crossover allows turn initiation to come easily.

Similar to a hockey stop, a highly dynamic turn will show an extreme buildup of force: little force between turns, a lot of force at turn finish. MARK ELLING NEAR THE PINNACLES, MT. BACHELOR

Continue this drill, increasing the crossover an inch at a time until the skis not only flatten and slip but actually roll far enough to engage the next set of edges. This is how your body mass movement can link carved turns together with minimal wasted energy and minimal skidding between turns.

### Cycle Turns

To polish your management of body mass from turn to turn, try skiing the way you might ride a bicycle at high speed. As your speed increases on a bicycle, your need to turn the handlebars decreases. Your turns are made more by leaning the bicycle to one side and then to the other. Pretend you are riding a bike and making these sorts of turns while you ski. Simply focus on leaning from one side to the other to start each turn. Don't worry about other tools; just tilt side to side. Try to move your hips, not just your head. Try this on moderate terrain at a comfortable speed, even though faster is easier than slower here.

### Ninja Turns

This imagery drill is a variation of the Cycle Turns drill, but it is adapted for more advanced skiers. Here the focus is not so much on learning to control body mass movements but on how you are moving your body mass. The name comes from the Kawasaki Ninja motorcycle, whose rider at times moves like a skier. Imagine the motorcycle racer making turns in a racecourse. The rider leans the bike into each turn, but he also jockeys around on the seat so that his knee scrapes the asphalt while his upper body remains in a more upright position.

This move mimics the way an expert skier drops her hips to the inside of a turn while maintaining an upright upper body position. To perform this drill, achieve Ninja-style speeds and make turns by shifting your hips to the inside of each turn. You can adopt a wider stance to enhance hip movement.

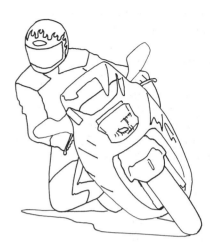

Similar to the relationship of a skier's upper and lower body, the rider leans less than the motorcycle.

## TROUBLESHOOTING BODY MASS MOVEMENT

Moving your body's center of mass back and forth across your skis is not magic. However, there are two problems skiers generally have with this tool.

For one, they remain static from turn to turn, never moving far enough toward the inside of the turn. This basically eliminates any need to crossover. This skier may look smooth, but she does not look or feel very athletic. To this skier, world-class racers whose hips almost brush the snow during a high speed turn may seem like athletes from outer space.

If you have this problem, think about *why* your body mass moves from side to side during turns. Remember that as force builds beneath your skis during a turn, you shift your hips and body mass away from your feet and toward the inside of the turn to reach a point of balance between tipping over and falling to the snow. A skier who does not make this movement probably has no need to, meaning she has failed to build force in her turn. This skier needs to create friction under her feet by increasing speed, outside ski dominance, edge angles, or all of the above.

A skier with this problem might need to work on the shape of her turns, since shape can lead to more efficient force buildup. The next chapter on turn size and shape will help.

This change is also related to lateral weight transfer. The skier begins pressuring the new outside ski and her hips shift away from the outside ski at the point of weight transfer. The fundamental beginnings of body mass movement start at the level of the feet.

The other common stumbling block in achieving good body mass movement is an inability to make the crossover move to start a turn. Skiers with this problem also tend to have problems with edge-release skills. Conquering their crossover problems will usually also solve their edge-release problems.

There are a few contributing factors to deficient crossover, most of which involve the tendency to hug the hill and remain in a position where the body's mass remains stuck in the inside of a turn. This is often manifested in CTS (Chronic Traverse Syndrome), where a skier makes one or two turns and then follows them with a long traverse across the hill. Usually this occurs at a steeper section of the slope while a skier looks for "a good place to turn." Her body mass has taken a dive toward the inside of the turn for safety reasons, and it does not want to come out. The primary factor at work here is fear.

To correct this, first master proper body mass movement on unintimidating terrain. Second, learn to control speed through turn shape and size to reduce that feeling of dread that may come when starting a turn on steep terrain. Then give the drills in this chapter another try. More specific information on body mass movement will be found in this book's final section, Getting Techno.

# Turn Size and Shape

I once thought that some elements of skiing were so basic that they were not worth the time it took to explain them to students. Turn size and shape were two of those elements.

I might have overlooked turn size and shape as performance tools of the expert skier had it not been for the students who asked, "How do I make those small turns?" The concepts behind turn size and shape are easily understood. They are only problematic when skiers, such as myself, forget about them altogether!

What I have continued to learn, however, is that while simple to understand and accomplish, properly shaped turns of varying size are critical to high performance skiing. The dynamics of flow and explosive energy in skiing cannot exist without good turn shape in an appropriately sized turn. I like to think of turn size and shape as a blueprint for good skiing, like skiing DNA.

## TURN SIZE

Skiers know why they vary the size of their turns. Either you want to make things interesting, or the terrain dictates the size of your turns: for example, small turns in moguls and large ones on gentle terrain. But skiers often fail to learn how to vary the size of their turns, and they end up using the wrong tool for the job. Understanding the basics of varying turn size

Round-shaped turns, like the letter C, are the key to smooth skiing, no matter what the snow conditions.

GREG RUBIN AT PAULINA PEAK, OREGON

is the first step toward mastering this tool. These basics involve your expenditure of energy.

Imagine yourself pushing off and sliding straight down a slope. What happens? You travel very fast down the run and no turns occur. Imagine pushing off again, but this time you add a slight amount of steering, edge, and outside ski dominance. What happens this time? A gentle, drawn-out turn takes place—a large-radius turn. Now imagine pushing off and steering your skis as rapidly as possible while laying your ski on edge and stomping on it. A tight, short-radius turn results.

Turns of every size occupy the space between these extremes. On a basic level, all you do to make a larger or smaller turn is decrease or increase the intensity at which you use your skiing tools.

A ski is designed to carve a turn of one particular size according to the ski's sidecut, and this is typically a large turn. The only ways to make a turn smaller than the arc determined by the ski's sidecut are to steer the ski through a smaller turn or bend it so it carves a tighter turn, or both. In a large-radius turn, you may simply stick your outside ski out and stand on it throughout the turn. In a small-radius turn, you need to both increase pressure on the ski to bend it farther and actively steer the skis toward the next turn. As turns get smaller, you have to make more adjustments and make them more quickly and more often.

One of the tools an expert skier uses to manipulate a ski and bend it into a tighter arc is lower body flexion and extension. Flexion and extension of the legs is a result of the buildup of force during a turn. But you can also use this motion to increase and decrease the force exerted on your skis.

By increasing the range of extension and flexion of your legs, or by flexing and extending harder or faster, you can increase the force buildup under your skis during a turn and prolong the float you feel at the start of the next turn. This enables you to bend your ski into a tighter arc during the control phase of the turn and

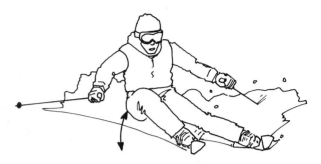

Long-radius turns take longer to develop and give you time to drop your center of mass farther to the inside of the turn.

guide the skis farther across the fall line at the start of the next turn. This action will result in smaller, quicker turns, and explains why an expert skier making linked short swings appears to use more lower body flexion and extension (see illustration, opposite).

## TURN SHAPE

Turn shape is one of the unsung heroes of skiing. The shape a ski draws on the snow during a turn is responsible for a skier's speed, energy, and control. We all like to think we make symmetrical, round turns—the kind of tracks we see slicing through powder on the pages of ski magazines—but unfortunately we butcher a lot of our turn shapes. We not only lose aesthetic points for this: the lines we draw in the snow have a major impact on how well we ski.

Turn shape dictates both how fast or slow you travel down the hill and how much force you build during a turn. Speed control has obvious merits, but some skiers fail to understand how turn shape relates to speed control.

Ideally, you enter a turn under control and pick up speed as you point your skis downhill. Then you control your speed as you finish the turn and slow down to the proper speed for starting the next turn. That is the ideal, but many of us go faster and faster until we slam on

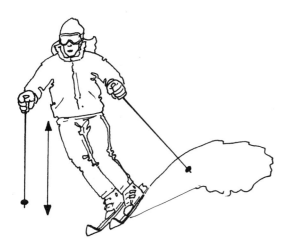

Short-radius turns require quicker movements of lower body flexion and extension to bend the skis into smaller arcs (rather than the large, lateral movements of the long-radius turn), and produce a taller stance.

the brakes somehow—with a skid, a partial hockey stop, or a long traverse. What we are doing is failing to finish our turns.

A turning path shaped like the letter C, with enough turn happening early in the turn and at the finish of the turn, makes for optimal speed control with the least amount of braking movements. These panicked attempts to slow down can throw your body into an unbalanced position.

Force is a tremendously useful tool in skiing. You already know how to use force to make a turn more powerful and stable, and force translates into smooth body mass movements and flow (other applications of force are discussed later). But this buildup of force during a turn cannot exist without proper turn shape.

Many intermediate skiers try to break through their performance plateaus by taking advanced lessons in bumps or powder, but they still fail to reach their athletic goals. What they need to do is learn about force at a basic level. A quick study of turn shape can make the difference between a skier who is always on the edge of breakthrough and the true expert.

A skier who skis straight down a smooth slope will not alter the amount of pressure, or force,

exerted by her skis on the snow. As soon as she begins to make a turn, she deviates from her straight-down path. This skier developed inertia when she was traveling straight, and friction and pressure will build beneath her skis when she starts to turn. Quite simply, making turns causes force to build beneath a skier's feet. Erratically shaped turns cause force to build erratically; sharp, abrupt turns cause force to build abruptly; weak, skinny turns produce little useful force. Smooth, round turns produce smooth and predictable force—that is, *useful* force.

Expert skiing is about dynamics, or constant change. The expert is continually turning and making body movements to complement the forces that build during turns. If you stop making smooth turns and insert a traverse into a portion of a turn, your efficient body mass movements will also stop. Consistent, round turns produce consistent body mass movements and rhythmic flow. Skiers who can't make continuous, round turns will have a difficult time generating the energy it takes to bend a ski, will not make smooth transitions from one turn to the next, and may struggle to make predictable turns in advanced skiing situations. Skiers need to focus on continuing movements throughout each turn rather than "just getting by" with short-lived movements. Continuing to steer the feet, shift the hips, flex or extend the legs, and swing the pole in smooth, continuous flow requires some concentration and an ability to move slowly and surely while traveling downslope at speed.

*You can feel*
**YOURSELF VARYING TURN SIZE AND SHAPE**

1. Different size turns feel as different as they look. Try isolating different ways of making larger or smaller turns and tune in to how they feel. For example, make some large turns by slowly pressuring one foot and then

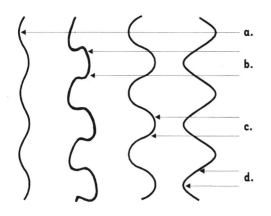

a. A snaking line without much deviation from the fall line may not have enough turn finish to generate a buildup of force in the turn.

b. A late-developing turn that runs straight and then hooks hard at the end of the turn will allow for too much acceleration and tend to have an abrupt, braking finish that fouls good body positioning.

c. Smooth, continuously arcing turns promote a predictable buildup of force and reliable speed control.

d. A traversing line with abrupt direction changes followed by straight runs causes "dead spots" in a turn where no force is generated.

the other. Note the rhythm of your weight transfer and how hard or soft you need to push to accomplish the large turn. Then make smaller turns using only pressure control. Does your rhythm get faster? Do you feel how you need to push harder against the ski? Continue the drill but use only your steering skills. First make large, then small, turns. Feel the way you increase or decrease steering in turns of varying sizes.

2. A well-shaped turn has one predictable feel: that of constant motion. In a smooth, round turn that is adequately completed, there is little time when the body is not making adjustments. Remember that your body mass moves throughout the turn—first toward the inside of the turn, then across the skis toward

the inside of the next turn. There isn't time for your body to freeze in place. Remember how you transfer weight from one ski to the other during turns. It feels as if you are marching very slowly in place without ever stopping. Even steering is continuous during turns.

*You can see*
### YOURSELF VARYING TURN SIZE AND SHAPE

1. Ski a run beneath a chairlift and try to make large, medium, and small turns. Then ride back up the lift and check your tracks.
2. With the sun overhead, ski beneath a chairlift and use the oncoming shadows of chairs as a slalom course. First try to turn around every chair's shadow. Then try turning around two chairs at a time while controlling your speed with good turn shape. Finally, try making two turns for every passing chair's shadow without accelerating, making sure to complete each turn for speed control.
3. You can judge your turns by following the tracks of a skier who makes well-shaped turns. Team up with a partner and have him make a series of turns of a specified size. Ski about one turn behind your partner and try to match his speed. Look to see if you follow his path all the way through the turn. If not, look to find the place where you get off the track. Focus your attention on that part of the turn.

## OTHER DRILLS

Here are some other drills that will help you improve turn shape and size.

### Dope Slope Slalom

This drill strengthens your ability to make smaller turns. On an extremely gentle slope,

There are infinite options for turn shape and size. Remember, round turns produce the most useful buildup of force for all-mountain skiing. SOUTH BOWL, MOUNT BAILEY SNOWCAT SKIING

compete with a friend to see who can make the most turns within a given distance. Because of the lack of steepness, you will need to rely on steering and exaggerated pressure control to make continuous small turns. Then try the same drill on steeper terrain and feel the way steepness generates enough force so you can make smaller turns more efficiently.

### Serpent Ski

This drill enhances your ability to vary turn shape smoothly, but the exercise is harder to perform than you might think. Imagine a snake shaped on the ground in a series of S-turns, with the biggest curves at the head's end and the smallest curves at the tip of the tail. Try skiing

this pattern. Start with enormous turns and make them progressively smaller until they are as small as you can make them. This is tricky, because bigger turns tend to generate more speed, which will become more difficult to control as your turns get smaller. This drill requires attention to turn shape, especially at the finish of the turn, so you can control your speed.

### U-Turns

This drill helps skiers who find they are continually speeding out of control. Ski straight down a wide run where other skiers are not nearby and begin making a turn. Then continue that turn and keep turning until you come to a complete stop. You may be facing back up the hill as if you skied a U-turn. Notice that you stopped. This is how finishing turns controls your speed. In the U-Turn drill you overfinish a turn and come to a stop. In normal turns, you do not turn that far. Instead, you slow down to a manageable speed.

### TROUBLESHOOTING TURN SIZE AND SHAPE

Being able to control the size of your turns depends on how well you use the tools of steering, edging, and pressuring your skis. If you have trouble making small turns and staying in control, you may want to strengthen these basic tools. Skiers rarely have trouble making large turns, but they may fear them because of the speeds they can generate. These skiers should remember that a good turn shape with enough of a finish phase will control speed—no matter how large the turn.

Modifying the shape of your turns should come easily. But if you find yourself making chronically erratic or jerky turns, there is a chance that your skis may be so poorly tuned that they are the culprit. If this is the case, pay special attention to the section on tuning in the chapter on skis.

# Using Your Poles

I have left the discussion on using your poles until the end of the Creating a Toolbox section because I want to de-emphasize the importance of poles in skiing. Most skiers rely too heavily on their poles, both for balance and for making turns. Skiers who use their poles as a type of crutch can develop other skill weaknesses.

Good pole use is important to an expert skier, primarily as a finishing touch. Think of effective pole use as an extension of all the good things you are already doing with the rest of your body. If your feet, legs, and center of mass do their jobs, then your hands, arms, and poles are likely to fall into place. Sometimes, however, a skier can use poles in ways that have a negative effect on his skiing. This is why I de-emphasize pole use: the less you do with them the better.

Pole use can be broken into two basic parts: the pole swing and the pole plant. These movements can help your timing, speed control, and transitions from one turn to the next. Before any of this can happen, you need to review the basics of hand position and how they relate to a sound stance.

*Natural* and *relaxed* are key words in hand positioning. Gone are the days of rigid, outstretched arms that made a skier look as if he were carrying a tray. Let your arms hang, shake them out until they are shoulder width apart (or a bit wider), and then relax. Swing them out in front of you to the point where you can see your hands with your peripheral vision. This ready position allows you to make smooth movements and have a good range of motion. Treat this as the neutral hand position you return to, just as you return to a tall, balanced stance between turns.

Even though I use pole plant as a universal term, the touch of your pole to the snow is not always crucial. Some situations demand a firm pole plant, and some call for a gentler pole plant. What is more important is the arm movement that leads up to the pole plant, which we call pole swing.

The pole swing is the movement of the arm and hand out of its neutral position. This is another one of those skiing heartbeats, because it happens every time you make a turn. The movement is subtle: a slight swing of your arm forward and up (the same arm motion you use when walking) and a small flexion of your wrist to flick the tip of the pole forward and out in front of you.

Your hand does not swing out to the left or to the right. It should swing directly forward. Learning to swing your pole straight forward now will help as you master angulation and counter-rotation, which I will discuss later.

As an expert skier makes smooth turns, her arms are continually moving. Each arm swings forward in time with each turn, as if she were walking. A skier's constant arm movement is like the movement of her feet: the feet steer and apply pressure to the skis continually without stopping or slowing to a fixed or stalled position.

Poles should be used quietly, enhancing good body movement patterns without detracting from other skills. Small movements of the arms and wrists are enough to put the pole tip where you want it.

How fast you swing your poles and how firmly you plant them depends on what kind of turn you make. Imagine that you are watching a videotape of a track star running. Focus on the runner's arm movements. Now run the imaginary video in slow motion. The runner's movement and his arms' range of motion are exactly the same in actual time and in slow motion. The arm movement in slow motion simply takes longer. This is exactly the way a pole swing changes when a skier goes from making small turns to large turns.

A large turn's pole swing can feel like a slow-motion move. Your arm swings the same distance it does in a small turn, but it swings over a longer period of time because the bigger turn takes longer to complete. The way your arm swings and the actual distance it moves are about the same in large and small turns. The size of the turn, however, dictates how long the pole swing takes.

Some skiers don't understand this, and they try to use a quick pole swing in larger turns.

This will work, but it produces a stop-and-go movement in the arms and in their turns. A smooth pole swing that keeps moving from the start to the finish of each turn allows you to maintain an effective flow of movement from one turn to the next without interruption.

At the end of the pole swing is the pole plant, when the tip of the pole makes contact with the snow. This touch of the pole to the snow helps you maintain a rhythmic cadence in your turns, gives you some kinesthetic feedback about the space around you, and can help you control speed and maintain a functional body position on steep terrain.

It is important to know which arm you should swing and plant with. This is simple to learn, but it still confuses some skiers. Here's one way to understand this: In a medium- to large-radius turn, the arm closer to the bottom of the hill is the swinging arm; in a medium- to small-radius turn, the arm on the same side as the outside ski is the swinging arm. These are simply two ways of saying the same thing. But one or the other is a better cue depending on what size turn you are making.

When making large turns, you generally are not concerned about reducing your speed in every turn. You let speed and energy flow from one turn into the next. Big turns are about going fast and generally are used on less-steep slopes. The pole swing matches the cadence of the large turn: it is long and drawn out, and the pole plant is very soft. In a large turn, you don't want to interrupt the flow of movement into the next turn, and the pole plant is therefore barely a tap on the snow. The placement of this pole touch in the large turn is also important: it occurs out in front, toward the next turn.

At the finish of a large-radius turn, the swinging arm (downhill arm) is still swinging. It reaches out toward the next turn as you transfer your weight to the new outside ski. This pole swing is an extension of your center of mass; as your center of mass crosses over your skis, your swinging arm goes with it. Pole swing and pole plant in larger turns are all about starting the

Watch the skier's left arm swing smoothly forward toward a pole touch at the transition between turns; then note how the right arm immediately begins its swing. Dragging pole tips can send the skier spatial information.

next turn. The arm's reaching movement enhances your crossover movement and makes the start of the next turn smoother.

The pole swing and pole plant must therefore blend in with what you are trying to accomplish in each turn. In large turns, the poles are used to redirect energy and aid in the flow of movement out of one turn and into the next. When you make small turns, you are trying to do something entirely different, and your pole use will be different.

The expert skier makes small turns because he wants to control his speed. He may be skiing a tight line, which won't allow for larger turns, or he may be on steep terrain. In small turns where speed control is the primary objective, he makes a more pronounced braking movement at the finish of each turn. This braking movement is characterized by a good turn finish,

where the skis are directed across the fall line and usually are accompanied by heavier edging. On a steep pitch, where this braking movement becomes more extreme, the skier's edging becomes more radical. This extreme edging movement is called an edge-set. The edge-set is like slamming the brakes on in your car. A good example of an edge-set is a hockey stop.

Pole swing and pole plant happen quickly in small turns. The arm swings forward at the start of the turn, and the pole is planted firmly just after the edge-set. As your braking movements become more dramatic, the pole plant becomes stronger and occurs more closely to the edge-set. The aggressive pole plant is used here as a brace that helps you slow down and regain control and balance before starting a new turn.

The tricky part about mastering pole use is that between the two extremes of very large and very small turns there are a million different-sized turns you can make. An expert skier matches the timing of his pole swing and the strength of his pole plant to the kind of turn he makes. Whether you employ the pole swing and pole plant you would use for a small turn or those you would use for a large turn is entirely up to you. There are as many different pole-swing and pole-plant combinations as there are turn sizes, and the only way to master how you blend poling with different turns is to practice. But once you master your technique in very large and very small turns, the rest will fall between those two extremes.

*You can feel*
### PROPER POLE SWINGS AND POLE PLANTS

1. Ski straight down a cat track. Don't think about your feet but feel how your arms and hands are hanging. Note how claustrophobic it feels (or should feel) to hold your arms pressed against your sides. Then note how awkward it feels to hold your arms wide, as

In short-radius turns, the pole is planted firmly just after maximum edging is achieved.

if you were hugging a redwood. Try to establish a comfortable position between these two extremes. Now begin swinging your poles. You can alternate them or swing them both at the same time. Feel the way your arm rotates at the shoulder and bends slightly at the elbow and feel the slight flick of the wrist that comes at the end of the pole swing.

2. Ski down a road or cat track as you did in the last exercise. Swing your poles alternately but vary your rhythm. Try swinging your arms smoothly and quickly, then swing them slowly. Approximate your timing for short turns and long turns. Feel the way your arms and hands move the same distance but at a faster or slower rate.

*You can see*
### EFFICIENT POLE USE

1. Make turns on gentle terrain. Watch your hands out of your peripheral vision to see if they disappear from sight after they return to their neutral position after a pole plant. If they disappear, concentrate on bringing your arms farther forward and out in front of you. This will make poling easier, help keep your stance centered over your skis, and aid in crossover movements. You can also watch for any sideways swing of your hands, which can throw off other body movements.

2. When you pole during short-radius turns, use peripheral vision to watch the spray from your skis. On very short, braking turns your pole plant will come at the same time as this spray of snow, or at the time of your edge-set. On turns not quite this small, your pole plant will occur just after the spray.

3. When you pole during large-radius turns, keep reaching with your pole swing until you stop seeing your ski boots beneath you and you see only snow and the bottom of the hill. Then gently begin a soft pole plant. The

disappearance of your ski boots indicates that your body mass has crossed over into the next turn and your pole swing's job has been accomplished. Touch your pole tip to the snow and start your next pole swing.

## OTHER DRILLS

Other drills that can help you maximize the use of your poles follow.

### Zipper Lines

This drill minimizes a tendency to swing your arm across your chest and toward your other arm when you are poling. Imagine that the zipper on your coat marks a force field that separates one arm from the other. Your pole swing should move out from your body, not across it. Cross-body pole swings can contribute to an over-rotated upper body, which can have a negative effect on your edging skills.

### Floaters

This drill focuses on pole use in large-radius turns. Make large, fairly fast turns and swing your outside hand all the way through the finish of the turn. Keep swinging that arm toward the next turn until that turn is started, but don't plant your pole. Then begin with the next arm. You should feel as if you are floating into the next turn and your arm is helping your body fall across your skis and into the next turn.

### Settle

This drill helps fine-tune your pole plant timing in smaller turns. It's important here to feel how your body flexes to absorb pressure during small turns and how your body bends laterally at the hips and flexes at the knees and ankles to create edge angles. This flexing produces an overall shortening of your body, which can

be described as *settling*. In small turns, you reach the bottom of your flexion at the finish of each turn, near the time of edge-set; your pole plant happens at this same time. Make several turns and focus on each turn's settling phase. Chant to yourself, "settle, settle, settle . . . " at the finish of each turn. Your pole plant should happen at the same time as the word—as if the settling motion itself was driving the pole's tip into the snow.

### Clone Poling

This is not the cow-tipping equivalent for genetics nerds. In this drill you simply follow a master pole-user and mimic his movements. Pole use is easier when you have a solid tools foundation and some understanding of pole function. You will master the skill only with practice. The best practice is done properly, and the only way to ensure you're doing it properly is to copy an accomplished skier. Try turning when, not where, your clone turns, so you can tune into the timing aspect of his pole use.

## TROUBLESHOOTING POLE USE

Improper pole use is not usually a problem all by itself. Generally, inefficient poling is caused by an underlying problem that involves a more basic skiing tool. Many instructors fail to look beyond a problem with poling because the poles are so easily noticed—like red flags that both reveal and conceal the real issue. The problem is diagnosing the root of the trouble, because it could be any number of things.

My best advice for skiers who have difficulty using poles is to wait: wait for a more basic problem to show up and then tackle that issue and see what happens to your pole use.

One way to accelerate this process is to ski without poles and note if any movements feel strange. Does it feel funny to start or finish turns? Can you steer easily? Is it difficult to adequately pressure your skis? Try to imagine what you might be doing with your poles to compensate for any trouble you are having. If you can fix the underlying problem without using your poles as aids, then your pole problems may fade away when you review the basics of this chapter.

On the brighter side, there is a chance that the only problem is the length of your poles. Too-long or too-short poles can have a negative effect. If you think this may be the case, look at the short chapter on poles in You *Can* Blame It on Your Gear! Sometimes.

# PART III
# You CAN Blame It on Your Gear! Sometimes

Skiers are inextricably bound to their equipment. The use of skis, boots, and poles is part of the poetry of skiing: the blend of the natural environment with athletic skill and human-made tools. Sports equipment has become a cultural talisman for the modern athlete, evidenced by the saying, "Whoever who dies with the most toys wins!" While most of us recognize that saying as a tongue-in-cheek expression, there is some truth to our dependence on high-tech equipment for supreme sports satisfaction.

Accept this fact: Quality ski equipment that suits your size and needs will help you become an expert skier at a faster rate. However, quality equipment is of no benefit if it is not properly prepared and maintained.

Back in the old days, if it didn't turn, you just kept it up in the air. MIKE O'SHEA
HIGH ABOVE THE CORKSCREW, MT. BACHELOR

If boots and skis are to us what wings are in dreams, then it's no wonder that large companies spend so much time and energy developing and selling ski equipment. For a skier, skis and boots are the magical tools that grant us access to a special world. Without them, we are earthbound.

Now, more than ever, ski equipment figures hugely into how well people can ski. In the past several years, the sport of skiing has seen significant changes in ski design, and both boots and bindings have benefited from the technological trickle-down. This gear improvement boom has opened the doors to aspiring athletes who wish to gain a mechanical edge over their previous levels of performance on the hill. The new stuff simply skis better, and skiers who es-

chew trying new equipment out of an old-school, purist mind-set will simply limit their performance, period.

In a sport as gear-dependent as skiing, dysfunctional equipment can ruin your chances to excel. This is much more crippling than any single bad habit. Bad equipment will affect everything you do in skiing. Every serious skier comes to a point in his skill development when he will ask: "Is it me, or is it my gear?"

Most of us suffer from a combination of skill limitations and the limitations of our gear. But what if your skill limitations were magnified, or even created, by poorly purchased, poorly manipulated, and poorly maintained equipment? Many of my students who displayed bad habits and ineffective technique did so because

If better gear gives us better wings, no wonder helmet sales are up. GREG RUBIN IN SURFER BOWL, MT. BACHELOR

they were forced to compensate for problems with their equipment.

The relationship between the skier and her gear is an experimental dynamic: change one thing and it can affect a half-dozen other things. Perfecting the skier-equipment dynamic is like tinkering with a hot rod. It takes time and practice to get it right. But when it works, the experience is so pleasurable that twice the amount of time and hassle would have been worth it.

This is the true artistry of the gear geek. Skis come from the manufacturer ready for use by the average skier; how many of us fit that mold? You will probably need to customize your equipment to match your body type, your skiing style, and your goals.

Getting your gear dialed is an experiment, but it should be a controlled one. Try not to change more than one variable at a time. When adjusting your ski boots, avoid making massive changes to every knob and screw. Instead, make one major change at a time and determine the result of that change.

When I finally made some minor but necessary adjustments to my gear, I began skiing the way I wanted to. Working out my equipment problems allowed me to start making turns where and when I wanted to, in any type of snow condition. I didn't go out and purchase wonder-gear: I discovered what it was about my equipment that was holding me back.

Your gear experimentation is also a process of eliminating excuses. If you address every aspect of your equipment, you can then be sure that any problems you experience with your skiing performance are directly related to your own skill level. This is a rare situation to be in, and this state enhances your learning by intensifying its focus: the responsibility for improving is yours alone.

This section is about being able to make informed purchases of ski equipment that are appropriate for the way you ski—and for the way you want to ski. More importantly, this section is about how to prepare, maintain, and manipulate your equipment to make it work the way you need it to.

The only way to ensure that you can't blame your skiing performance on your gear is to go through this section, item by item, and attack each possible gear problem that you come to.

Don't give up. Glory awaits.

# Skis

In recent years I have taught skiing, guided skiers in the backcountry, tested ski equipment for *Ski* and *Skiing* magazines, and worked in a ski shop, which has given me an opportunity to ski a lot of different skis, in a lot of different conditions. And while skis have changed dramatically over the past several years, I am still convinced that brand doesn't matter that much. We all have favorite brands, and some manufacturers may produce more good skis than others, but that doesn't change the fact that there are great all-mountain skis available from just about every maker out there.

With that said, how does one go about finding that perfect ski? It helps to know a few essentials, and a little bit of the new history on ski design.

First, it has evolved away from the *straight*, or *traditional*, ski in favor of what's currently being called the *shaped* ski. But I say currently with good reason, for design trends will always remain in flux regarding skis. New ideas about ski equipment are making it onto the ski shop floor every couple seasons, so it's wise not to talk about current models but rather to understand design trends that have been proven effective and will be around for the long term.

For example, the first generation of new-school skis were referred to as *parabolics*, but that terminology has already faded from cool ski vernacular. So remember that it's not so much the jargon of the day that's important as the actual design changes that have come to

pass. These changes are not mere fickle shifts in fashion but real improvements—evolution, if you will—and even though the names will change down the road, again, these core design elements will remain relevant to modern skis.

Given that, go back a few years to the straight ski and recall that snowboarding was really starting to take off. We have to pay respects to the boarders (and snowboard designers)—and especially to the alpine race snowboarders with their hard-plate bindings—for tipping off ski manufacturers to what could be done on snow. I can remember watching from the chairlift as good snowboarders carved pure, tight arcs below, drawing clean circular lines in the snow with little effort and no skid. Their secret was more shape, and it came to the boarders first because their boards were wider than our skis. Snowboard designers had more material to play with, and shape and width are now the keys to modern all-mountain skiing. Thanks, jibbers.

## THE ESSENTIALS OF FINDING THE PERFECT SKI FOR YOU

The process of finding the best ski for your needs as a skier has changed, but it really has become easier. In the past our choices were GS, slalom, or mogul skis (or perhaps some kind of blend of those). These skis were designed around an event that involved big turns, short turns, or bumps, respectively. We had to guess whether one or the other might best suit our personal kind of skiing. This was tough to do, especially if the salesperson hadn't had a chance to demo all the models offered at the shop.

Now skis are designed around how and—more importantly—*where* a skier will use the ski. The design elements of shape and width have changed our ski menu a bit, to the point that it's pretty easy to find a great ski if you know what you want to do with your ski and can find a good ski shop with smart salespeople.

The types of skis out there now are more defined. There are skis designed for carving turns on firm, smooth surfaces, aptly called *carving skis*. There are really wide skis that offer lots of surface area for flotation in powder and softer snow called, not surprisingly, *fat skis*. There are skis that fall into the middle ground between these first two types and are pretty good both on groomed slopes and out in the junk; these in-between skis are called *mid-fats*, or *all-mountain* skis. Within each category, a manufacturer will offer several versions that will be geared toward different ability levels and body weights.

There are still specialized skis out there. There are still race skis that are designed around the needs of a particular event. Mogul skis are available for the specific job of hammering down through bumps. Twin-tip skis are the call for half-pipe and terrain-park specialists who employ backward, or *switch*, takeoffs and landings.

Often, some design elements from specialty skis will find their way into other types of skis. For example, many manufacturers are experimenting with adding the turned-up tail of the twin-tip ski to other skis in their line, giving rise to hybrids like the *twin-fat*. You get the picture. There will always be some crossover between categories and blurring of the boundaries, and this is good. But for an understanding of our current ski menu, go with the simple road map provided above.

So which ski will work best for you? Well, get one pair of each if you can't decide and if money is no object. Owning a couple pairs of skis would be nice—say, a ski for hard snow days

and a pair for powder and crud. Yet most of us can't afford that kind of quiver, so we search for the perfect ski—the all-conditions tool that does everything perfectly. Well, you *can* find that ski, but you need to know yourself and perhaps be willing to compromise a little bit.

## Knowing Yourself and Skis

If you're not planning to try different skis before buying them, you'll be relying on a salesperson at a ski shop as your primary source of information (see Ski Demos and Alternative Information Sources on pages 74–76). If you've got a sharp salesperson, you will still need to know your skiing-self. Why? A good salesperson is going to try to find you the perfect match for the way you ski and where you ski, because if you're happy with his recommendation, it's likely that you'll be back to spend more money. And this may be cash in his pocket, if the shop offers a sales commission.

Different skis for different jobs. Know what you want them to do. MT. BACHELOR SKI AND SPORT

A good ski salesperson tries to get a picture in her head of where and how a customer likes to ski, so be able to answer her questions with specifics. When I'm helping a ski-buying customer, I ask a few basic questions: Are they looking for a ski that sticks to groomed trails, or goes everywhere on the mountain? What percentage of the time do they spend skiing groomers versus skiing off-piste? Are they expert, intermediate, or somewhere in between? Have they tried any skis recently that they either liked or hated, and why?

The answers to these questions will help narrow down the options for the buyer. Typically, skiers looking for a ski that goes everywhere on the mountain will end up with a mid-fat of some kind. But if the skier is the kind of athlete who wants all-mountain performance yet in reality spends 80 percent of her time carving on groomed trails, then a salesperson may consider the "carvier" end of the mid-fat spectrum. Conversely, some mid-fats are predisposed to superior powder and crud skiing, but they suffer on hardpack, and some skiers would rather sacrifice performance on ice because they'll be inside having a beer if it's that hard. Make sure you know the answers to these kinds of questions before you go to the shop.

There are lots of good skis out there, but they all have their own flavor, or performance characteristics, that will make the difference between a good ski and that perfect match for the skier. A good salesperson may have skied all the skis on the wall and be able to attest to how they ski. I'll go so far as to try to find out *how* a customer skis. Do they have a tall, tight-footed stance, or a wider, more angulated one? Do they tend toward a large- or small-radius turn? How do they ski powder, with small bounding turns or with wide sweeping ones? Do they want to ski in the trees or stay in wide-open spaces?

Knowing yourself will help a salesperson identify the best choices for you. And if he or she is good, the salesperson will also tell you where you may find the ski lacking. Often, knowing the weak point of a ski is a great bit of information if it happens to be the one kind of skiing you hate to do.

I used to be pretty down on ski shop salespeople, and now I am one myself. Oh well; I suppose it's karma. I've come to understand that there are truly inspired ski shop technicians and salespeople, some pretty uninformed ones, and some downright rude and condescending ones. Find a shop with the staff of the first sort and reward them with your purchases—even if you could save a few bucks down at the discount sports store.

## SKI DESIGN ESSENTIALS

You don't need to be a mechanical engineer to know something about how a ski is designed. It's really pretty basic stuff, and having a handle on how changes in a ski's design will affect how it feels on snow will help you in your quest to find a great ski. It may also help you explain why some other skis you've tried in the past didn't turn your crank.

### Shape

Shape is a funny term to make such a big deal of. Skis are still the same basic shape: they're long and sort of skinny, with a slippery bottom and a front and back. What's the big deal?

In fact, shape is nothing new. It's just a new word for *sidecut*, or the hourglass-like shape you notice when sighting down the length of the ski's base. Our old traditional, or straight, skis weren't really straight. They had sidecut, or shape—just not very much of it. New skis employ more sidecut, so they are considered to have more shape, and hence the name: *shaped* ski. They were called hourglass skis and parabolic skis at their inception for the same reason: they had more sidecut.

The big deal about more shape is that the curved edge running along a ski from the tip to the tail is, more or less, an arc segment. Do you remember that term from high school geometry?

An arc segment is just a chunk of a circle, and in the case of the shaped ski, that arc segment is stuck onto the side of a ski. When you tip a shaped ski onto its edge, the edge engages the snow and the ski begins to follow the path defined by the arc segment built into the ski. When people talk about *turn radius*, they are speaking of the theoretical circle that the ski designer stole the ski's shape from. In the days of straight skis, the circle was huge. Now it's smaller.

It's worth mentioning *how* a ski designer gets more shape, and there are two ways. One is to make the ski's waist narrower; the other is to make the tip and tail wider. Since traditional skis were already narrow-waisted, tips and tails got wider. This has mainly had a good effect on skiing (more on this in the section on width).

But more shape is not always better. The first generation of shaped skis, the parabolics, were radically shaped and made poor all-mountain skis for a couple reasons. First, dramatic sidecut profiles can produce a ski that tends to "lock" onto a carved turn whose turn size is not easily varied. This makes for fun carving on groomed slopes, but it can be a drag in off-piste conditions, where changing turn size and being able to occasionally skid a turn is important.

The parabolic ski's tip and tail were also very wide, and the waist of the ski was as narrow as ever. In soft snow, such as untracked powder, the wide tip and tail would float more than the narrow waist would. During a turn, this allowed for too much ski flex and produced an over-turning ski that tended to whip through the turn too quickly and essentially trip up a skier.

The amount of shape still matters with modern skis. Carving skis designed to stay on smooth, firm surfaces will incorporate more shape and narrower waists. All-mountain skis—such as mid-fats and fat skis—will tend to offer a little less shape and wider waists, to conserve even flexing in deep snow. All-mountain skis with radical shape will often excel in carving

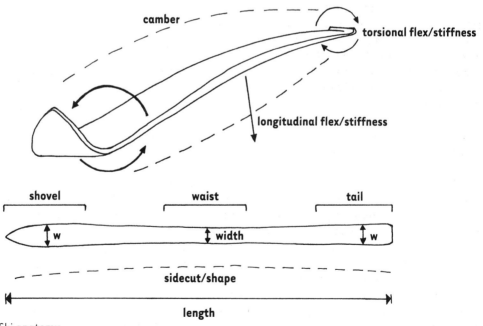

Ski anatomy.

applications and suffer a bit in powder. Straighter mid-fats rule in crud and powder, but they can lack performance for carving.

As a rule of thumb, skiers who utilize a tall, tight-footed stance and don't roll the ski onto a steep edge (this is an old-school style) do not typically like radically shaped skis; these skis tend to engage turns more aggressively than expected and they feel unpredictable when flat. These skiers often prefer less dramatic sidecut. However, skiers who have adopted a wider stance and can achieve more aggressive edge angles tend to appreciate the tighter radius carved turns that come with highly shaped designs.

Skiers new to shaped skis need to realize that the new ski designs are built to turn. When the edge is engaged, they turn. Period. So these skis are made to be kept on edge and not run flat. Skiers can't expect to be able to stand tall with their skis flat and cruise at speed to the bottom of the chair without a bit of instability. To them, the shaped skis will often feel squirrelly; remember, they want to turn. Keep them on edge, even just a bit, by following a snaking path—a little left, a little right—instead of going straight as an arrow.

## Width

Fooling around with a ski's width was never really a consideration—except in fat skis—until the shape boom struck. Once designers started increasing shape by widening the ski's tip and tail, the door was thrown wide open for big changes in skis. The key was surface area. Not only did the wider tip and tail increase sidecut and allow for easier, more athletic carved turns: the increased width also pumped up the overall surface area of the ski.

Extra surface area made for instant improvement in softer snow, as long as the ski didn't have too extreme a shape, as mentioned above. The fact that a ski with more surface area would float better in powder and soft crud was nothing new: all-mountain skiers had been getting more

Wider is better in softer snow. MARK ELLING ON COW'S FACE, MT. BACHELOR

surface area for years just for that reason, except they were doing it with added length. Now, skiers who used to ride on 205 cm skis could achieve that same amount of surface area (or more) at drastically shorter lengths. (We'll discuss this more in the upcoming section on length.)

Currently, widths define different types of skis. Carving skis are the narrowest. The powder and crud specialists—the fat skis—are the widest. Mid-fats occupy the in-between widths. This has made finding an all-mountain ski easier for skiers because they can actually see the difference from one ski to the next.

Different widths have also opened up a new dimension in powder skiing (see the Powder chapter in Getting Tough: Advanced Situations)—and it's a vertical component. Wider skis float higher on soft snow; narrow skis sink deeper. Depending on how a skier wishes to ski in powder, he or she can select a certain width ski.

Old-school powder hounds who are used to skiing fast to generate planing speeds for flotation, and who rely on deep diving moves in the snow to help control their speed, may not like full-blown fat skis. They are hard to push down deep into the powder and tend to jump up to the surface and begin to plane at much slower speeds.

However, skiers who never had much success in the deep stuff will probably love the wider skis in powder. Their buoyancy factor floats the skis right to the surface where a skier can cruise—almost as if she were skiing on groomed snow.

A whole new kind of all-mountain style has been born with the greater width skis. Many skiers are "surfing" the powder with a fast skiing style that incorporates big turns and slashing transitions; this was virtually impossible with skinny skis for most of us. The increased width, which offers new stability at speed in powder, has made this possible. Now skiers can feel what snowboarders have been crowing about for years.

## Length

Just about every skier out there knows by now that skis have gotten shorter. Big guys over 220 pounds who used to cruise on 207 cm traditional skis are out ripping around on shaped skis ranging anywhere from 190 cm, on the long end of the spectrum, down to 155 cm for a slalom racing ski.

Length used to be an important part of graduating to expert-level skiing, and there were some psychological factors at work there too. The longer the ski, the better you were: that was the thinking back in those days. To have some-body suggest that we might like a shorter ski was insulting. Back then, my answer was, "Short skis suck."

Well, times have changed and so have skis, and it helps to understand why skis have gotten shorter. When shape increased so did width, and with increased width came increased mass. Suddenly, with the added width, 190 cm skis could feel like 220 cm downhill boards. To make a wider ski feel right, it simply had to be shortened. Technology has also improved, and core designs and materials for ski production have gotten better. Specifically, new materials and construction can make skis more torsionally rigid without increasing their longitudinal stiffness. This makes skis feel more stable at high speeds and on hard snow without feeling unwieldy (see also Stiffness, below). It used to be that to get stability on hard snow at high speed, one needed to go long. Now skis are stable at extremely short lengths.

So how do you choose the right length in today's market? It pays to know a few basics and to be able to trust your demo technician or salesperson.

Skis are being built for a particular application and with a range of skier weights and ability levels in mind. For example, carving skis are built to operate on a firm surface where flotation (which is a function of surface area) isn't important. Mid-fats are built to operate everywhere on the hill, including powder. Carving skis will come in shorter lengths than the mid-fats, because they don't need the surface area for skiing on soft snow. It's pretty common to see the longest length available in a mid-fat running around 190 cm, while the same manufacturer's carving ski may top out at 180 cm.

Skiers should realize that designers are building skis to suit a person of a particular weight. That 190 cm mid-fat is built to handle a skier who is 6 feet, 4 inches tall and weighs 250 pounds, as well as the super-aggressive skier who goes 50 mph and drops 40-footers on a daily basis. You may not fit that bill. Even though you used to ski 205s, you might be happiest on a 184 cm ski now. Have an open mind and listen to your technician or salesperson.

The basic rule still applies: The length that falls between the ski that feels too long and the ski that feels to short is just right. Simple, huh? Remember, a too-long ski doesn't like to make your short turn and only seems to work well if you ski fast. A too-short ski feels overly pivotal and feels unstable at higher speeds. Find the happy medium.

### Why Should You Go Short?

Why not?, is usually my first answer to this question. Shorter skis are easier to steer because of the reduced swing weight, which comes from not having as much ski hanging out at the tip and the tail. Shorter skis carve better at slower speeds because the skier's weight is distributed over a reduced edge-contact length: more pounds per inch along the edge equals more edge grip. And shorter skis are proportionately lighter, which makes for less fatigue at the end of the day.

Short skis are now extremely stable, as long as they're on edge. Olympic and World Cup slalom specialists—who are not small people—are skiing 155 cm skis! So, stability and power are obviously not compromised at shorter lengths.

My advice is to go as short as you can for the kind of skiing you're going to do. Taking the kind of skiing you plan to do into account is important: your particular skiing application may require more length, so be sure to discuss your needs with the technician or salesperson (see also Why Shouldn't You Go Short? opposite).

Be aware that skis are made with varying degrees of stiffness to accommodate skiers of varying ability levels and weights. Big guys or gals

Shorter, narrower skis are best for carving hard snow. CHRIS SMITH IN THE CORKSCREW, MT. BACHELOR

can go short, but they need to be careful not to get too soft a ski in a short length. A ski still needs to support the skier's weight to feel stable (see more on this in the section on stiffness, below).

### Why Shouldn't You Go Short?

There are a few reasons to go long. If a skier wants a ski to float a little better in powder and crud, she needs to conserve surface area. The fatter the ski, the shorter she can go to maintain workable surface area. Narrow skis make up for that loss in surface area with added length.

For example, in order to get the same feel of flotation in powder with Rossignol's current all-mountain line, I could ski the Bandit XXX (fat ski) in a 178 cm; the Bandit XX (mid-fat) in a 184 cm; or the Bandit X (narrow all-mountain) in a 191 cm.

If your favorite ski happens to be a narrow one, but you want to use it in powder, be sure to go with a length on the longer end of the ski's recommended length range for your weight and ability. If you love that ski on the groomed slopes, great; that might be your ski. If it feels too long for enjoyable cruising and bump skiing, then go shorter and live with the ski's lack of surface area in powder. It's still got tons more surface area than your old skis probably did.

For skiers who like to rip through variable snow conditions (tracked-up powder, chunky crud), a ski that's too short can fail to provide enough of a fore-aft platform for aggressive skiing. Variable snow can offer a bumpy, stop-and-go surface that tends to pitch a skier forward and backward. A little extra length will smooth out that bumpy ride and allow the skier to remain centered. Short skis are workable in this kind of environment but will give you much less margin for error.

For skiers who are super aggressive and ski extremely fast in all-mountain conditions, a longer ski is still the ticket. But these skiers will lose performance on the mellow end of things.

For example, a 190 cm mid-fat may be designed for a big dude over 200 pounds; but Harry the Hucker likes to go big—even though he only weighs 165 pounds. Harry's going to

like this ski when he's in softer snow and when he's skiing at mach speed: he can bend the ski well if the snow is soft, or if he generates extra centrifugal force against the ski by traveling at high speeds. But when Harry slows down or tries to make a crisp, short turn on hard snow, the ski may feel a bit long and unwieldy. But for this kind of skier, losing performance here is often worth the advantage of using a longer ski at high speeds in crummy snow.

### Stiffness

A ski's stiffness is a hard thing to see, because stiffness is a product of how the ski is constructed. Its inner core and outer shell, or laminate structure, are what determine how stiff or soft-flexing a ski will be.

It's good to understand that there are two types of stiffness: longitudinal and torsional.

*Longitudinal* stiffness is how rigid or soft-flexing the ski is under the downward pressure of the skier. Imagine suspending the ski between two moguls—one holding the tip, the other holding the tail—so the middle of the ski is completely off the snow. The ski that's stiffer longitudinally would better support the skier's weight; the longitudinally soft ski would bend more so the waist might almost touch the snow between the moguls.

*Torsional* stiffness is a measure of how resistant to twisting a ski is. For example, if you held a ski's tail firmly between your feet and grabbed the tip with two hands, you could twist the ski. A more torsionally rigid ski wouldn't twist at all, and a ski that was softer torsionally would twist a fair bit.

It used to be the case that ski manufacturers manipulated longitudinal stiffness to make a ski either more stable at speed or more forgiving for easy cruising. Stiff skis were stable; soft skis were easygoing. But the stiff ski wasn't user friendly and the soft ski wasn't stable at speed.

Now ski designers have found that stability is more a matter of how torsionally stiff the ski is. If a ski resists twisting when it's on edge, it will feel stable and smooth. This has been a good development for skiers. A ski can be built to have softer longitudinal flex, which makes a ski easier to bend and more forgiving, yet retain good torsional rigidity, so the ski stays stable on harder snows and at higher speeds.

When a salesperson or demo technician explains that two skis may have exactly the same shape but that one is considered an expert-level ski while the other is more geared toward intermediate through advanced skiers, she's indicating that there's a difference in construction and stiffness in the ski. While all skis are softer in longitudinal flex than they used to be, the rule still applies: The stiffer ski handles high speeds better; the softer ski is more forgiving.

This matter of different degrees of stiffness can be a little tricky, and here's why. The expert will like the stiffer ski because it remains stable at high speeds. The intermediate would not like that same ski because he isn't used to traveling fast enough to generate the force needed to work the stiffer ski. Typically, the expert would not like the intermediate model with softer flex because it will overbend and feel a little noodle-like to him.

However, what if that intermediate skier was packing a few extra pounds? He might prefer the expert-level ski because its stiffer construction would support his weight better than the softer intermediate ski could. Likewise, if the expert skier was lighter than average, he or she may prefer going to a little softer ski and fully enjoy a ski that was designed for intermediate to advanced skiers.

It helps to have a salesperson or demo technician that understands this. You can simply ask the shop employee how a skier might decide between the expert and advanced level skis. If the salesperson fails to address the skier's weight in addition to ability level, politely seek help from somebody else.

### Ski Viagra

The general rule on ski length is, the longer the ski, the stiffer it feels to the skier. If a skier goes to a ski that's too short, that ski will not be stiff enough longitudinally to support his weight. The skier will essentially squash the too-short ski so it is overly bent, which allows the tip and tail to start losing full contact with the snow.

In the quest to make shorter skis work better for bigger skiers, ski designers have found ways to beef up or stiffen even the shortest of skis. Usually these short, stiff skis employ some kind of plate or thicker construction in the mid-body and are designed for use on firm, smooth snow. This provides the extra rigidity that other skis of the same length would lack.

Skiers should realize that this kind of "souped-up" ski is designed to be skied in shorter-than-normal lengths; to ride such a ski in your regular length would make things tough on yourself. Likewise, if you use this kind of ski, don't expect your buddies of equal weight and ability to go that short unless they're also using a stiffened model.

## SKI DEMOS AND ALTERNATIVE INFORMATION SOURCES

The basic idea behind demo programs is to "try before you buy." Demo centers offer many different brands and models of skis for skiers to rent (or "demo") for a fee that's usually higher than a regular rental. These models are most often new skis that the shop has for sale. Many demo programs offer the ability to apply one or more days' demo fees toward a purchase, so you're really not out a dime if you're interested in buying skis and don't mind purchasing them from that particular shop. Making use of demo shops is also a good way to get some decent skis if you're traveling and haven't brought your own skis (remember to bring your own boots, though).

Working in a ski demo shop has really driven home the value and risk of having a chance to ski on a pair of skis before you buy them. The value is obvious: you get to see if you like the way the skis feel on snow. The risk is less obvious, and it comes down to both tune and selection. If you demo a great ski that is either badly in need of a fresh tune or has been tuned improperly, you will not like it, no ifs, ands, or buts; unfortunately, this is a variable that is out of your control. Likewise, if you are unable to try a ski of your choice in the proper length, you won't have a real feel for how that ski at the right length might have performed for you.

However, if the demo shop maintains its skis well and offers decent selection, a demo program is a great way to go. I recommend compiling a long list of potential skis with the help of salespeople and other sources (below) before dropping in on a demo shop. They won't have all of them; but if they have at least one, that's a start. Once you've tried that ski, you can return it and give the demo technician some feedback on how you liked or disliked it. She should be able to give you another ski to try. It may not be on your list but it may be the perfect ski for you, so give it a shot.

Midweek, nonholiday times during the early season are the best times to demo. The gear selection is good, the competition for skis is low, and retail stock is better before the Christmas holiday. It's a drag to find your perfect ski and then be unable to apply your demo fee toward its purchase because the ski in your length is already sold out.

## Some Ski Demo Tactics

If you're really serious about using a demo program to help you find a great ski, treat your time on those demos like a true ski test.

After warming up for the day, take three or four runs on each pair of skis and search out a wide variety of terrain on those runs. Make big turns, make little turns; ski fast, ski slow. Try all your tricks. Use the same, or similar, runs for each ski you try, and don't test any more models once you're tired. Just ski the rest of the day on something for fun. Some people say they wouldn't be able to tell the difference between one ski and another. That's just not true. A skier

may not be able to articulate what she liked or didn't like very clearly, but everybody has an opinion and every demo customer finishes the day with a favorite.

Try to reserve at least the first ski you're going to try for the day with a demo technician prior to your arrival. Once you're there, see if you can't finagle a reservation on the second pair of skis on your list. This is pretty uncommon, so prepare to get shut down; but it's worth trying. Remember these magic words whenever you don't get the answer you want: "Would it be any different if I brought a six-pack of beer with me?" You'll be amazed at the wonders this will work, but don't ever welsh on a beer promise: that brings very bad luck.

Always ask the demo technician how close to the ski's center your boot's center mark is when he sets the demo bindings. Unless you're trying to change your fore-aft balance for some specific reason, you'll want the boot's center mark to align with the ski's center mark. Some technicians can "forget" to get you right on, so it doesn't hurt to check that you're centered.

Once you've narrowed your search to a final ski, try it in another length if you can. Usually skiers can choose from two or even three length options in a given ski model. One may feel too long; the other may feel too short; and one's usually just right, so it's nice to know you've got that one.

## Magazine Buyer's Guides

Every season ski periodicals produce consumer guides to the new crop of skis, boots, and bindings that have become available. These issues are big sellers for the magazines because skiers want good information to help guide their purchases, because skis certainly aren't cheap anymore! There are pros and cons to these ski magazine guides, and I should know: I've both written for them and have worked as a tester.

The real benefit of the buyer's guides is the information gathered from on-snow testing: readers can see what different testers thought of different skis. Magazines that actually put together a diverse group of testers who get on the skis to see how they do are the ones worth looking at. *Skiing, Ski,* and *Ski Press* magazines do a good job of conducting actual ski tests to generate the data for their reports. Other magazines fudge on this to save money, and they simply publish rewritten versions of what manufacturers say the skis will do. In my opinion, this is not as helpful to the consumer.

The problem with the buyer's guide concept is twofold: space and advertising. There isn't enough space in the magazine to give accurate reporting on every ski they tested, so editors have to cut the reviews short, and choose not to review certain skis in the manufacturer's line. The magazines also make their money on advertising dollars, and ski manufacturers spend a lot of money on ads with the magazines throughout the year. Even though editors do the best job they can to be objective, there is a certain amount of pressure to refrain from slamming any manufacturer's product. Haven't you noticed that just about every ski gets a medal?

Using the ski magazine guides as one of your sources of information to help you in your purchase is a good idea. They are not gospel, and they have some inherent flaws. But this is a good way to get a general idea of which skis may suit your needs.

Along the same lines, you can also seek out skiing Web sites that offer similar product information and sometimes offer test data (for sources, see the appendix).

## BASIC FACTS ABOUT TUNING

No ski will do what it is supposed to do unless it is tuned properly (and tuned on a regular basis during the ski season). This means that a brand-new but poorly tuned pair of top-of-the-line boards often will not perform as well as a well-tuned pair of rental skis. The new skis have more performance potential than the rentals, but their potential is compromised by poor tuning, while the performance of the well-tuned rentals has been maximized.

The issue of ski tuning, however, is sometimes regarded with disdain. When I discuss tuning with other instructors, I find many of them rarely bother to maintain the tune of their skis, either on their own or with the help of a shop. They claim it takes too much time and makes little difference. Many students of mine have never had their skis tuned since the day they purchased them. It is difficult to persuade them to learn to tune their own skis, much less to pay a professional to do them; these skiers have never experienced how much better a ski can perform after it has been tuned well.

Tuning your skis is a lot cheaper than buying new ones, and a good tune can work wonders for your skiing. If your skis are currently in bad shape, a good tune might solve problems in every aspect of your skiing.

Learning to tune your own skis can be fun, if you have the time and desire for a hobby that not only improves your skiing but saves you money in the long run—and gives you an opportunity to swill beer and breathe toxic fumes. Learning to tune skis well takes practice and patience, and preferably a pair of rock-boards to start experimenting on, but it's worth doing. An older but still relevant self-help guide is *Alpine Ski Maintenance and Repair Handbook* by Seth Masia (Contemporary Books), or find the new bible by Michael Howden called *World Class Tuning* (available at www.skitools.com). Another good tuning resource is the Tognar (pronounced "tone-ar") Toolworks catalog, which is packed annually with good deals on tools, videos, books on ski tuning, as well as lots of tricks and advice (see the appendix at the end of this book for more information).

There are ways to get around having to tune your own skis. You can pay a ski shop to do a full tune on them. A full tune usually includes a base grind with either a belt sander and/or a stone grinder; an edge tune, which should include edge deburring, edge beveling, and sharpening; and a hot wax. This option is pricey but worth the money if the shop technician is good. Ask local instructors and coaches who they would recommend. You can also ask the shop to do a less involved tune—at a less involved price—and use your local shop for the majority of the work and add the finishing touches yourself. For example, I'll often have a shop perform a light belt sanding and a stone grind, and then I'll do the edge tuning and hot waxing myself.

Whether you do all the work yourself, have the shop do it all, or find a workable arrangement somewhere in between, you will need to know what you want done to your skis. Even if your bias is to stay away from files and wax, read the following tuning information so you can be part of the tuning process. You can compare tuning to working on your own car: we all know what happens when we give a mechanic carte blanche.

## Base Profile

Base profile is one of the most important elements of a well-tuned ski, but it is by far one of the most overlooked. The base profile is the shape, or topography, of a ski's base and edges in relation to each other. Sight down the underside of a ski and use a true bar or roll pin (a straightedge) to examine the flatness of the ski's bottom. Note how the base material relates to the metal edge attached to it. This is the base profile.

We are looking to see if the bottom of the ski is flat, base-high, edge-high, or a combination of these conditions. A perfectly flat ski with both edge and base at the same level is the ideal foun-

If your skis are tuned badly, it's no fun keeping them on snow. Here's a nice base profile. BEN FERGUSON IN DEAD WOOD BOWL, MT. BACHELOR

dation on which we will add other helpful ingredients. Anything other than flat will require some attention. Note that with both terms, *base-high* and *edge-high,* I am referring to an upside-down ski (like one on a tuning bench).

## Base-High

A ski that is base-high means that the actual sliding surface of the ski, the base, protrudes into the snow farther than the edges do. This is very common and can be caused by seasonal storage, poor tuning, or chronic edge wear without frequent maintenance. Regardless of the cause, a ski that has become base-high has become unstable and difficult to control. Because the ski's edges are recessed below the level of the base material, they don't contact the snow when the ski is flat. This condition can be likened to a car whose tires are overinflated.

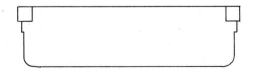

The base profile: bottom surfaces of base material and edge material are flush.

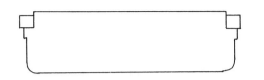

This ski is base-high.

### *Curing the Base-High Ski*

You need to take the level of the base down so your edges and base contact the snow at the same time. You can do this yourself with an aggressive scraping tool like a 4 mm steel scraper or base planer, but it's not very much fun and it can take a long time. A better idea is to take your skis to a local shop and have them grind your skis flat. They will likely use a wet belt sander and then possibly a stone grinder. The belt sander is a better option for you if cost is an issue; a stone grinder costs the shop thousands of dollars and they will pass that cost on to you. For an ideal tune, a stone grind after the belt sanding is worth the extra few bucks as it puts a good structure on the skis' bases (see Structure below).

## Edge-High

An edge-high ski is one whose edges protrude into the snow farther than the base does.

Skis tend to become edge-high if they are stored for the off-season without a coat of wax to seal chemical moisture into the base. The loss of moisture in the base shrinks it, leaving the metal edges standing higher than everything else. Unlike the slippery, unstable feel of the base-high ski, the edge-high ski will feel like your old Flexible Flyer sled with metal

This ski is edge-high.

runners. The edge-high ski has edges that stick down into the snow below the level of the ski's base, and they effectively act as runners. Just as runners make a sled go straight, the edge-high ski goes straight and won't make smooth turns.

### *Curing the Edge-High Ski*

An edge-high ski can also be a candidate for the ski shop. However, this condition is not as hard to fix by yourself with an 8-, 10-, or 12-inch mill bastard file (if it's a sharp one). File the edges down until they are at the same level as the base material. Use a true bar or roll pin to gauge when your ski is flat, or stop filing when you notice yourself taking down small amounts of the base material along with the edge material. A good rule of thumb when filing down the edges of the edge-high ski is to simply keep filing until you feel the file stop cutting into the metal edges. As soon as the file skims smoothly across the base without contacting the edges, you're done. Be careful not to bend the file as you work the length of the ski, as this can produce an unintended bevel.

## Structure

A ski's base is not perfectly smooth when it comes from the factory. It actually has fine grooves cut into the base material. These grooves make up the base's structure, and the job of structure is to help the ski slide smoothly and quickly across the snow.

As snow melts beneath the ski, which is under the pressure of a skier's weight, water can *sheet* under the ski's base and cause suction. This slows the ski down. The fine pattern of microgrooves of the base's structure acts like the treads of a car's tires, providing a way for water to get out from under the running surface. Often, in the spring, savvy tuners will apply a more aggressive pattern of deeper grooves to handle the extra water that ends up under skis on a warm day.

You can produce a structured base by hand several different ways, such as using a groove-producing tool called a *rilling bar* or even sandpaper wrapped around a file. But the cost of a stone grind at a good shop is well worth the price, for the modern stone grinder produces the best quality structure out there. After the stone grind, you can finish the rest of the tune—the edge tune and hot wax—yourself, or have the shop continue the work.

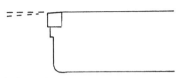

A little bit of base-edge bevel.

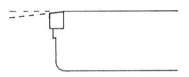

A little more base-edge bevel.

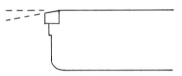

A whole lot of base-edge bevel.

## Beveling

Beveling involves the ski's edges. To bevel in ski tuning means to shape at a slant rather than at a right angle. You can change the shape of an edge to change a ski's performance.

There are two surfaces in a ski edge: the one that faces down toward the snow, called the *base-edge,* and the one that faces the left or right, called the *side-edge.*

### Base-Edge Beveling

This reduces an edge's contact with the snow so your ski behaves differently. A ski with base-edge beveling is not the same as a base-high ski, where the edges are recessed below the level of the base. In a base-edge bevel, the edge is shaved away in half- and full-degree increments. A 0.5-degree bevel is conservative and a 3-degree bevel is large.

Base-edge beveling eliminates the "grabbiness" of a sharp, unbeveled edge and gives a ski a more "loose" feel underfoot. Beveling allows you a greater margin for error, because a beveled edge does not engage the snow as readily. A base-edge bevel will strengthen your skills in steering and edge release. It will also let you

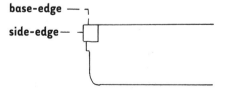

The edge material's base-edge and side-edge.

generate more power during a turn because the base-edge bevel requires extra body mass movement to the inside of the turn in order to create the appropriate edge angle. This movement allows you to create a greater buildup of force because you will not be so easily tipped over into the next turn.

More than just about any other element of the ski tune, base-edge beveling can change the way a ski feels. Many skiers don't like the way their new skis perform until they have been retuned with a little more base-edge bevel. Any ski that feels too long, too slow from edge to edge, or tends to "hook" during the turn should be treated to a bit more base-edge bevel.

**Applying a Base-Edge Bevel.** One benefit of base-edge beveling is the predictable feel it produces in a ski. You can edge your ski a small, preset amount in every turn before your edge begins to engage in earnest. Most tuners maintain an even base-edge bevel from tip to tail, but

Using a good file guide makes base-edge beveling simple. MT. BACHELOR SKI AND SPORT

you can vary the bevel along the length of the ski for differing effects. I tend to use a 1.5-degree base-edge bevel, which I find produces a smooth, predictable ski that works well in variable snow and during aggressive edging movements. Many skiers find a 2-degree bevel too loose underfoot, as the ski must roll a little farther over before it engages. An appropriate amount of base-edge bevel is both a subjective thing and dependent on the particular ski, so don't expect to always run the same tune. As a general rule, when trying to find the best bevel for you, simply remember that too little bevel will not produce noticeable change and will leave a ski feeling "hooky," or as if the edge is prone to engaging too early and with too much grip. This can also make a ski feel slow edge to edge. Too much bevel will make a ski feel base-high and too slippery.

If you are going to do your own beveling (which is easy to do), purchase a file holder that

you can set at half-degree increments. This way, you can produce a consistent bevel and find exactly the amount of base-edge bevel you prefer. When experimenting with manipulating the base-edge bevel in your tune, start with small changes. Start by increasing the base-edge bevel on your ski (which came from the factory with a set amount) in 0.5-degree increments. As you tune and then ski, you'll find an amount of base-edge bevel that feels right to you—not too edgy or grabby, and not too loose and "turny," or overly pivotal.

### Side-Edge Bevel

A side-edge bevel has less influence than a base-edge bevel on your ski's performance, but it is an important element, especially if you are running a base-edge bevel on your skis. A side-edge bevel makes your edge sharper: beveling the side of the edge makes the edge angle more acute.

Side-edge beveling is most commonly used in conjunction with base-edge beveling. For example, a ski with a base-edge bevel of 1.5 degrees needs a side-edge bevel of 1.5 degrees to bring the edge back to its original right angle. A 90-degree edge is plenty sharp, but some skiers like to run a more acute edge, say an 89- or 88-degree edge (sometimes even sharper) for extra hold on firm snow and ice. This is done by increasing the amount of side-edge bevel beyond the amount of the ski's base-edge bevel.

**Applying a Side-Edge Bevel.** If you purchase a base-edge beveling device, check to see if the device also has the capacity to produce a side-edge bevel. Otherwise, be sure to purchase a side-edge beveling tool in addition to the base-

A side-edge bevel.

edge beveling tool, preferably by the same man-ufacturer so that their degree or half-degree in-crements are standard. If you are having a ski shop do your beveling, let them know what you want: for example, X amount of base-edge bevel and Y amount of side-edge bevel to produce an edge angle of Z degrees.

## Edge Sharpening

This is one of the more basic elements of ski tun-ing, and one that produces less earth-shattering results in your performance. But edge sharpen-ing is often neglected, and some skiers' edges are so dull that the skis are almost useless in cer-tain snow conditions. Edge sharpness is crucial for making powerful, stable turns on firm snow. If your skis (especially your outside ski) consis-tently skid sideways during turns, you may have dull edges. Generally, an edge should have a 90-, 89-, or 88-degree edge (or some half-de-gree in between). This angle is produced by the base-edge and the side-edge.

Skiing all day on hard snow can wear down a ski's edge. This rounding of your edge is all it takes to make a ski feel dull. You will need to resharpen your edge to solve the problem. Bur-ring is another problem. Every time you nick a rock, even a small one, your edges record the abuse. Rocks take small chunks out of a metal edge, resulting in recesses and jagged edge ma-terial. This rough piece of edge can create drag on the snow and make turns feel less smooth, even grabby.

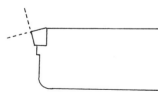

This ski's edge angle has been brought back to 90 degrees with base-edge and side-edge beveling. This edge is sharp enough for most skiing.

These edges are dulled and burred.

### Curing the Dull Edge

The result of base-edge and side-edge beveling is a sharpened edge that needs to be maintained with a hand file. To maintain edge sharpness, pass your file along the side-edge from tip to tail. File away a small amount of edge material without changing your bevel angle. This re-moval of old edge material restores your finely honed edge. Some skiers with a fine touch and steady hand can do this without a file guide, but most tuners use file guides. If the skis have been beveled, use the same amount of bevel to sharpen as you used to set the degree of base-edge and side-edge bevel.

Dealing with burrs is more difficult, because the metal can be hardened, or tempered, by its traumatic contact with the rock. Using a file may not work. In these cases, the edge should be de-burred with a whetstone—or better yet, with a diamond stone—purchased from a ski shop. Af-ter deburring the base-edge and side-edge, file the base-edge and side-edge until sharp. Some-times deburring with a diamond stone is all it takes to resharpen the edge, so don't make ex-tra work for yourself by filing if this is the case. Also, there's only so much edge material avail-able to work with, so only edge-tune when you need it—and tune only enough to get the job done.

A good way to tell when an edge is sharp enough is to pass the top of your fingernail across the edge. Your edge is sharp if it scrapes off a bit of your nail. This test gets you in the ballpark and you will get a feel for how sharp you like your skis' edges. Keep in mind that too sharp an edge will make a ski feel "hooky" and overly long. Often, aggressive beveling will leave a micro-burr along the entire ski's edge. If the edge feels too sharp, like the edge of an opened tin can, deburr with a soft and not-too-rough whetstone called a gummy stone just a bit, to take the razorlike sharpness down a bit.

There is one final trick to achieving a sharp edge. On any ski, the edge material is bonded to the sidewall, or side of the ski. There often is a small ridge of plastic material that runs parallel to the edge. This plastic can prevent your file from cutting into your edge properly. This will be apparent when plastic dust the same color as the sidewall shows up on your file. Shave that ridge down so you can cut into the edge material.

You can use the square end of the file (away from the pointy tang), or the edge of a 4 mm steel scraper, to scrape along the length of the sidewall. Place a corner of the file's end (or scraper's end) on the plastic ridge and run it along the length of the ski like a planer. A continuous curlicue of colored plastic should come off the ski. Repeat this several times for each edge. Then file the edges until they are sharp.

If you continue to get more colored dust than steel shavings on your file, rescrape the sidewall. Some tuners will use really rough files, called *body files* or *panzer files*, to do this. You can also purchase specialized sidewall planers to do this job right, but they are pricey. If you appreciate good tools, go for it. But the first method I mentioned will work for the rest of us hacks.

## Detuning

Detuning used to be a big part of the ski tune, but it's less important now, and even problematic. A detune was the strategic dulling of the skis' edges at the tip and tail of the ski. This aided the ski in entering and exiting the turn smoothly. This was very important in the days of long, straight skis that weren't the easiest things to turn.

Now, with shorter, more shaped skis that flex easier, the detune as we knew it then just isn't as necessary. In fact, the detune of the old days would make a good shaped ski perform pretty badly. This is good news for us tuners, because detuning was a kind of subjective art that was hard to convey.

The detune isn't exactly extinct, just limited in its use. Currently I detune only the tip of the ski where it doesn't contact the snow. I do this for safety reasons: in case I take a beater, I don't want to get cut by a sharp tip. The same goes for the tail of the ski, if it is turned up off the snow. If I find that a ski feels extremely "hooky" in the shovel, I may just barely detune the first inch or two of the edge where it begins to contact the snow. Generally though, modern shaped skis won't need this.

### Doing the Perfect Detune

For whatever reason you may need to detune, this is still easy to do on your own—even if it is a variable art. For dulling the tip and tail where the edge no longer makes contact with the snow, just use a file and round off the sharp edge so it can't cut you.

For any detuning you wish to do to the edge where it contacts the snow, use a whetstone, diamond stone, or gummy stone. Hold whichever tool you use at a 45-degree angle to the edge and make short strokes from the tip or tail toward the middle of the ski. You should make very short strokes and try to dull the edge less toward the end of your stroke so that the edge becomes progressively sharper at the end of your detune. Remember, less is more—and nowadays, this may not even be necessary.

## Waxing

Waxing waterproofs a ski. Skis don't slide on snow as much as they slide on snowmelt. On a micro level, the pressure a ski exerts on the snow creates heat. This melts the snow's ice crystals and produces minute water droplets. A waterproof surface makes water bead and roll off the surface. The wax on a ski forces the water beneath it to bead, and these beads work like small ball bearings on which the ski rolls. The lack of adequate wax causes water to sheet along the base of the ski, which causes suction and slows the ski.

A ski's performance is based on the assumption that it will slide smoothly on the snow. The suction that slows a ski can foul your balance. Just as a driver who hits the brakes too hard sends passengers flying forward, the unwaxed ski sends you too far forward. Unwaxed skis wreak havoc in powder and soft crud: the ski's deceleration forces your balance forward, which drives the skis into the snow and sends you onto your face.

### How to Wax

Waxing is nontechnical and easy to do, and it smells good. All you need is an old iron without steam holes, a Plexiglas scraper, some wax, and a Fibertex or Scotch-Brite pad, which is similar to a dish-scrubbing pad.

Snow temperature determines which wax you use. If the temperature at your ski area is very consistent, you can trust the advice of a local shop technician. However, if temperature varies, buy universal wax, which is an all-temperature wax produced by many manufacturers. If you want high performance and you are a weather watcher, you can wax every few days according to the current snow temperature.

Buy your Plexiglas scraper at a ski shop to ensure it is flat. Any stiff plastic, however, will do in a pinch. Metal scrapers work, but they can chatter and cut small chunks into the base material that are difficult to smooth out without belt sanding.

Heat the iron to the point where it melts wax on contact but does not make the wax smoke. Smoking wax indicates that your iron is too hot, which could damage your ski's base. Drip wax along the ski's base (you will learn from experience how much is enough), then iron the wax into your ski's base with circular or back-and-forth strokes. Keep the iron moving. You need to cook the wax into the base, but you don't want to overheat the ski. Count how many passes it takes at the shovel for the topside of the ski to warm just the slightest bit. (Test it by touching it with your hand.) Use that many passes (or fewer) for the rest of the ski's base.

After ironing the wax in, let the skis sit until the base is cool to the touch. Then scrape off the wax with your scraper. The important wax is the wax you cooked into the porous base of your ski: that's the wax that keeps your skis sliding. Be sure to scrape wax off both the base-edge and side-edge. Then buff the base with tip-to-tail strokes with your Fibertex or Scotch-Brite pad for an even finish. The Fibertex or Scotch-Brite pad also helps pull some of the melted wax out of your base's structure. Some tuners use fine brushes made of nylon, brass, or horsehair to get even more wax out of these fine grooves for really lightning-fast skis.

# Boots

Of all the equipment decisions you make as a skier, those involving your ski boots are the most important. Most of the fundamental skills of skiing, as you learned in the first half of this book, involve the movements of your feet and legs. Those foot and leg movements eventually end up in one place: your boots.

Your ski boot is the link between your body and your skis. Boots are designed to translate leg and foot movements to your skis. Ski boot design today is very advanced and the basic system is functional. But the system is flawed, because we can purchase whichever boot we choose, in whatever size we choose. Then we are free to decide whether we will manipulate and maintain that boot's fit and features.

Unfortunately, even the most skilled skiers often buy boots the same way they might buy a microwave: right color, right price, nukes popcorn—I'll take it. But in a way, buying boots is like getting married; if you're not careful, you can make your life miserable for a long time.

Salespeople at ski shops may or may not be very helpful when it comes to your search for the perfect boot. *Help* is the key word. No salesperson or bootfitter can tell you which boot is the right one for you because they can't feel what you feel when that boot's on your foot. This is the root of all boot-buying evils: you have to decide for yourself whether it's the right boot or not.

A good bootfitter should serve more as a facilitator during your boot search, guiding you toward boots that match your needs both in comfort and skiing performance. She should be able to ask some basic questions about how you ski and about your general fit preferences, then take a look at your foot shape and come up with some ideas on which boots may suit you best.

However, finding good bootfitting help can be tricky. Ask around in your group of skiing acquaintances and see if the same shops or bootfitters are named repeatedly. These quality shops have earned a good reputation for a reason, and they will save you a lot of strife when it comes to choosing your boots and then getting them dialed. You should buy boots at a shop that treats you right before the purchase and after. Even if their boots are a few bucks more, you'll be better off in the end. Trust me.

That great ski shop may not be close to home for you, so it's best to learn how to fend for yourself when it comes to finding boots. Learning how to buy the right boot involves understanding the basics of what constitutes a good fit, understanding the features of ski boots, and knowing how to use those features to maximize your skiing potential. Then you need to learn how to customize your boots' fit (or find the right bootfitter to help you) so you can live happily in them throughout the winter.

## BUYING THE RIGHT BOOT FOR YOU

After helping shop employees fit and sell ski boots for years and then eventually becoming a

The right boot with a perfect fit will give you more than comfort and control: it will give you courage. MARK ELLING IN THE ROCK GARDEN, MT. BACHELOR

There are a lot of good boots out there, but the best boot for you fits *your* foot. MT. BACHELOR SKI AND SPORT

professional bootfitter myself, it has become clear that too often boot buyers fall into two categories. The first shopper is interested in a particular brand of ski boot; he will not be satisfied until he has stuffed his dogs into that brand's model that he thinks best suits him. The other shopper is not looking for a brand name, but he wants the cushiest, fluffiest slipper of a ski boot he can find. The first customer is either loyal or foolish. The second one has the right idea, but he will never achieve a performance fit in a ski boot.

The first rule in ski boot buying is that comfort is king. A ski boot that hurts in the shop will really hurt on the hill—and the fit is not likely to get any better with time. Foot pain ruins skiing. Any expert who brags that foot pain is the price of being a good skier obviously is not as good as he could be if he had a better fitting boot.

However, you should look for the most comfortable fit you can find in a boot that is the right size for your foot. This is the second law of boot buying: Buy the boot that fits, not the one that feels the most comfortable. This is not a contradiction of the first rule, but a necessary clarification.

For example, let's assume that a size 6 is the proper size for a woman shopping for a ski boot. The size 6 hurts her feet, so she tries on a size 7 and achieves the comfort she wants. But even though the larger boot is more comfortable, this boot is the wrong size. Many skiers buy their boots a size too big because the proper size is not comfortable. If the boot is the right size but it isn't comfortable, then it isn't the boot for you. Period. Try another boot that is also the right size but may fit differently, and then another, and another, until you find a great match for your feet—one that's comfortable and fits. What a concept.

How do you speed up this process? It helps to know the basics of bootfitting. The two leading factors that influence boot fit are a boot's length, or size, and the boot's shape. The ideal boot for you is the right length, has a shape in the lower boot that matches the shape of your foot, and offers an upper boot that matches the shape and movements of your lower leg.

### Shell Sizing

A boot's true size is determined by the length of its outer, plastic boot. This outer boot, or shell, will not stretch or get broken in, and therefore the shell size represents the real size of the boot. A boot's liner is the foam and fabric inner boot that actually touches your foot. This liner will stretch and get broken in and packed down during the first several days of solid use and throughout an entire season. During this process, the liner conforms to your foot to customize your boot's fit to the shape of your foot. After this process is over, your boot will feel roomier. It is always difficult to gauge how much a given liner will "pack out." This is what can make sizing a boot and its liner a matter of guesswork.

The best way to eliminate much of the guesswork that comes from wondering how much a boot will pack out is to choose a size based on the part of the boot that won't change, the shell.

Either you or the shop salesperson should make sure you have the right length boot by *shell sizing* it before you try the boot on. To do this, remove the liner of the boot so you can place your longer foot (if one is longer than the other) in the boot shell, either barefoot or with a thin sock on. Once the shell is on, touch your longest toe gently against the front of the shell. It's preferable to do this while sitting down. With your longest toe touching the front of the boot, sight down the back of the boot using a small flashlight to determine the distance between your heel and the plastic shell directly behind it. This distance determines whether the boot is too large, too small, or just right.

The amount of space between the heel and the shell should typically fall between a ½ inch to 1 inch. A ½-inch gap between heel and shell is going to be a very snug fit, and a 1-inch gap is on the roomy end of the perfect fit spectrum. Where you fall within the ½-inch to 1-inch range

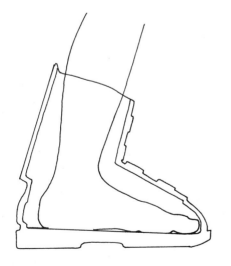

With the big toe barely touching the front of the boot's shell, look for a $^1/_2$- to 1-inch gap directly behind the heel.

is up to your own judgment, although most elite athletes and professional bootfitters prefer a ½-inch gap (or even smaller).

This last choice shouldn't be glossed over, for the difference between a shell measurement of a ½ inch to 1 inch is massive. The ½-inch shell fit produces the kind of tight fit that translates into superior ski control. It's like the rack-and-pinion steering of a sports car: serious drivers, and skiers, have to have it. But until this boot's liner packs out a bit, it's going to be tight. Some skiers just can't tolerate feeling the end of their toe jammed right up against the end of the boot.

A full inch or more behind the heel during a shell fit indicates that the boot will become too roomy after the liner packs out. The boot will require some work at that point to make it perform like new again, or the skier's feet will be swimming. This boot will ski the way my 1976 Land Cruiser drove—with enough play in the steering wheel to be scary.

Where you are willing to settle on length is up to you and depends on how tolerant you will be of a tight fit. With a few more bootfitting years under my belt I have come to realize that many more bootfitting problems down the road will stem from boots that are too large, so do yourself a favor and follow this rule: go as short as you can, comfortably.

### *Judging Length*

At some point, after taking a peek at your shell fit dimension, you'll try on the boot. Before you freak out and kick the thing off your foot and call it quits, here are a few things to remember.

First, boots' liners are often built to be a little shorter than the space they occupy inside the boot shell. Boot companies do this at times by accident and at other times as a matter of course so the liners don't accidentally get wrinkled inside the shell at the factory (wrinkled liners that sit in a warehouse for six months to a year don't sell well). So, you can anticipate the boot will feel too short, at least initially. If you're confident after a shell fit that you have enough room in length, tolerate the short liner for 5 or 10 minutes. It should warm up and begin to stretch.

Also, keep in mind that a custom footbed will often shorten the length of your foot as it supports your arch. (You will learn more about custom footbeds in the chapter on alignment.) A foot with a high arch that collapses inside the boot due to lack of support can elongate by ¼ inch or more. And realize that it's possible to grind out a few millimeters of extra room just in front of the longest toe and behind the heel, if necessary.

The general rule remains that when standing tall, with a little weight distributed to your heel, you should feel your longest toe touching the end of the boot. This can be anywhere from just barely touching to just plain crammed against it, depending on your tolerance for a tight fit. When you shift your balance forward and press the boot's tongue with your shin, that pressure should be relieved, anywhere from completely relieved to the point where the longest toe feels only light pressure.

Your boot will pack out, even in length, but not by much. Most of the room will be gained in thick foam areas like the ankle pockets. Remember, comfort is king.

## Last Shape

Finding the right shell size is just the beginning. Every boot manufacturer makes a different shaped *last*, or footprint. Boot designers create a boot mold for a model foot they envision as the foot they want to sell boots to. Because different boot companies have different design teams and theories on what makes a good boot, they end up producing a boot with a last shape that will be different than a competitor's boot. Sometimes, a boot company will produce sev-

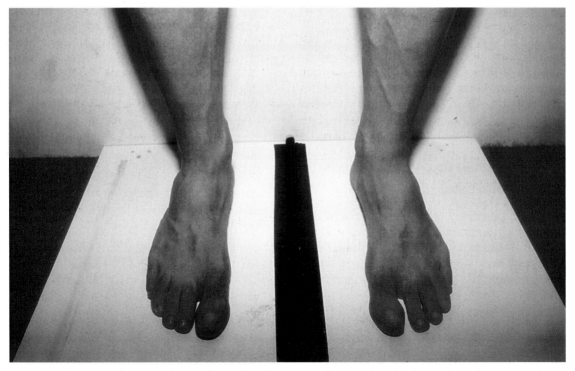

Everyone's feet are unique in shape. Try to find a boot that matches the shape of your foot.

eral different last shapes in its boot line to accommodate a wider variety of feet. Remember that last shape refers to the general shape of the lower boot. Skiers should strive to find a match for their foot shape both in the lower boot as well as the upper boot.

The primary factor to look at in the lower boot's last shape is its volume, or the overall mass of the foot that the boot was designed to work with. Some boots are high-volume boots for thick, wide feet. Other boots are low-volume boots for thin, narrow feet. Some boots fit feet that are not fat or skinny but of moderate volume. Still others fill the gaps in between. Look at your own feet and think about volume.

A good bootfitter will know which brands accommodate a foot like yours, so seek this kind of professional help at a good ski shop. Design trends will change from year to year with boot manufacturers, and a good bootfitting staff will stay on top of those changes. A boot brand that never suited you in the past may have changed, so stay open-minded and try on any boot that may suit your needs.

Overall volume is your first consideration, but you also need to consider where a boot's volume is located. Some boots are designed with a wide toebox (the space that houses your toes and the ball of your foot), and others have a narrow one. Look at your own feet to determine where they have the most and least volume. If your foot has a wide ball, wearing a boot with a narrow toebox is going to be uncomfortable. If the forward section of your foot is narrow and you choose a boot with a wide toebox, your skiing performance will suffer because of the sloppiness around your foot's ball and toes.

Performance and comfort are optimum when your boot shell fits closely along your foot and is cushioned by the inner boot, or liner. If excess space exists between your foot and your boot shell, skiing performance will be hampered. This is because the transfer of movement from your foot to the boot and eventually to the ski will be slowed. However, if your boot's plastic shell comes too close to your foot, you will have pain—especially when that pressure is on a bony spot. Try to find a happy medium between these two extremes, but keep in mind that too much pressure in an isolated spot, such as a bony prominence, can usually be easily fixed by a good bootfitter.

### Judging Shape

Unlike determining the proper length, which you can do with a flashlight, deciding if the lower boot's shape suits your foot is a subjective matter. A few tips will help you make good decisions about the lower boot that houses your foot.

A properly snug fit in the lower boot should feel like a very firm handshake on every nook and cranny of your foot. A good handshake neither feels limp-wristed, nor does it crush the bones in your hand. A good fit in the lower boot should feel pretty darned tight but without cutting off circulation or causing numbness. A snug boot is a warm boot, but a boot that is constrictive of blood flow will lead to cold toes.

The snug nature of the fit should feel very evenly distributed, and each part of the foot should be held with a similar amount of pressure. Some increased pressure is OK if it's right on a specific, bony prominence and a good bootfitter can assure you that it's fixable after the purchase. A too-tight fit in a general area—such as the forefoot, toes, or heel—may be workable. But a better bet would be to find a boot that fits those areas in the same, evenly snug manner as the rest of the foot.

### The Upper Boot

There's a lot of complex stuff going on in the upper boot: it has to flex forward with the skier's leg in a fashion that matches the biomechanics of ankle and knee flexion. The upper boot's amount of forward lean is the controlling factor for a skier's fore-aft balance. The upper boot needs to be oriented laterally in a way that suits skiers' anatomy and alignment, so that edging movements remain balanced and efficient. The upper boot may have adjustments for different fit or performance effects. And don't forget that the upper boot still has to close around the skier's lower leg in a way that's comfortably snug.

What's the moral of that little story? Don't forget to seek a good match for your needs in the upper boot as well as the lower. Different manufacturers provide different shapes in upper boots, the same way that they produce different lasts in the lower boot. Find bootfitters who can correlate your needs in the lower boot with your needs in the upper boot and ones that offer boots that accommodate both. Finding an ideal match for yourself in the upper boot is not any harder than finding a good fit in the lower boot—but there are a couple extra variables.

Before evaluating these finer points, be sure that the upper boot's closure around your lower leg is snug and evenly distributed, just as we discussed with the lower boot. There should not be any biting or chopping sensations along your shin or at the back of the calf. The calf muscle should not feel constricted at the boot top, and the boot should feel evenly snug along the entire length of the lower leg. Conversely, there should be no gap present in front of the shin or behind the calf.

### Judging the Upper Boot's Flex

Every ski boot is designed to flex when a skier presses his or her shin into the boot's tongue. But some boots are stiffer than others. It used to be that a better skier gravitated toward a stiffer boot, but that rule has changed a bit. With the newer skis, you don't have to exert as much pressure on the ski's shovel to get a turn started, so boots have gotten softer in forward flex. The movements involved in turn initiation are more lateral in nature with modern skis, so the direction of energy transmission in boots has changed: boots are rigid medially and laterally, or side to side, to help with solid edging movements. They simply don't need to be as stiff in forward flex anymore.

This doesn't mean that everybody likes a soft boot. Boots have gotten softer across the board, but skiers still have preferences and needs that lead them to boots of different flex characteristics. There are two basic things to consider in determining whether the upper boot's flex is right for you: the nature of the flexing movement itself and how much the boot flexes under your weight.

A boot should flex in an ergonomic fashion that moves in concert with the way your lower leg moves during ankle and knee flexion. The entire upper boot should move with your lower leg as it drives forward in the boot. The boot's flex, ideally, should feel as if it were being generated nearest the part of the body that's doing the flexing, the ankle. An upper boot that seems to hinge or fold somewhere along the middle of the shin isn't what you're looking for. When you flex the boot, the pressure along the lower leg—from the top of the shin to the instep—should remain evenly distributed rather than bite into any one part of the leg more than another.

The basic guideline for determining whether a boot's too soft or too stiff goes like this: The boot that's too stiff will not move with the lower leg during flexion; instead, a gap behind the calf is produced. The skier can't flex the too-stiff boot, only the liner's tongue; this is only wasted movement inside the shell of the boot, just like the slop in the steering of my Land Cruiser. A boot that's too stiff will hold the skier in a non-flexing stance that's static and unworkable for smooth skiing in softer snows.

A boot that's too soft will allow a skier to overflex the upper boot and drive the upper boot's bottom buckle strap into the dome of the lower boot, thus squashing it. The only thing stopping the boot from flexing farther is this collision—which causes bad things to happen both in fit and performance.

The right amount of flex is found between these two parameters, and the fine details come down to your personal preference.

The ski boot should flex with your movements but still support a tall stance. BRIAN ELLING ON ED'S GARDEN, MT. BACHELOR

### Judging the Upper Boot's Forward Lean

There's no rule for determining whether an upper boot is built too upright or too forward for your stance and style of skiing; you have to *feel* whether the boot's right for you. However, the matter of forward lean is fundamental to your achieving proper fore-aft balance on skis. Here are a few guidelines to help you identify workable forward lean.

A boot should support your stance: it is the base on which you stack your skeletal frame. While your stance should feel tall and natural, you should feel as though you can settle your weight, using your shin, against the tongue of the boot and be essentially "propped up" by the boot. Ideally, functional forward lean will allow you to relax against the boot and remain tall and balanced, with your weight evenly distributed from the ball of your foot to the heel.

A boot that's too upright will not allow you to settle into a slightly flexed skiing stance; it will force you to stand tall. Tongue pressure against the shin will feel too aggressive and tend to push you back into a straight-legged, backseat stance. You'll also feel too much pressure under your heels.

A boot that offers too much forward lean will not support you in a tall, balanced stance. To relax your weight against the boot and have it support you will require more than average ankle and knee flexion. This results in an overly squatty stance that taxes the quadricep muscles. This type of boot does not provide enough support to allow you to relax into a tall stance, propped up a bit by your boot.

In the ski shop, if you find that a particular boot makes you feel too bent-legged or your thighs begin to burn just being in the boots, try to find a better match for the sake of your fore-aft balance. (The Fore-Aft Alignment section in Getting Techno will help if you have to deal with a boot that has too much forward lean.)

If a boot feels just a shade too upright in the shop, it will probably be fine. Most bindings have a certain amount of *ramp*, or high heel, built into them, which should make enough difference in your stance so you feel balanced during skiing.

### Judging the Upper Boot's Lateral Alignment Bias

The upper boot's lateral alignment bias may sound pretty complicated, but it's not. Simply put, you don't want to buy a boot that makes you feel too bowlegged or knock-kneed when you're standing in those boots on the ski shop's hard, flat floor. People have differently shaped legs, and the angles of their legs are different too. Some skiers' knees tend to "knock" in toward each other; some skiers' knees tend to "bow" out away from each other. Boot manufacturers make boots that may suit these angles better for some than others.

Ideally, the lateral bias—or the way the upper boot tilts inward or outward—should match the angles of your legs perfectly, or at least come close. Most boots offer *lateral upper-cuff adjustment* devices to help skiers achieve that match. You can make sure the boot's lateral upper-cuff adjustment range is sufficient before you settle on the boot. If your boot doesn't offer enough adjustment range, a good bootfitter may have some ideas for how to get around the problem.

Issues of lateral alignment can get complex, and the chapter on alignment will give you more information. But on this score, just remember to question boots that make you adopt a really bowlegged or knock-kneed stance when you stand on a flat floor in your normal skiing width.

## Boot Buying (and Tweaking) Tactics

When I shop for a new boot, I can spend three hours at a shop trying on boot after boot. I eventually narrow my selection down to two or three pairs and spend 15 to 20 minutes in each boot. Then I'll go to a shop that carries different brands and repeat the process. I shop during the week when there are few other shoppers, and ideally during the early season before the holiday rush. If it's helpful to the salesperson, I offer to fetch, rebox, and put away the boots I try on. You may feel like a jerk spending half your day playing with ski boots, but being a true gear geek takes guts.

At some point, you'll need to decide on one pair. Understand that almost no boot feels perfect, especially if you have only a half-inch of space in your boot shell. A few knobs and bone spurs on your feet may hurt to some degree. But this pain should only be tolerated prior to purchase. Most hot spots and minor pressure points can be alleviated with custom bootfitting, which you can do yourself or have done by the shop. Many shops offer a guaranteed fit to customers who purchase new boots, so don't go to a larger size. Fix the small pain problems.

I will talk about custom bootfitting later. There are, however, some kinds of boot pain that are very difficult to deal with. They should

be considered red flags to warn you away from a particular boot.

Problems that cause shin pain are difficult to fix. A boot that bites aggressively into any one part of your shin may be customized to distribute tongue pressure more evenly along the shin, but that is about the extent of your options. If you have chronic shin pain, you should try to find a boot that does not hurt your shins in the shop—even if it means doing extra fitting elsewhere on the boot.

Boots that cause heel pain are also problematic, due to the lack of available space for major adjustment. There's a bit of space for grinding away plastic from the boot's shell, but some other sorts of bootfitting tricks are not possible on heels if the alteration affects the way the boot's heel functions in the binding. You may be able to ease minor heel pain with customization. But if a boot hurts your heel badly to begin with, you may end up with that pain throughout the season.

I'm also wary of boots that kill my ankle bones. Boot liners can be manipulated to deal with minor ankle discomfort, but sometimes the way the lower boot and upper boot come together can be a problem. Rivets and connecting hardware can often make bootfitting tough if your ankle problem happens to be right on that spot. If your ankles aren't perfect in the boot you're about to buy, make sure the problems are fixable.

If you think you need to modify the boot you've chosen, consult with the shop's bootfitter before making the purchase. Shops have different tools and experience in bootfitting, and your shop may or may not be able to make that particular boot work for you. If you've found the best boot for your feet and your shop can't handle the modifications you need, don't despair. In most skiing communities, there are one or two shop technicians who moonlight as bootfitters. And there are ski shops that offer bootfitting services for similar fees. If your feet are giving you a lot of trouble, it will be well worth the money to seek out these professionals.

A performance fit with adequate comfort is the foundation for becoming an expert skier and for maintaining that level of expertise, because nothing works if your feet hurt.

Don't forget that there are ski shops out there that demo boots. This is a way to see how a boot will perform in a colder environment and under the kind of skiing movements that are hard to simulate inside. My experience with boots is that if a particular boot fits right, flexes right, and accommodates my alignment needs, it's a winner. But, as they say, the proof's in the pudding: if you can try a boot before you buy it, go for it.

## YOUR BOOTS' BELLS AND WHISTLES

The above information should drive your decision-making process when choosing a new ski boot, but many high-performance boots also come with an arsenal of bells and whistles. These extras can affect your buying decision. What's important to know is how to use these options to get the most out of the boots you choose to buy. The following are some of the most common and useful gadgets that come with boots. Included are descriptions of how these features can help your skiing and how you can manipulate them for best results. Always ask about a boot's features when you are considering a purchase. A lot of salespeople will simply forget to tell you about them. Also be sure you understand how they function when you buy them.

### Lateral Upper-Cuff Adjustment

The lateral upper-cuff adjustment (often mistakenly called lateral canting adjustment, or something similar) is indispensable for many skiers. This adjustment allows the upper boot to shift medially and laterally. This enables a boot to match the bone angles of your lower legs. A knock-kneed or bowlegged skier can make necessary adjustments for his anatomy.

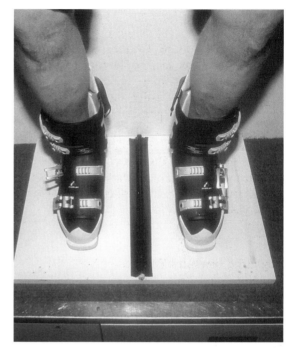

This bowlegged skier needs to use the lateral cuff adjustment to help match the upper boot to his leg angles (more on this subject in the chapter on alignment).

This feature is crucial for achieving proper alignment for most skiers. The alignment chapter later in this section explains the benefits of using the lateral upper-cuff adjustment and methods for manipulation. Look for a boot that has as much lateral upper-cuff adjustment range as possible. Many boots offer an adjustment on the lateral hinge-point of a boot (the outside, where the buckles are). Boots that offer adjustment on both the lateral and medial (inside) sides of the boot will often provide greater adjustment range.

### Flex Adjustment

This mechanism alters the amount of resistance to the forward movement of your lower leg due to flexion of your ankle. The means by which the boot's flex is changed may vary, but it's always pretty simple: make it softer or make it stiffer.

This is a good adjustment to have on a ski boot for the simple fact that temperature can affect the stiffness of any boot. Sometimes, boots will feel too stiff on a really cold day and too soft during the spring. This is the only reason I tend to mess with a flex adjustment, but that's enough reason for me.

Always ask about this feature and identify which mode the boot is in when you try it on. It would be a shame to give up on a boot because it felt either too soft or too stiff simply because you didn't know it had a flex adjustment.

### Forward Lean Adjustment

While this option is becoming more scarce, it can be a lifesaver for skiers who are having problems getting their fore-aft balance dialed. For a skier who can't tell whether a boot is too upright or leaned too forward, having this adjustment can be helpful in learning which stance works best for him.

Skiers who know they have problems with limited ankle flexion (for example, some skiers can't flex much past a 90-degree angle in their street shoes without having their heels lift off the floor) should consider boots with forward lean adjustment. Being able to straighten a boot up does wonders for keeping the heel solidly in the bottom of the boot without having to add heel lifts. (We'll discuss this later in Some Boot-fitting Basics.)

### Ramp-Angle Adjustment

Ramp angle may be one of the lesser known adjustment functions, possibly because few boots offer it. But be happy if your boots have this feature: it is one of the most helpful and convenient customizing tools available.

Ramp angle is the *high heel* factor in boots. Ski boots offer a certain amount of heel lift, so your foot is not sitting perfectly flat on top of your ski. This function aligns your center of mass in

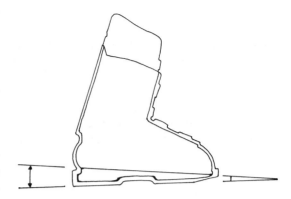

Ramp angle is the degree of tilt to the boot shell's floor, or boot board.

the middle of the ski, which is one of the most fundamental tools of the expert skier.

Boot designers envision a skier with a certain center of mass, and they choose the amount of ramp angle for that hypothetical skier. Many of us do not match the designer's model, so we are at an immediate disadvantage in our skiing.

Making ramp-angle adjustments can place your center of mass farther forward or backward. Skiers with a ramp-angle adjustment on their boots need only to turn a screw. If you don't have this adjustment, there are other ways of shifting your mass forward and aft (see the sections on Fore-Aft Alignment in the Alignment chapter and the Getting Techno section).

### Arch Height Adjustment

This may sound like a pretty cool adjustment feature, but I'm not too into it. Why? It's not that skiers don't need arch support: it's that they need *custom* arch support that suits the nature of *their* arch. The way to get that kind of support is with a well-made, custom footbed. A footbed provides support to the bottom of your foot, and a custom footbed is designed to sit on top of a smooth, flat surface (for more on footbeds, see pages 115–18). Most boot boards (the bottom or floor of the boot's shell, also called a *zeppa*) are flat. But boots that offer an arch adjustment have some kind of non-flat boot board that must be made flat for use with a custom footbed.

If you plan on getting any kind of footbed at all, remember to remind the technician that you have the custom arch adjustment in your boots. He or she will remove it or adjust it, to make the boot board as flat as possible. The technician making your footbeds will probably not need the reminder, but I've forgotten about these gizmos from time to time.

## Ski-Walk Adjustment

Who knows how long these gadgets will stick around, but a lot of skiers like them. The ski-walk adjustment (also known as the ski-bar adjustment or Joey Switch) allows the boot's upper cuff to hinge rearward to put your boot into a walk mode. You can then make more natural walking movements—say, across the largest ski-area parking lot on the face of the earth.

Generally, you won't find this feature on higher end boots for the simple reason that ski boots should not flex backward. The mechanism that allows the walk mode will often render the

ski boot lacking in rearward support. If you're considering this feature, be sure a boot with a ski-walk adjustment feels rigid when you lean back while you're on your skis (click in at the ski shop, if you want). Better yet, demo the boots. A boot that flexes in the opposite direction is a no-go.

## Power Strap

It seems silly to even mention power straps, but there are a lot of boots out there that don't have them. The power strap is the Velcro strap at the top of the boot that makes for a snug fit at the top of your shin and calf. Without one, there can be too much movement inside the liner of the boot—movement that bears no effect on the ski. You gotta have one.

Skiers with skinny calves (or those folks whose boots never seem tight enough at the very top) can try running the power strap around the front of the liner, *inside* the plastic overlap, and then buckle up over the top of the power strap. This will make the liner snug around the lower leg, so any leg movement will transfer directly into the shell and—in turn—the ski.

Seek a good bootfitter to help you get your boots dialed. If he seems a little dazed, that's normal. MT. BACHELOR SKI AND SPORT

A product that's gaining in popularity is the Booster Strap, which is an elasticized aftermarket power strap that uses a metal cam-strap or plastic ladder-lock buckle to cinch the strap tight. In my experience, it works really well.

## SOME BOOTFITTING BASICS

While many ski shops offer custom bootfitting, some do not. Expert skiers should therefore know some of the simple things they can do themselves to achieve a snug and painless fit. It also helps to know what can be done to customize the fit of a ski boot; that way, you can get exactly what you need when you have a ski shop do the work for you.

When it comes to bootfitting, your prime directive is to pack your feet as snugly as you can into your boots and eradicate all discomfort—no matter how minor. This is a lofty goal, but it's something to strive for. Some of the following bootfitting tips can be done with basic tools, such as scissors, dense foam, and duct tape. Specific bootfitting materials for do-it-yourself fixes can be purchased from a ski shop or through ski tuning catalogs, such as the Tognar Toolworks catalog (see the appendix for more information). I recommend using the right materials rather than cobbling together some odd pieces and parts. Other bootfitting projects will require help from a ski shop.

If you need a shop's help, do all the prep work you can before going to the shop for one or two specific jobs. Some of these tactics will be described below. This approach limits the shop's involvement (which keeps the price down), enables you to get your boots back quickly, and affords you valuable hands-on experience in altering your own boots. However, don't be too fixed on your plan of attack when it comes to working on your boots. A good bootfitter will often have a better way to solve your problem, so be willing to let him work his magic.

Here we'll look at several common fit problems and the most promising solutions available

to you. Again, comfort is king. My general advice is to make yourself a walking bootfitting experiment until your boots are comfortable and snug. Get after any problems right away: don't wait until you're on the hill and in excruciating pain. If you can get your boots dialed at the start of the season, you can enjoy them pain-free for a few seasons down the road.

### Volume Problems: The Boot's Too Tight

First of all, tight is good. An extremely snug fit will improve your skiing performance more than just about anything else when it comes to boots. So be sure to make the distinction between a very snug boot and a boot that's truly too tight. You may not want to render a decision on the tightness factor until the boot's been skied on several times and broken in a bit. However, a boot that's too tight is one that cuts off circulation, causes numbness, or produces pressure directly on the bones of a particular part of the foot.

Typically, a boot isn't too tight everywhere—just in a certain area. It's important to start paying attention to exactly where the boot feels too tight. Skiers will often tolerate discomfort in one area of the boot throughout the day, so it becomes difficult to identify where the problem actually started. Boot pain can spread, so pay attention to where it starts and remember that. In my experience, it's rare that a boot is too small—unless the skier's foot is still growing and he has simply outgrown the boot.

Shell sizing is key for double-checking if a boot is simply too small. If you've ended up with a boot that gives you a mere ¼ inch in a shell fit, you've got your work cut out for you. But if there's more room than that in length, you'll probably be fine. Here are a few "too tight" scenarios and their common solutions.

### *The Boot's Too Tight in Length*

Unless a skier has a reason why she shouldn't feel her toe touching the end of the boot, the longest toe should touch the end of the boot while she stands tall, with some weight on her heel. Some skiers like just a faint amount of pressure on the end of the toe, while others prefer a real tight fit where the toes are up against the end of the boot firmly. The toes really shouldn't have to curl under to survive, and if your longest toes are sore from being jammed against the end of the boot at the end of a day of skiing, you should do something about it.

Don't start grinding on the boots until you've exhausted a few easy fixes first. Keep your toenails trimmed. Keep your upper boot buckles and power strap as snug as possible, to retain your instep and drive your heel into its pocket; this keeps the toes pulled as far back away from the front of the boot as possible.

Make sure that you have some kind of custom footbed in the boot, as support for your arch will shorten the length of your foot (unless, of course, your foot is truly flat). When your arch collapses for lack of support, your foot becomes elongated. Be sure that whatever footbed you use is cut or ground to match the length and forefoot shape of the stock insole that came with your boot. An overly long footbed can curl up in the end of the liner and make the boot feel shorter. Also check that your footbed tucks seamlessly into the back of the heel pocket. A footbed that doesn't seat deeply in the heel pocket will shuttle your foot a little forward and make your boot feel short.

Consider grinding the forefoot area of your footbed a little thinner. This gives the toes more room vertically. And sometimes the toes are riding too high in the lower boot and are meeting the boot shell where it begins to curve and cover the top of the toes. Also consider using a heel lift, as long as that won't hurt your fore-aft alignment (see Fore-Aft Alignment: Project Delta and Attention Skiers with Limited Ankle Dorsiflexion in the Getting Techno section). Heel lift can put your heel into a deeper part of the shell's heel pocket, which can pull the toes away from the front of the boot.

After all these first-strike options have been exhausted, see your bootfitter about grinding.

Before I grind, I'll check the boot's liner to make sure there's no extra thick material at the front of the toebox; if there is, it can be thinned. After that, it's time to grind the plastic shell directly in front of the longest toe(s). The plastic is actually pretty thick right there, and it's common to be able to grind at least a couple millimeters of material away. This doesn't sound like much, but it's often all your toes will need. It's wise to remove the boot board in the bottom of the shell before grinding the toebox, so it doesn't get trashed.

As a last resort, the heel pocket of the shell can be ground so that the heel moves aft. But it's possible to render the heel a little loose after grinding, which then has to be dealt with as a loose heel problem (see the section on correcting a loose heel problem on page 100).

### The Lower Boot's Too Tight in Width

It's common to have too tight a fit at the widest part of the ball of the foot. Usually, the boot's simply not wide enough at that spot. First make sure that your custom footbed matches exactly to the forefoot shape of the boot's stock insole. Then proceed with any of three main courses of action.

If the boot is a bit snug over the top of the foot as well, then the boot board in the bottom of the shell can be ground down. This lowers the foot in the shell, an area where the shell is often a bit wider. A bootfitter should ensure that there's material available beneath the boot board, and keep in mind that this is generally considered a permanent alteration. If the boot is too tight only in width, and not on the top of the foot, the shell can be made wider by grinding or by heat-stretching the shell. You can aid your bootfitting technician by prepping your boot as described in Hot Spots on pages 103–5).

### The Boot's Too Tight Across the Top of the Foot

More often than not, a ski boot can be too tight across the tops of the toes, or it can be too tight across the top of the middle of the foot, where skiers often have bony prominences. The approach to fixing the problem depends on where the problem is.

For boots that are too tight across the tops of the toes, the idea is to minimize the material directly under the forefoot. For example, the footbed should be ground as thin as possible without damaging its structural integrity. And the boot board (if it's removable) should be ground in small increments to lower the foot away from the top of the boot's shell where it's pressing against the toes. It is possible to do some grinding on the boot's shell over the top of the toes. But the shell overlap and toe dam (which keeps water out) is often in the way, and these areas may or may not be conducive to grinding.

For boots that are too tight across the middle of the foot, the boot's tongue itself is often the culprit. Many ski boot designs utilize a fairly rigid plastic on the boot tongue. Even though the plastic is padded with foam, it's often so stiff that it can't flex to accommodate bony spots on the top of the foot. Find where the tongue hits the problem spot and mark the plastic on the tongue. This general area can be thinned with a Dremel tool, grinder, or some shaving device. Don't thin the plastic too much; thin it just enough so it starts to flex a bit.

### Upper-Boot Tightness

If you are experiencing tightness along the sides of your lower leg or around your calf, there are a few alterations you can make.

Your calf or lower leg may be thicker than the largest buckle setting. Trade those buckles for larger ones that you can set for a wider lower leg. Most buckles on the upper boot now offer predrilled or premarked holes so you can move your buckles to a wider setting.

If this does not relieve the tightness, look for ways to reduce the amount of material between the plastic shell and your skin. Built-in plastic shims are sometimes placed along the sides or back of the calf area on a boot shell. They can also be incorporated into the liner itself. Removing these pieces will let you gain some space.

Be careful that this material is not crucial for the boot's lateral stiffness or for overall stability and function. If this is not apparent, be sure to ask for advice from a good boot technician at your local shop.

Another option is to raise the calf a bit higher out of the top of the boot using heel lifts. Raising the calf lets the boot cuff meet a narrower part of the lower leg. This works well if the heel lifts don't negatively effect the skier's fore-aft alignment (see Fore-Aft Alignment: Project Delta and Attention Skiers with Limited Ankle Dorsiflexion in the Getting Techno section). The boot cuff itself can be lowered by cutting off the top edge of some boot shells, but this is a bit more extreme.

The final option for dealing with lower-leg tightness is to have a shop technician thin the plastic at the top of the boot shell to allow for some flex, or she can cut expansion slots into the upper shell of the boot. These slots are usually cut vertically from the top edge of the plastic shell into a large, drilled hole that prevents the slot from ripping further. However, this weakens the boot and renders it less precise in transmitting your movements to your skis.

### Volume Problems: The Boot's Too Loose

Most boots that feel too loose have been improperly sized to begin with. A properly sized boot will feel almost unbearably snug for a week or so and then pack out to a comfortable tightness. After my boots pack out, my toes still gently touch the front of the boot but are not as scrunched as they were initially. Skiers with long, skinny feet, however, may have to buy a boot that suits their foot's length but leaves the rest of the foot with excess room.

Shimming is the name of the game for a boot that's too loose. Where you place shims depends on where the extra room is. There are also different kinds of materials for making shims, and I will discuss some of them here. We're assuming here that skiers have a good, custom footbed. The custom footbed can make a boot feel more snug for two reasons: it may be thicker than the stock insole and take up room, and/or the way a footbed stabilizes a skier's foot will make a boot seem tighter.

### The Boot's Loose Along the Entire Foot

If your boot feels loose everywhere along your foot, a full-length shim of dense material placed on top of the boot board, under the liner, will elevate your foot so it occupies a narrower space in the dome of the lower boot. This will also take up space along the sides of the foot. Start by using shims that are ¹⁄₁₆ inch thick. Stack the shims progressively until a snug fit is achieved, or simply use a thicker shim.

The shim should be made of a noncompressible material, such as hard plastic or some other dense material, so your foot movements will transfer through the shim to the bottom of the boot and ultimately to your ski. Soft shimming material, such as foams or thick cardboard, will absorb movements that you want to transfer to your skis. The best way to go for full-length boot board shims is to purchase exactly that from a ski shop or catalog. These are often called insole shims or Bond-Tex shims.

Be sure to cut the boot board shims to size so that they fit perfectly on the bottom of the shell. If they're too short, they'll slip back and forth a bit. If they're too large anywhere, they'll curl up a bit and potentially alter the fit.

### The Boot's Loose Around the Ankles

Shimming with softer material in the spaces around your ankle bones (called the *medial maleolus* on the inside of your foot and the *lateral maleolus* to the outside) will prevent your ankle from rolling from side to side in your boot. Use foam that's ³⁄₁₆ to ¼ inch thick with one sticky side. You can purchase this dense, bootfitting foam at most ski shops. Some comes precut in ankle-friendly shapes that you can customize easily.

Note where your ankle bone and adjacent tendons protrude and avoid putting pressure on those points with your shim. If your shim material isn't precut, cut out modified dough-

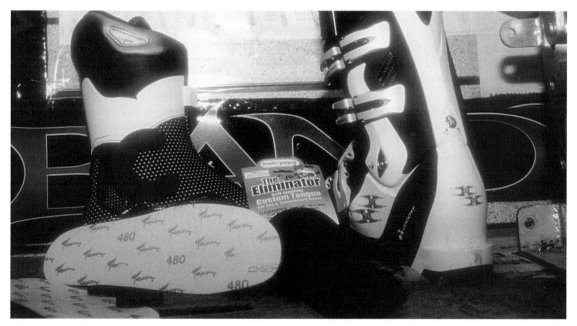

Different bootfitting products: Bond-Tex shims, C pad, Eliminator Tongue. MT. BACHELOR
SKI AND SPORT

nut shapes, which may look like horseshoes, letter Cs, or hockey sticks, and stick them to the liner while your foot is still in it (or mark where your ankles are on the liner). You usually want to shim both the inside and outside of your ankle, to keep your ankle centered in the boot and prevent it from shifting to one side.

Place the liners back in the shells and put the boots on. Wear them for a few minutes before deciding if the shims did the job. You should be able to determine if there is still excess room to be taken up or if you have created too much pressure on some points that were already snug. Add or cut away shimming material as needed. Repeat the process until a comfortably snug fit is achieved.

If your shimming feels as if it is altering the natural positioning of your ankle, reposition your shims or decrease their size. If the problem persists, remove all shims and take your boots to a shop. Be sure to tell them about the ankle placement problem.

### The Boot's Loose Around the Heels

Dealing with loose heels, or complaints of *heel lift*, is more complicated than one might think. The real trick—and one that's been missed by many bootfitters for years, including me—is to determine whether a skier's heels are lifting off the bottom of the boot because the heel pocket is loose, or whether they lift off *because they have to.*

It's very common for a boot's heel pocket to pack out and become loose. This is fixed with shimming, which we'll discuss. But first, it pays to know that some skiers will notice loose heels right from the start in a new boot, especially when flexing the boot.

Many people have limited ankle flexion range that prevents them from standing in the kind of ankle-flexed position required in ski boots. A person with limited dorsiflexion (which is the opposite of pointing one's toes) can't flex his ankles enough to keep his heels on the bottom of the boot. This skier, if he were to stand barefoot on a hard floor, could not bend his knees forward very far before his heels would begin too lose contact with the floor. The ankle gets to the end of its range, the lower leg keeps moving forward (as it would during ski boot flex), and the heel has to lift.

The only way to fix loose heels for this person is to reduce the amount of flex required by the ski boot by making it more upright, if this can be done, or by bringing the boot board up under the heel with the use of heel lifts. The heel lifts are placed on the boot board, under the liner. The distance the heels raise during deep flexion is the amount of heel lift needed, which is generally up to a half-inch. No other fix-it strategy will do. Note that most people can increase their dorsiflexion range through stretching exercises, but some cannot. A good bootfitter should be able to tell to what degree a skier's dorsiflexion range is limited. Or you can try standing on the floor with as much flex as required by your boots during skiing and see if your heels stay firmly against the floor.

Shimming along the outside of the liner, behind the ankle bones, is the trick for your run-of-the-mill loose heel pocket. Both the medial and lateral side of the liner will need shimming. Feel around the ankle bones and find the void space that falls between the ankle and the Achilles tendon, as well as the space just below the ankle bones. These spots are where you want to add your sticky-backed bootfitting foam. Use a J-shaped piece to run behind and under the ankle bone without exerting pressure on the bony spots or upon the Achilles tendon. An ideal fit will be snug but very comfortable. Remove foam where it's uncomfortably tight until you've got it dialed.

It is possible to use heel lifts under the liner to bring a skier's heel up tighter against the top of the shell's heel pocket, but keep in mind that heel lifts alter fore-aft alignment. This change may be a good thing, and you'll have killed two birds with one stone. But it may not be (see Fore-Aft Alignment: Project Delta and Attention Skiers with Limited Ankle Dorsiflexion in the Getting Techno section).

### Upper-Boot Looseness

Many skiers have skinny calves and skinny lower legs. If this sounds like you, be sure that you buy boots that offer upper buckles with predrilled or premarked buckle holes, so you can gain a tighter fit after the boots pack out a bit. This tends to do the trick for most folks; but for those skiers who experience a lot of slop in the upper boot, there's a slick new way to take care of it.

A company called Masterfit Enterprises (listed in the appendix) has developed a simple bootfitting product called the Eliminator Tongue that solves quite a few different boot-fitting problems, one of them being a loose upper boot. The Eliminator Tongue is a medium-density foam insert that runs along the boot's tongue, between the tongue and the skier's shin. The tongue tapers both in width and in thickness and is designed to run from the top of the shin all the way to the foot's instep. It can be installed with Velcro, which sticks right to most boot tongue fabrics, or it can be permanently affixed to the boot's tongue with contact cement.

### Shin Pain (aka Boot Bang)

Shins can be tricky because the tibia runs close to the skin, providing a bony mass that butts up against the tongue of the boot where a lot of pressure can be exerted during skiing. It's worth mentioning again that skiers must buy boots that feel great on the shin. Don't settle for just an OK fit along the shin: get a super fit on the shin, even if it means you'll have to deal with some minor problems elsewhere on that boot. Some boots simply don't fit and flex right for your shin, and those boots will make your life hell. So don't go there.

Sometimes shins get sore on the first day of the season because that kind of pressure is unique to skiing; this typically goes away. Sometimes skiers' shins get sensitive because the movement of flexing in a ski boot rips hairs out of the lower leg. I actually shave my legs from

the boot top down during the ski season. This works well, but looks pretty stupid! Unfortunately, bad boot bang comes from an imperfect interface between the shin and the boot, and that can be tougher to solve.

Occasionally, the boot liner's tongue is too stiff where the boot needs to flex, and pulling the liner out and working the tongue through some rigorous flexing will often be enough to make it more supple.

However, more often than not, shin pain is the result of being in too large a boot. The boot fails to contact the shin with evenly distributed pressure from top to bottom because it's not small enough to approach all these spots. As the skier flexes, her shin will impact the top of the tongue more than the rest of it, and this spot gets sore. The only way to solve the problem is to get better tongue-to-shin contact in all those other spots, to spread the pressure more evenly. Using the elasticized Booster Strap, which we mentioned earlier, can help achieve that fit, as can the Eliminator Tongue.

Some skiers have problematic shins, either due to bone mass issues or nerve irritation. The Eliminator Tongue is thick enough that its backside, or the side that meets the boot's tongue, can be ground to produce cavities or channels. This allows for a way to lighten the pressure in a particular problem area while keeping the rest of the shin snug.

### The Boot's Too Stiff

It is typically easier to make a stiff boot softer than it is to make a too-soft boot feel more substantial; but not having to do either is your best bet. Don't make a boot-buying decision that requires major alteration to the boot's flex if you can avoid it.

There are two main ways to soften a boot's forward flex. The first and most often successful way is to shave a little material off the bottom of the bottom buckle strap on the upper boot. Sometimes, this buckle strap comes into contact with the lower boot during flexion. The boot isn't too stiff as much as its flex range is limited by the collision between the bottom buckle strap on the upper boot with the lower boot. Taking some plastic off the bottom of the strap using a mat knife or grinder will increase the flex range and make the boot feel softer.

The other way to soften a ski boot is to cut the inner shell. Pull the liner out of the boot and look at the shell. You may see slots marked for cutting that will soften the boot's flex. Sometimes a shell already has a V-shaped slot cut in the back that is blocked with a bit of plastic; once the plastic is removed, the V can close during flexion and provide increased forward flex range. Generally, a bootfitting technician will have to do the cutting for you. Try to find a technician who is experienced with softening boot flex. If this is done incorrectly, the manner in which the boot flexes can be altered for the worse.

## Black Toe

Unfortunately, a lot of skiers know what I'm talking about when I mention black toe. Too many folks bruise their big toe during the ski season badly enough that the nail bed turns black, and the toenail often falls off sometime in the summer months. It doesn't feel good— and it looks pretty gross.

Skiers who lose their big toenail because their boot is too small are in the minority. Most black toe comes from being in a boot that's too big. This allows the foot to slide fore and aft, jackhammering the big toe into the end of the boot when the skier gets into the backseat in the bumps, or upon landing a jump.

Boots that are really too short can be dealt with, as we described above in The Boot's Too Tight in Length, pages 96–97. Boots that are too big can be dealt with as described above in various ways, but of particular use here is the Eliminator Tongue. This does a good job of shoving the foot back into the heel pocket and keeping it there—even when the bumps

get the best of you. Your big toe will thank you.

## Arch Cramping and Aching

Pretty much any problems associated with the underside of the foot are either created or solved by footbeds (it's usually the latter). As you'll read about footbeds in the chapter on alignment, most skiers' arches need some kind of support. Even very flat feet tend to benefit from a little arch support. The key is to have an appropriate amount of support under the foot.

The medium- to high-arch foot that doesn't have enough support beneath it can spasm after being put under the kinds of stress we create during all-day edging movements. An under-supported arch renders the foot less stable in the ski boot, and we unconsciously put our feet through contortions during skiing to make them feel solid. This kind of foot movement makes them seize up.

The vast majority of skiers benefit from footbeds. Here are a pair of trim-to-fit, or premolded, footbeds on the left and a pair of moldable cork custom footbeds on the right, both by DownUnders. MT. BACHELOR SKI AND SPORT

Low arches that receive too much support from poorly built footbeds—or from pre-molded, off-the-shelf footbeds—will react negatively as well. You can't force an arch into a flat foot; a flat foot needs appropriately low support to feel comfortable.

## Da Burnin' Balls

Most skiers won't know what I'm talking about here, and that's good. Consider yourself lucky if you're raising your eyebrows right now. The unfortunate few who know exactly what I mean have felt the tingling begin under the balls of their feet and build (either quickly or throughout the day) to a mighty crescendo of flaming foot torture. It's not just uncomfortable: it's downright debilitating when it gets bad.

To simplify, it's a nerve situation that is exacerbated by ski boots that put the metatarsals (the bones in the ball of the foot) in an unsound position. Essentially, the metatarsals are happiest in a bit of a crested orientation—in the same way that the knuckles of your hand reside in a somewhat arched position when your hand is held out and relaxed. If the metatarsals are squashed flat or squeezed side to side by a ski boot, the nerves that run through the bone structure of the forefoot can riot and light the fires.

The narrow boot that squeezes the forefoot side to side is the easy one to fix: just make it wider, as we discussed above, and as we'll cover in the next section on hot spots.

The forefoot that is squashed flat is usually flattened for one of two reasons, or at times both.

First, skiers who have limited ankle dorsiflexion and don't deal with the issue with heel lifts will have heels that lift off the bottom of their boot. This puts the skier's entire weight on the balls of his feet, rather than spreading the load evenly across the whole foot. The forefeet get all the load and the balls start burning. Often, simply dealing with the dorsiflexion issue by adding heel lifts solves the whole problem. (But

as I've said before, any time heel lifts are added, fore-aft balance is affected.)

The other reason the balls burn is that the foot's *transverse arch*, or the hollow that runs side to side just behind the ball of the foot, isn't being properly supported. If this arch collapses, the bones flatten and the balls of the feet can get fired up. This type of foot needs a little support for that lesser-known arch with what custom footbed technicians call a *metatarsal pad*, which is built into your custom footbed. This is a more technical operation, and you'll need to find a technician who knows what you're talking about. But search for that person; she may be your salvation.

Some skiers are dealing with both these situations, and they'll have to deal with two variables simultaneously. This is a bit more difficult. But once these skiers get their boots and footbeds wired, it's smooth sailing.

## Hot Spots

A hot spot is any specific location of pain or uncomfortable pressure caused by your boot. Any place where your foot comes into closer contact with the boot shell than it was meant to can become a hot spot. This is not a general problem with boot fit; it is a localized one caused by the shape of your foot or lower leg. Hot spots can result from bony protuberances on the feet—usually around the heel, ankle, or forefoot—or they can be caused by any overly wide portion of the foot.

Ignoring a hot spot is a bad idea. Hot spots are usually places where the boot is putting pressure directly on bone. Our body senses that this bone mass is under stress and attempts to fortify it by first sending some swelling and, later, some calcium deposits. If not dealt with, a hot spot can turn into what's known as a bone spur, which can require surgical removal in the worst cases. Don't blow off a hot spot and keep skiing.

The way to deal with hot spots depends on how bad the hot spot is, and how bad a hot spot

The first step in eradicating a hot spot is finding it and marking its location on the liner. MT. BACHELOR SKI AND SPORT

is depends on how much pressure the boot's shell is putting on that bony part of the foot. If you are experiencing only minor pressure and discomfort, the sensitive part of the foot can be "blocked" away from the shell by padding *around* the sensitive area. This is generally called the doughnut method because the padding around the hot spot can start to look like a doughnut. More often, the pad is C-shaped and arcs around the problem area.

To apply the doughnut method, pull your boot liner from the shell and put the liner on your foot. Stand with your foot flat on the floor and poke around with your fingers to find the painful spot. When you find it, make a mark with an ink pen that shows the size of the entire painful area. Now feel around the painful spot to see if there is some available void space, or non-bony parts, surrounding the hot spot. You will place the sticky-backed bootfitting foam in this area—and who knows what kind of weird doughnut it will end up looking like? Put the liner back into the boot and see how it feels. If your padding has *added* pressure to the spot, figure out where that extra padding is located and remove some of it, a little at a time.

If the spot is still problematic after trying the doughnut, it means that more drastic action is required. The options are grinding, punching, or stretching the shell.

A bootfitting technician can grind plastic material from the inside of the shell in exactly the spot where the shell comes too close to the foot; but the amount of material available to grind away is generally small. However, it's common that the amount of space gained by grinding is enough to solve the problem forever. The real trick is making sure the grinding is done in the right location.

Find the hot spot on the boot's liner; you may already have made a mark. If not, use a ballpoint pen, a felt-tip marker, or even lipstick to mark the hot spot area on the liner. (Be sure to use plenty of ink if you're using a pen.) The idea is to put the liner back into the shell, wear the boot for a bit, pull the liner back out, and be able to see a mark that's been transferred to the inside of the shell. This is something you can do ahead of time, before skiing, and then pop into the shop toward the end of the day to have your tech-

A shop can spread the shell and grind for hot spots, even in the toebox. MT. BACHELOR SKI AND SPORT

nician grind the spot that has been transferred by your skiing to the inside of the boot. Sometimes I'll ink several different spots that I suspect may be problematic, then ski for a few days before pulling my liners out to grind the shells. By then, I'll have a regular road map to follow.

If grinding won't provide enough relief for the hot spot, it's possible to *punch* a boot's shell by heating up a specific area to the verge of melting the plastic, and then clamping the shell in a device that produces a bulge in the plastic—essentially, a cave for the skier's bony spot to hang out in. The difference between what many technicians call a *punch* and a *stretch* is that the punch is a tidy, isolated bulge. The heat stretch of a shell is more of a broad-sword approach to widening a large portion of the boot, usually in the forefoot. There are some devices out there that can do both at once.

There are some locations on a boot that are hard to heat stretch or punch. Any riveted hinge points or overlapping plastic layers can prove difficult. Your bootfitter will be able to tell you how "punchable" your hot spot is.

Both punching and stretching require heating the shell substantially and then rigging some kind of gizmo inside and around the boot. This means that working off an ink transfer inside the shell is more difficult to see. I prefer to use a mark made on the outside of the shell. The best way to locate this mark is to put the boot on, buckle it up, and start whacking on it with a hammer to find the hot spot. When you think you've got it pegged, make a small dot with a pen, then go at it some more to see if that's the *exact* spot. If you're not on target in locating the hot spot, you can make things worse. Be sure your mark is visible and communicated accurately to the technician who will do the work.

I tend to punch or stretch at least 33 percent more than I really need to, because the stretched plastic tends to relax a little over time. Also realize that your boots will begin to look freakish after undertaking this process. Don't be bothered by this: it's the true sign of a comfortable boot.

You can bulge the shell's plastic to accommodate your foot's knobs and bony spots. MT. BACHELOR SKI AND SPORT

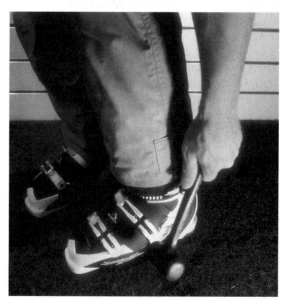

For shell punches, it's best to locate the hot spot's epicenter on the outside of the shell by tapping with a hammer, then marking the spot for a technician. MT. BACHELOR SKI AND SPORT

# 12

# Poles and Bindings

## POLES

There is little to talk about when it comes to the physical ski pole. The use of ski poles can be a tricky thing, and this subtle skill is only mastered after a lot of practice. But the poles themselves are not complex pieces of equipment, so this discussion will be brief.

When it comes to buying poles, pole length is the only truly important consideration. You can follow your gut reactions when it comes to weight, grip style, construction, and price; but don't ignore the finer points of finding the perfect length.

A too-short pole will force you into an overly flexed or hunched stance and will cause you to develop a contrived, reaching pole swing as you bend over slightly and reach toward the snow to achieve a solid pole plant. A too-long pole can cause an overly tall, stiff stance or impede smooth pole-swing movements, which in turn can cause problems with body mass movement. And long poles simply ruin your skiing potential in bumps.

To find a pole of the correct length in a ski shop, grasp a ski pole upside down so the basket rests on top of your fist, against your thumb. Flex your legs slightly into a skiing stance and plant the pole grip just in front of your feet. Keep your hands in a skiing position so that the pole's shaft stands more or less straight up and down. Without moving, look at your elbow. The angle created between your forearm and upper

arm should be about 90 degrees. Once you put your ski boots and skis on, your poles will seem a little shorter and your elbow angle will be a little greater than 90 degrees. Remember that some bindings with a lot of lift will make your poles seem even shorter.

Ski with your poles and make note of the following situations. When you ski bumps, can you "ski through" your pole plant by simply breaking your wrist, just as if you were using a hammer? If your entire arm is lifted slightly, then your poles may be too long. Do you find during short turns that the pole's tip touches the snow prematurely or behind the point where you want it to? This may also be a clue that your poles are too long. Poles that are too short will make your bump skiing easier, but they will alter your balanced stance in other terrain.

You can take your poles to a shop and have them shortened if they seem too long. A ½-inch difference will feel like a major change, so try to make no more than ½-inch adjustments at a time (unless you are absolutely positive). Sometimes a ¼ inch is all it takes. When you find that perfect length, measure it and remember it. You can size your next pair of poles immediately. Some shops will try to tell you that you can't shorten composite poles, but you can. It requires careful hacksawing instead of using a pipe cutter, but it can be done.

You can shorten your own poles if you want to, but you'll need to come up with a way to get the grips off. The best way that I've come across

Using your poles is always more fun than buying your poles. JURGEN FENNERL ON THE MORAINE, MT. BACHELOR

is to have a notch cut into a solid piece of shop furniture, such as a bench or even an exposed wall stud. I have a couple different sized notches to use, depending on the width of the shaft. You want the notch sized so you can just barely slide the pole shaft into the notch, but the notch should be too small for the grip to make it through.

Slide the pole through the notch, then grab the pole tightly and give it a hard yank; the grip will smack into the wooden barrier and pop right off. You may have to heat stubborn grips with a blow dryer or heat gun to coax them off.

Put the grip back on after shortening the pole by pushing it on with your hand; then turn the pole upside down and whack the top of the grip straight onto the floor: a few good shots and it will be on all the way.

Many skiers have turned to adjustable-length ski poles, both for ease of experimentation in finding the perfect length and for convenience during travel. Some of these poles can function as avalanche probes as well, giving skiers another tool in the backcountry or while cat- or heli-skiing.

## Although Length Does Matter . . .

While your primary concern when it comes to poles is getting the right length, it can pay, literally, to know something about their construction. Poles bend and poles break. It makes sense to avoid both if you can. Poles are currently made either of aluminum or of composite material, like the material found in golf club shafts.

Aluminum poles can bend or snap in half during a crash. Composite shaft poles will not bend, but they can break. Many skiers opt for aluminum for the sake of affordability. But they should consider paying a little extra for the stiffest and lightest grade aluminum pole that fits their budget, for the more rigid poles tend to get bent less often.

Composite shaft poles are becoming as affordable as aluminum and can offer skiers greater longevity since they won't bend during

Buying your poles is, well, pretty easy. MT. BACHELOR SKI AND SPORT

falls. However, nicks and cuts made by skis' edges on the pole shaft near the basket can weaken the pole and cause it to snap prematurely. I like to wrap the bottom four inches of the shaft, just above the basket, with electrical tape to help prevent this from happening.

Last but not least, consider finding a pole that has a decent-sized basket or comes with two interchangeable sizes. Bigger baskets are key for skiing powder and for getting around in deeper snow. Small baskets dive too deep in soft snow and can both slow you down in your travels toward fresh tracks and mess with your balance once you're there.

## BINDINGS

I used to think that the binding's function was merely to hold the boot to the ski and to release when needed. But times have changed. While it may have been that a binding was simply an expensive fastener in the past, new technology in skis and boots has brought on a new kind of binding. Now, bindings can affect how your ski performs—and mostly for the better if you know what to look for.

The traditional binding, while essential, has always been a hindrance to a ski's ability to do its job. A ski is designed to bend into an arc, like a small section of a large circle that the skier rides on during a turn. When a binding clamps a boot onto that ski, the binding can't help but prevent the ski from bending into the true arc it was designed to achieve. The traditional binding produced a nonbending, or dead, spot on the ski that limited the ski's performance.

As shaped skis have evolved—with deeper sidecut, softer flex characteristics, and shorter lengths—skiers are bending skis even farther. To prevent the binding-induced dead spot, binding manufacturers are developing binding systems that allow for more unhindered flex in the ski and, in turn, better performance.

Some bindings just allow for more flex in the ski; others can even enhance or manipulate a ski's flex to give a ski performance characteristics it wouldn't have without the binding. Many manufacturers are developing ski-binding systems in which a ski is matched with a particular, integrated binding to achieve this kind of added performance. But whether the binding is part of a "system" or made for use on any ski, the goal of managing ski flex remains the same.

There are a few things you need to know about choosing the right bindings and then getting the most out of them once you've purchased them.

## Buying the Right Binding

The binding purchase is often left to chance or made as an afterthought to a well-planned boot and ski buy. This is not wise, for today's bindings can affect your skiing performance and are truly a piece of safety equipment that merits a little consideration. Finding a good binding isn't tough, as long as you know what you're looking for. You will have to rely on a good salesperson at a ski shop to guide you through what's offered in current models, but you'll be ahead of the game if you ask about the binding's features regarding retention, release, lift, and performance enhancements.

### Retention Features

Accomplished skiers need to seek a fine balance between a binding that comes off when it should but otherwise stays on no matter how stressful the skiing environment may become. There are times when a ski that pops off prematurely or during in-control, high-impact skiing can present more danger to the skier than a binding that doesn't release properly.

Some bindings in a manufacturer's line will have design characteristics that allow for better retention during high-performance skiing. The binding's toepiece may have limited release modes or the heelpiece may boast a higher-than-average elastic travel range. And some bindings offer improved means of maintaining constant forward pressure in the binding during extreme ski flex and rebound. All of these elements have

Bindings are more than just a clamp between boot and ski. MT. BACHELOR SKI AND SPORT

been shown to help increase retention in bump-and-jump skiing.

### Release Features

Every skier wants his or her bindings to release when they need to, and every binding on the market has gone through stringent safety testing to ensure that they will. But every model is different, so it doesn't hurt to find out what release features each binding offers.

You should know whether the binding offers upward release (in addition to standard lateral release) in the toepiece, as well as what directions the heelpiece will allow the boot to escape from the binding. Some bindings offer designs that claim to increase release in slow rolling or twisting falls; these types of falls could fail to release a skier from the binding, which could cause an injury.

Often overlooked by the buyer is the type of antifriction device, or AFD, used in the binding's toepiece. The AFD is the part of the toepiece that the boot sole will ride upon. Its function is to allow the boot to slide smoothly out of the binding, no matter what kind of ice or grit may be present under the boot. Mechanical AFDs incorporate some kind of moving parts that roll or glide laterally to help the boot exit the binding. Fixed AFDs do not move, but they use a slippery, tough material like Teflon to reduce friction between the boot and binding.

### Lift

It's getting hard to find a binding that doesn't offer some kind of lift or plate to suspend a skier a little higher off the ski. In the days of the straight ski, bindings were typically mounted with the toepiece and heelpiece riding on the ski and independent of each other, with a low profile that allowed the boot sole to come very close to the *topsheet,* or top surface, of the ski. Modern bindings are more connected structures, with plates, pieces, and parts running between the toepiece and heelpiece. These *lifted* bindings let the boot ride higher off the top of the ski for a few different reasons.

Primarily, a lifted binding helps prevent what's called *boot out* from happening during extreme edging movements. During a deeply carved turn in which a skier rolls the ski far onto its edge, the boot can begin to hit the snow surface. If the boot hangs too far out over the edge of the ski, it can actually pry the ski's edge back out of the snow, causing the ski to break into a skid, or "boot out." A lifted binding suspends the boot higher off the ski and provides a little extra clearance between the boot and the snow during radical edging. This kind of deep edging movement may seem out of your reach. But shaped skis make it more of a reality for good skiers than ever before, so it does matter.

Lifted bindings also make the skier's legs longer in the same way that elevator shoes make a person taller. This amounts to having a longer lever with which to tip the ski over. Many skiers report marked improvements with their edging quickness and power through using a lifted binding. And as skis become wider, extra levering power becomes more necessary.

Many skiers may have had bad experiences with the first generations of lifted bindings. Those early designs had a tendency to make a ski feel overly heavy and stiff in the waist of the ski. These first lifted bindings also felt precarious at times, and they seemed to do more harm than good. But my experience is that lifted bindings are vastly superior now and they offer far more benefit than they used to. Skiers shouldn't be afraid to mount them on their next pair of skis.

### Performance Enhancements

Some bindings offer nothing in this regard, while others pack a ton of bells and whistles into a small device. Here are a few common features to look for.

First, some kind of vibration dampening means is popular in bindings. This can be as simple as using rubber or another elastomeric material in the base of the binding, or it may involve more complex gizmos. The idea behind vibration dampening in bindings is to keep the ski's edge carving smoothly.

Other bindings offer ways to manipulate the amount of rebound energy available in the ski. Some increase the rebound energy, for extra snap and acceleration when coming out of turns; some mellow it, for a more dampened feel. The choice of which way to go would depend on your skiing style or on the nature of the ski you plan to mount with such a binding.

There are a few bindings out there that offer *switches* that can be placed at different settings to alter the way the ski performs. Most of these switchable bindings utilize mechanisms in their lift plate systems to change the way the ski flexes, which in turn changes the way the ski performs.

Finally, there are bindings that allow for a range of movement fore and aft on the ski. This is a handy feature for skiers who are tuned in to being centered on their skis or for skiers who never feel as if they're far enough forward on their skis. Fore-aft adjustment in a binding is also the ultimate tool for keeping your ski tips from diving in extremely deep powder.

There are other ways to manipulate fore-aft alignment (see the section on Project Delta in Getting Techno, pages 212–14), but shifting the binding forward or backward of center on the ski is very effective. Unfortunately, most of these fore-aft adjusters offer adjustment increments that are pretty large (5–7 mm). For the truly techno, an increment of a couple millimeters at a time would be preferred.

### Some Other Considerations

After you've narrowed down your binding selection, don't forget to look at the binding's indicator setting range, also formerly known as the DIN range. Your binding will be set at a certain indicator setting based on information you provide to your technician: height, weight, age, Skier Type classification, and boot sole length.

Ideally, a skier's setting should fall somewhere in the middle of the binding's setting range. Don't buy a binding with a range of DIN 6–14 if your indicator setting is 6, if you can help it. Typically bindings with lighter setting ranges are less expensive, so there's no reason to buy more than you need.

Also consider how you plan to travel with your skis and determine whether you need a ski bag or binding protector. Leaving skis on the roof rack for road trips will coat bindings in fine grit and road grime, and this can impede smooth binding function.

To keep your bindings working consistently from season to season, back off the spring tension for both the heelpiece and toepiece during the summer. Just remember where to reset them the following winter, or have them reset by your ski shop.

## A Primer on "Prerelease"

Skiers are often so concerned that their skis will come off prematurely, or *prerelease,* as it's often referred to, that they are willing to turn their binding's indicator setting up to potentially dangerous levels. Not wanting a ski to pop off

Prerelease can make things a little too exciting. BILL SHEPPERD ABOVE THE WHO-DA-THUNKS, MT. BACHELOR

during aggressive skiing is understandable. But as I mentioned above, there's an appropriate balance between retention and release. Here are a few tips to help you find that middle ground.

Skiers should understand that the information they provide to a binding technician—height, weight, age, boot sole length, and Skier Type—is what will initially determine how the binding will be set. Skiers who experience binding release in situations they feel did not merit a release should follow a few steps to keep the ski on without jeopardizing their safety.

The first step is to confirm with the technician that the subjective information you provided is correct. Then the technician should double-check to make sure your settings were properly determined and set. How the technician sets a binding's forward pressure is critical here: if the setting is too loose, the binding can often release prematurely. Be sure the technician checks that the forward pressure is within the specifications.

If this first check doesn't find anything amiss, a skier must make a decision: to continue skiing with the binding as is; to consider changing his or her technique to put less stress on the binding system; to have the binding torque tested; or to make a change in the binding indicator settings.

Torque testing is the way a ski shop makes sure a binding is releasing properly at a given setting. This route is worth taking if you are concerned that the binding may not be functioning correctly—especially if it's always one ski that tends to pop off. The shop can set that ski's binding higher to match the release values of the other ski if the test shows that it's necessary.

Skiers who decide to increase their binding's indicator setting have a couple options. One way is to revise your Skier Type information, if possible. For example, a skier who selected Skier Type II and subsequently had repeated unnecessary releases could choose to reclassify himself with the technician as a Skier Type III. This will bump up the indicator setting substan-

tially. Many accomplished skiers who already classify themselves as a Skier Type III don't realize that they can reclassify themselves as a Skier Type III+ and achieve this same kind of across-the-board increase in their settings.

The problem with revising Skier Type information is that the jump in indicator settings can be large—at times taking a skier from, say, an 8.5 all the way to a 10. It's hard to know whether this will be just right or too high for safe binding releases. What if somewhere in between would be better for you?

The other way you can increase your indicator settings to find a safe middle ground between retention and release is to simply tell the technician what indicator setting you want, above and beyond your intial, problematic setting. The key here is to make small changes above your chart-determined setting and see how they work out. *Take note that here you're taking responsibility for your own decisions.* The shop technician will probably ask you to sign some kind of waiver in order to do this for you.

My personal rule of thumb is to make an increase to my initial setting by 0.5 and continue skiing. If I continue to release prematurely, I try to determine which ski I'm releasing out of and whether it's the toepiece or heelpiece. If you haven't had a torque test performed, it's a good idea to do so if one ski is always coming off. Then I increase the culprit (heel or toe) by another 0.5 and continue skiing. I have always had luck in quickly finding a point at which my bindings stay on, yet still release in a crash. With my current Rossignol binding I actually ski at my chart-determined setting and have had no problems. Be careful with indiator settings—these are your knees!—and remember to seek good advice from knowledgeable binding technicians.

You can find a lot of interesting binding information, including information on "prerelease," on the Vermont Ski Safety Web site at www.vermontskisafety.com (see the FAQs for skiers).

## A Binding Alternative

Backcountry skiing (off-area, no lifts) has continued to gain popularity in recent years among alpine skiers for a few reasons. First, if done safely, backcountry skiing is a great way to get some exercise and good skiing. It's also a way to find fresh powder after the resort's been completely tracked out—and that phenomenon is becoming far too common with the advent of wider skis. In addition, skiers are getting into the backcountry simply because they can, thanks again to new skis that make off-piste conditions easier to deal with.

The only real detail keeping most alpine skiers out of the backcountry is the lack of a good way to go uphill. Hiking in ski boots through powder only to "posthole" up to one's waist isn't fun, and snowshoes are slow going. Many alpine skiers have turned to telemark skiing in order to gain the uphill touring advantage. But you don't have to take up a new sport to get into the backcountry: you just need a new binding.

Alpine touring, or *randonnée*, bindings have been around for ages, but only recently have they been improved to the point where a skier could consider using an alpine touring binding as her everyday binding for on- and off-area skiing.

An alpine touring (AT) binding is designed to allow the heel to disengage from the ski and hinge at the toepiece so a more natural walking motion can be achieved, much like cross-country skiing. With the use of climbing skins, which are adhered to the base of the ski to provide grip on the snow, the free-heeling aspect of the AT binding allows a skier to walk right up a hill while staying on top of deep snow. When it's time to descend, the AT binding's heel is locked down (just like a regular ski binding), the skins are removed, and off you go.

In my opinion, the best AT binding on the market today for aggressive alpine skiers is the Fritschi Free Ride binding distributed by Black Diamond Equipment (see the appendix). Fritschi has developed a wide indicator setting range (from DIN 4–12), and the Free Ride comes equipped with a functional ski brake, multiple elevator settings, and an option for a ski crampon for ascending hard, spring snow.

Many AT aficionados use specialized, lightweight alpine touring boots that have the benefit of a higher flexing "touring mode" and a Vibram (lugged) sole for scrambling. But there's no reason why you can't use your regular ski boots, especially for day trips.

There are devices out there called touring adapters, which click into your existing bindings and offer a similar free-heeling effect. But between the regular binding and the adapter, weight becomes an issue. In my experience these adapters can feel precarious and can be a hassle to deal with.

Alpine touring bindings allow for backcountry ascent and descent.

# 13

# Alignment

Alignment, also called *stance balancing,* is the term used to describe the way a skier's feet, ankles, lower legs, knees, and hips stack up on top of one another and how ski equipment influences this stack of body parts. There is a biomechanically sound way for your body parts to meet and move with each other. For example, for correct posture in everyday life you must keep your back in an erect position, not arched or hunched. A biomechanically sound position can prevent injury and produce effective and powerful body movements.

In skiing, proper alignment describes a skier whose feet, ankles, lower legs, and (by extension) knees and hips are stacked on top of his ski boots in a manner that maintains a biomechanically sound relationship among these body parts. Proper alignment ensures that these body parts are in a position that will allow them to work effectively, thus reducing pain, fatigue, or injury. Proper alignment also maximizes these parts' potential for pressuring, twisting, and levering powerfully within ski boots.

With good alignment, your skis tend to ride in a neutral position, which is close to flat if you are sliding down a level run. Poor alignment negatively affects the way your skis ride on the snow. Misaligned skiers can have one good turn and one bad turn, experience difficulty entering or exiting turns, or struggle in certain terrain for no apparent reason.

Without knowing it, many misaligned skiers are riding on skis that are always on edge. Even

small changes in edge angle can effect major changes in what a ski will do. Misaligned skiers are at a mechanical disadvantage because when they assume their skis are flat, they are wrong.

When your alignment is right, the skis go exactly where you want them to. LIZ ELLING AT MONTANA SNOWBOWL; PHOTO BY R. MARK ELLING FOR KIRK DEVOLL PHOTOGRAPHY

With the advent of shaped skis, misaligned skiers are in more trouble than ever. New ski designs make skiing easier because skis engage in turns with minimal work: just tip the ski over and it turns. Imagine what a crazy ride shaped skis would be if your edging movements were out of your control. Many skiers find shaped skis hard to enjoy because their alignment is out of whack, but most of them don't know it: they just keep skiing their old, straight skis because they go, well, straight.

Achieving proper alignment is not difficult. However, there is still quite a bit of ignorance regarding the importance of proper alignment. You will find many good skiers, instructors, shop managers, and even coaches who minimize the importance of alignment. It's often the case that these skiers never had any experience with an alignment issue, so they never perceived a *need* to mess with it. Usually, skiers who scoff at alignment tend to have bodies that are naturally neutral, or not out of whack with their equipment. They don't know what the fuss is all about. Don't bother trying to explain to these folks that you need help: they can't help you anyway. Find ski industry professionals who know about stance balancing from firsthand experience and have dedicated time and energy in mastering this odd science.

In my experience, achieving proper alignment is a combined effort between your own abilities to experiment with your boots and a ski shop's ability to give you the products and assistance you need. Some trial and error is involved, but this effort can be fun. You will get immediate feedback from your experiments: either your adjustments will work or they won't.

Finally, note that as a general rule the term *alignment* refers to stance balancing in the lateral plane, which involves the nuances of edging and the correction of knock-knees and bowlegs. However, there is a front-to-back component in proper alignment, which I'll address later in this section. Proper fore-aft balancing with your ski equipment is less talked about, but equally important.

## STARTING FROM THE GROUND UP: FOOTBEDS

Good alignment starts with your feet and ankles. These body parts serve the same function as the foundation of a new house. A solid foundation at the level of your feet and ankles can do the most good for your alignment; poor foot support and ankle alignment will cause the most trouble.

A well-made custom footbed designed for skiing will provide support to the bottom of your foot for increased comfort and transmission of energy to your ski. It will also put your ankle into a biomechanically sound position in your ski boot and begin building a foundation of good alignment for skiing.

### Different Kinds of Footbeds

There are several different types of footbed-like products out there. Some are better for your skiing than others, and some cost more than others. You can find footbed products to suit your budget and your performance needs, if you know what you're looking for.

Every new boot comes with a *stock insole*. This is the soft but flat piece of foam that your foot rests on in the boot's liner. The stock insole doesn't offer much performance enhancement, but it comes in the boot.

Next in line, moving up the ladder of expense and performance, is the *premolded* or *trim-to-fit footbed*. The trim-to-fit is an insole that offers substantially more arch support than a stock insole. The trim-to-fit also has a deeper heel cup that helps hold the heel and ankle in a stable position. The problem with premolded footbeds is just that: they have been prefabricated for an average foot that isn't your foot. Their benefit is affordability. If you can't swallow the cost of a custom footbed, buy these.

*Custom footbeds* are skiing insoles that are custom-fitted to your foot's shape and to your alignment needs. They are made by a technician at a ski shop or by a bootfitting specialist and are

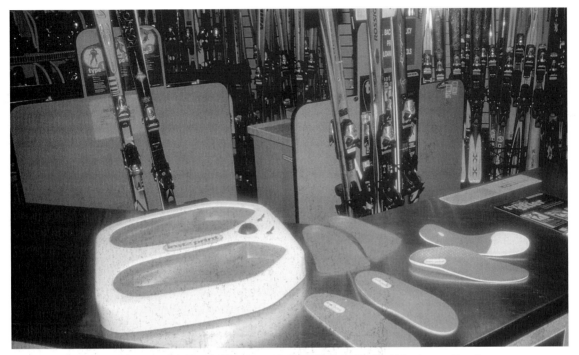

The Insta-Print custom footbed system: molding device, footbed blanks, posting foam, and finished footbeds. This is an example of a semi-weight-bearing production method. MT. BACHELOR SKI AND SPORT

designed for use in a ski boot. The processes by which the footbed is molded to your foot can vary widely, as can the materials that the custom footbed is made of. While there are different theories regarding which processes and materials are best, many of these arguments are semantic in nature. What matters most about the custom footbed made for a ski boot is *who* makes it. A good footbed technician can offer you a perfect fit for comfort and performance; a hack can make your feet cry and make your performance suffer. Ask around to find a good footbed builder.

*Orthotics* are custom insoles that are prescribed for your feet by a podiatrist and either built by a podiatrist or by a certified pedorthist (a footbed builder who can build an insole to the specifications of a podiatrist's prescription). These are not necessarily the ultimate products for a skiing application, unless you know you

have extreme foot-care issues or you already see a podiatrist. The prescribed orthotic is often not suitable for use in a ski boot, for some podiatrists or pedorthists are not skiers and they don't know what you really need. Orthotics are also expensive (running around $400 a pair now), but they are sometimes covered by insurance. If you want to go the prescribed orthotic route, be sure that your podiatrist or pedorthist knows how to make a skiing footbed.

## What Does a Custom Footbed Do?

A custom footbed first accommodates the shape of the bottom of your foot, taking up the void space around your foot's contours. If this void space under your foot isn't filled or supported in some way, it translates into slop, or lost energy, inside your ski boot. Stock insoles are notorious for letting your foot's fine-tuning movements get lost before they make it to the boot, not to mention the ski. A custom footbed that fills this void space and takes up this slop will instantly give you better control over your ski.

The custom footbed also supports the foot's arch in a manner that is comfortable and maintains the natural shape of the foot. A foot inside a ski boot can be put under pretty severe stress from turn to turn; without proper arch support, a foot can be put into some unnatural positions. The foot's arch can collapse, which stretches tendons and muscles more than normal, and the foot can twist in its attempt to render itself stable in the boot. These contortions can lead to an achy, cramping foot. The support of a custom footbed can stabilize your foot and support your arch enough so your foot can essentially relax inside your boot, even during high-energy skiing.

The custom footbed also cradles the heel in a heel cup that, in conjunction with a flat underside, keeps the ankle from rocking side to side in the boot. This provides better edge control, but it also affects a skier's alignment. The heel cup holds the ankle in a more set position than the boot's original stock insole. Ideally, the custom footbed holds the ankle in a biomechanically sound position that sets the skier on the road to good alignment.

## How Do You Know Your Custom Footbed Is a Good One?

If you're in the market for a custom footbed built at a ski shop or by a bootfitting specialist, you should know a few basics about beds. First, expect to pay from around $80 to $200 for a pair, depending on where you're located and the celebrity status of who's making them. If the technician is good, the $80 beds can be just as good, or even better, than pricier ones built by a less-skilled technician.

Again, when it comes to custom footbeds, the material used to make the footbed is not nearly as important as the skill of the technician making the bed. But the process of production is

worth discussing. There are three types of procedures for molding, or casting, the footbed: weight-bearing, non-weight-bearing, and semi-weight-bearing.

A weight-bearing production method requires the skier to stand up and put all his weight on the bed in order to mold it to the shape of his foot. Non-weight-bearing procedures will take a cast, or mold, of the foot without any of the skier's weight on it. Semi-weight-bearing procedures will take some or most of the weight off the skier's feet while the footbed is cast, usually by molding the footbed while the skier sits.

Weight-bearing production is not looked upon as favorably as the other, less weighted options because the skier's weight can cause his feet to overpronate (collapse medially) or over-supinate (roll laterally) during the molding process. A well-built footbed will prevent both of these foot movements and will be built to hold the ankle in a more neutral position. Semi-weighted and nonweighted methods avoid the pronation and supination issue, and these processes tend to produce more effective footbeds. Keep in mind, though, that a good technician may be able to address these issues using weight-bearing production methods.

Be sure to ask about the process. It's a good sign if the technician can tell you how his system will produce a footbed that holds your foot in a neutral, sound position.

### A Few Custom Footbed Consumer Tactics

If you're not sure about where to have your custom footbeds made, ask around at your favorite ski area. Talk to ski instructors and ski patrollers. These folks are on their feet all day, every day. They've probably had several different kinds of footbeds made by technicians in the area and can give you a few leads.

Talk to the technician who will actually be building your footbeds and quiz him or her on the process. If there's no mention of looking at your feet and discussing your past history with foot pain or alignment issues, it's cause for suspicion. The technician's understanding of your foot shape and arch height is critical to the production of a good footbed. And if he or she knows what kinds of foot problems you've had in the past, it's a good bet that those problems will be easier to fix this time around.

Ask to see a footbed that's being worked on at the moment, or one that's just been completed. (Don't look at the display model; who knows who built it?) You should take note of a few simple details. The footbed should not be just a one-ply sheet of material that took the shape of a foot. This kind of bed feels more comfortable than the stock insole, but it doesn't do anything to keep your foot from rocking back and forth in the ski boot. The void spaces under the arch and around the heel should be filled in, or *posted*, with whatever material the footbed's posting material is made of. (This could be cork or foam of varying densities.) Check that the posting material ends or thins out right behind the ball of the foot and that the posting material under the heel is ground flat so that the ankle is rendered stable. The footbed itself should not rock side to side if you weight it down a little bit.

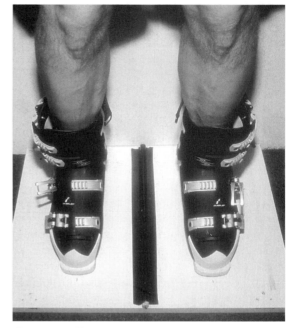

The upper cuffs need to be adjusted toward each other. MT. BACHELOR SKI AND SPORT

## NEXT IN LINE: UPPER-CUFF ADJUSTMENT

This next step in the alignment process will help you even if you don't have custom footbeds or orthotics. But this step will be most effective with these inserts, and I will discuss it with the skier who has custom footbeds or orthotics in mind.

A good footbed will hold your ankle in a biomechanically sound position, but it cannot stop your body from standing the way it naturally stands. The lateral upper-cuff adjustment lets the cuff of your boot shift to the inside or to the outside (medially or laterally) to accommodate a tendency to be slightly knock-kneed or bowlegged.

Put another way, lateral upper-cuff adjustment matches the cuff of your boot with your

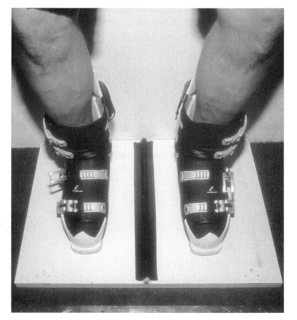

The upper cuffs need to be adjusted away from each other. MT. BACHELOR SKI AND SPORT

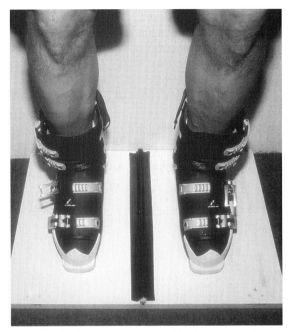

The lower leg is properly centered in the upper cuffs.
MT. BACHELOR SKI AND SPORT

lower leg's bone angle, so your lower leg does not press against the inside or outside of the boot but sits in the middle of your boot cuff.

If you center your lower leg in your boot, your leg will not affect your ski's edge angle—until you want it to by making an appropriate edging movement. Being slightly off center with your upper cuff in relation to your lower leg can cause major problems. I notice immediately if my boot's lateral cuff-adjustment screw becomes loose and the cuff shifts out of position slightly—even as little as a couple millimeters.

You make the cuff adjustment in your plastic boot shell with the liner removed. You will need a hard, level floor, a partner, and a few tools. Remove your boot liners from the boot shells and take your custom footbeds out of the liners. Place the footbeds inside both boot shells, insert your bare feet into the boots, and stand on your footbeds. Buckle your boot shells to simulate their shape when skiing. Position your boots at the width they usually are when you're skiing. This should be about hip width.

Try to establish your natural stance and maintain this stance width; keeping a consistent stance width is important in achieving proper alignment. You may want to measure your natural stance width and record it for convenience during your alignment work. A piece of masking tape stuck on the floor in front of each boot with a mark indicating the center of the boot toe makes keeping the stance width consistent a snap.

Try to center your feet in your boot shells with equal space in front of, behind, and to the sides of your feet. Your partner may need to reposition your boots so they point straight ahead, and not in a pigeon-toed or duck-footed direction. Your partner should now mark the floor at the center of each boot's toe. This marks your natural stance position. Now stand as if you were skiing, with your legs slightly flexed and your hands out in front. Look straight ahead and keep your balance distributed evenly on both feet. Your shins should not touch the fronts of your boots.

Your partner should check the amount of space between the sides of your lower leg and your boot shell. If these gaps are equal on both sides, no adjustment to your upper cuff is needed. If the gaps between your leg and your boot shell are not equal, adjust your upper cuff. (This often requires you to step out of your boot shells.)

Loosen the cuff-adjustment screw, which is usually located at ankle height on the shell, on the side of the boot where your buckles are. Some models have two, or even three, adjustment screws. Once the screws are loosened, shift the cuff to match the bone angle of your lower leg. It is difficult to make an accurate adjustment on the first try, but give it your best shot. Then retighten the adjustment screws, put your shells back on, buckle them, reset your stance width using the marks you made, and assume your skiing stance. Have your partner look at how your lower legs sit in your boots. You may need to readjust the upper cuff and repeat the process until you've got it right. Once your lower leg is centered, be sure your adjustment screws are tight, replace your footbeds in your liners, and put your liners back into your boot shells.

## The Right Feel

When the lateral upper-cuff adjustment has been properly set for your lower leg angles—or your *geometry*, as some folks will call it—you should feel balanced and symmetrical when you stand in your boots. Assume your normal skiing stance width on a hard, flat floor and let the bottom of your boot shell ride flat on the floor. Your legs should not feel as though they are being forced into an extremely bowlegged or knock-kneed position.

If you feel like a cowboy when you stand on the floor, with really bowed-out legs, when you get on snow and start skiing, you're going to be working with more inside edge engagement than you want. Most skiers find their bodies seek a certain stance during the dynamic movements of skiing. Even though the flat floor rolls the knees apart, when you're on the

Contrary to what many say, you can feel a mismatch in the upper cuff, especially in soft snow where the skis will go where your boots force them to. PETE TASHMAN AT MOUNT BAILEY SNOWCAT SKIING

hill (especially if the snow's soft), you will pull your knees into your normal skiing stance. This is what gives you too much inside edge and produces a feeling that your turns are overly hooked or causes your skis to cross. This skier will often feel that he needs to ski in a tighter-than-usual stance to get his skis to feel right.

Conversely, the skier who feels forced into a knock-kneed stance by her boots when she stands on the hard, flat floor will discover that her skis tend to overengage the outside edges during skiing. When she stands in her normal, athletic stance while skiing, she moves her knees farther apart than they were on the flat floor. This is why her outside edges engage more than they should and produce slippery-feeling skis that tend to catch edges or drift away at the start of a turn. This skier will find that adopting a wider-than-normal stance makes her skis feel better under foot.

Feeling a little bowlegged while standing on the hard, flat floor in your skiing stance width is OK. This means that you will engage your inside edges just a touch when you're cruising on a flat road in your normal stance. Most good skiers like to be aligned a tiny bit inside (say, 0.5 degrees to the inside, which we'll talk more about later). Some skiers, myself included, prefer to be dead flat.

### When Your Upper Cuffs Won't Match Your Lower Legs

Some boots don't have any upper-cuff adjustment at all, and many others won't have enough adjustment range to accommodate the angle of your lower legs. There are a few options for skiers in this situation.

First, you can leave the problem alone and search for a different ski boot the next time around (if that time is not too far off), one that offers enough upper-cuff adjustment to suit your alignment needs. But if you would rather work with the boots you have, then you have three options.

Some highly technical bootfitters will increase your upper cuff range by dismantling your boot and doing some creative cutting and grinding.

Another way to deal with a mismatch in the upper-cuff adjustment is to look at canting, which we'll discuss later.

The third way to deal with a misaligned upper cuff is to fill the gap between the boot shell and lower leg so the skier's leg becomes centered in the cuff. For example, if there's more space to the outside of the lower legs when the skier stands in his boot shells, it's possible to fill that gap with bootfitting foam stuck to outside of the liner. This way, the boot will not be forced quite as far to the inside during skiing, which would roll the skis onto their inside edges.

I've had pretty good success with this option, which I call the lazy man's canting method. But keep in mind that although this step can help achieve a flatter riding ski, it may not deal with other alignment issues involving the knee, which we'll discuss later in this chapter. Filling the gap between the liner and the upper cuff can also negatively affect the boot's fit along the side of the leg.

### CHECKING (AND UNDERSTANDING) YOUR ALIGNMENT

For most skiers, a well-made custom footbed and a properly adjusted upper cuff is all it takes to become balanced. But if the footbed and upper-cuff adjustment didn't get you there all the way, there are a few other methods to achieve the kind of alignment that allows for maximum performance. How do you know if you're dialed or need to take additional steps to solve your alignment issues? It helps to have an easy way to check your alignment; but first, it helps to understand the goal you're striving to reach.

There are two essential things that good alignment offers a skier.

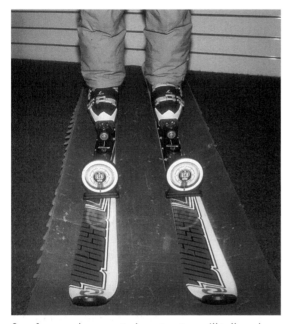

On a foam pad, carpenter's protractors will tell you how the rubber meets the road. MT. BACHELOR SKI AND SPORT

1. Sound alignment provides a solid column of body parts on which to stack the load that builds during a turn.
2. Sound alignment provides skis that ride flat when they're supposed to.

Ideally, a skier can have both these things.

The strong *drive train*—or sound alignment of the foot, knee, and hip—is best evidenced by a knee that aligns properly over the foot while in a skiing stance. The so-called *center of knee mass*, or center of the tibial plateau, should align just to the inside of the center of the boot. This is usually checked by a savvy alignment technician using a plumb bob, an L square, or some other alignment-checking device. This relationship between the center of the foot and the center of the knee basically represents the strongest column of body parts with which to push against a ski.

The other part of proper alignment is to achieve skis that actually do ride flat (or just a

hair on their inside edges) when the skier thinks they're flat—for example, while cruising down a flat road in a tall, neutral stance. Whether or not a skier's skis are running true can be checked with various devices at the ski shop. My current favorite is a combination of a few different methods; I like it because it's simple.

While clicked into her skis, the skier stands on a foam sleeping pad on a flat floor that is plumb and not sloping in any way. The foam allows her skis to roll from side to side, the way they would meet the snow when the skier adopts her normal stance. Two Devil Levels, which are carpenter's circular protractors, are then placed on the tops of her skis, one level for each ski. Be sure that the levels sit on a flat part of the skis' topsheets. A helper looks at the levels and can read by degrees and half-degrees how the skis are riding. A simple straightedge across the skis' topsheets will allow you to see, in general, how the skis meet the snow; but the levels give you an objective measure for each ski. Multiple trials are recommended to find an average measurement for each ski.

Ideally, the plumb bob-type testing (static assessment) will show a sound alignment of the knees, and the Devil Level test will show that the skis are riding flat or a half-degree to the inside. There are some devices that measure both the knees' position *and* the skis' flatness at the same time. Remember that it's not the contraption that matters, it's the ability to check the knees and the skis.

## Upper-Cuff Tweaking

After setting a skier's upper cuffs, I then check the alignment of the skier's knees. If the knees are within acceptable limits, but I find after a Devil Level test that the skis are just a hair off, I will often reset the skier's upper cuffs, if there is available range.

Simply looking at the upper cuffs and setting them as best you can the first time around is a means for gross adjustment. But you can't see a half-degree difference just by eyeballing the cuff adjustment. So after checking how the rubber meets the road, so to speak, with the Devil Levels, it's possible to make more finely tuned, micro adjustments to the upper cuff to achieve perfect alignment.

The key here is to make very small readjustments so the knee's good alignment isn't altered. A lot of folks think they won't feel the difference between half-degrees. But trust me, you will.

## What If I'm Not Properly Aligned?

In the above tests, you might discover that you are riding too far on your inside or outside edges, or that one ski is fine while the other is out of whack.

If you find you ride too much on your inside or outside edges, you are at least symmetrically out of alignment. The information in the rest of this chapter will help you.

If you discover your alignment is *asymmetrically* out of whack, you have some special hurdles to overcome. There are two primary causes.

Your feet, ankles, or knees might differ from one side to the other. This could be something you were born with or the result of an injury or another experience that altered the body parts on one side. You should see a podiatrist or orthopedic specialist who is familiar with the equipment needs of skiers.

You could also have one leg that is longer than the other. Having legs of different lengths can wreak havoc with a skier's alignment. Your hips work like floating islands that rest on top of your legs' femur bones, and your feet have to touch the ground; so the difference in length shows up at the femur head. A skier with legs of equal length has femur heads that match up heightwise, and his hips float in a flat, level position. A skier with one longer leg has femur heads that create a slanted platform for the hips to rest on. His hips consequently drop to one side, and his body must move to compensate for this hip tilt. This kind of compensation causes unnatural edging movements that tend to roll one ski onto its inside edge and the other onto its outside edge.

If you are experiencing problems with asymmetrical alignment, first have your legs measured by a health professional. Ask the person to measure you several times to ensure accurate results. If you do not find a length difference, consider seeking a podiatrist's help. If there is a length difference, you likely will need to either shim your bindings on one ski (which will always be used for your short leg) or you can have one boot sole shimmed like an elevator shoe. The latter option is best because you will be able to use any pair of skis (demos, for example). But this option is a more specialized process and you may need to search a bit for a bootfitting specialist who deals with this. It's also possible to use a heel lift on the boot board of the boot for use on the shorter leg. This is also a simple way to check how shimming may help a skier's alignment.

A veteran of leg-length problems and many bootfitters have advised me to use a shim of a thickness equal to one-half the difference in leg length whether or not you shim the bindings or the boot sole. This will help reach a middle ground between achieving equal leg length and working with what your body has become used to. Your first time skiing after attaching the shim (or heel wedge) may feel strange, but give it time. If any joint pain results from altering your stance with a binding shim, or your alignment is not improved, you may want to continue to deal with an unshimmed ski or boot.

Be sure to recheck your alignment using both the Devil Level and plumb bob-type methods using the shimmed ski or boot sole, to see how the shimming affected your alignment. Don't be intimidated by the seeming extreme nature of this solution. It's actually very easy and the results are simply amazing for skiers who have been dealing with leg-length discrepancies.

## CANTING

Skiers whose alignment problems don't disappear with good footbeds and a careful adjustment of the upper cuffs look to *canting* as the next step in achieving proper alignment. Canting is altering the angle at which your boot meets your ski with thin, wedge-shaped plastic shims that are mounted between your ski and your bindings, or by custom-grinding your boot's sole to achieve the same result. Canting cannot be done effectively until you have acquired good footbeds or orthotics and completed the process of upper-cuff adjustment.

There has always been a fair amount of confusion about the concept and application of canting. This is because it's a science that's not cut-and-dried, for the subjective variables of each skier's alignment needs tend to throw mathematical truths out the window. What I have learned recently from some really good alignment technicians is that the theories don't matter as much as the *results* of sound canting practice.

For the sake of discussion, let's imagine that we're dealing with a skier who is misaligned so that he is overengaging his inside edges. Canting provides a means by which to alter how the boot meets the ski so that we can solve his alignment problem. We'll discuss cant wedges as opposed to boot-sole grinding, for the sake of simplicity. The question at hand—and the one that always trips people up from a theoretical perspective—is, where do we place the fat side of the cant strip?

Do we place the fat side of the strip to the outsides of his skis, leaving his leg angles where they are but essentially flattening his skis' angle on the snow? This option is commonly called *filling*.

Or do we place the fat side of the strip to the insides of his skis, with the thought that this will tilt the legs away from each other and produce a more sound knee position and flatten the skis? This canting option is generally called *moving the knee*.

The answer could be either, depending on where the skier's knees are aligned and depending on how "cantable" the skier is. The entire concept of moving the knee is dependent on the skier's anatomy. Some skiers have enough space within the joints of the leg that their knee can be moved. Other skiers don't have that joint space and they aren't candidates for moving the knee.

The golden rule of canting now, at least for me, is that our theories and predictions don't matter; the results do. What this means is that an alignment technician can test the fat side to the inside and look at what happens to the knee's position and what happens to the Devil Levels; then he can test the fat side to the outside and look at those results. The idea is to have the skis ride flat and keep the knee in a sound position. Whichever canting method produces a better combination of those two goals determines how the cant should be placed.

My second rule of canting is that if I have to make a decision between a knee that's in the right spot or skis that ride flat, I'll always opt for skis that ride flat. Flat skis make for better skiing; perfect knee alignment is just the icing on the cake for me in terms of power, leverage, and longevity. I strive to have both, but I couldn't care less about power, leverage, and longevity if it means my skis will cross or catch edges with every turn.

### Cant Strips or Boot-Sole Grinding?

Canted plastic strips that get mounted between the binding and the ski are canting's old standby. But the new wave in canting is boot-sole grinding, which has been around for a long time in World Cup and professional race circles. There are pros and cons for each method.

The plastic cant strip is handy because it isn't permanent. If the alignment technician made a mistake or some variable in your alignment recipe changes (for example, new footbeds or new boots with more upper-cuff range), you can remove or change the cant strips. The downside to cant strips is that you are trapped by them: you'll ski well on skis that have the cants, and you'll suck on everything else. Don't plan on using demo skis—and hope the airlines never misplace your skis.

In boot-sole grinding, the bottom side of the boot is ground at a new angle—the angle that would have been produced by the cant strips. This method is superior in terms of convenience, for you can grab any ski and be dialed on it. However, the downside of boot-sole grinding is that it is permanent—unless the technician has a way of redoing it. Be sure that the footbed you're using isn't going to change for the life of the boot, and be sure that you trust the abilities of the bootfitter who will do the boot-sole grinding.

Be aware that boot-sole grinding changes the interface between boot and binding, which can alter binding release. While technicians do their best to return a ground boot to workable specifications, skiers must realize that they are choosing to have this procedure carried out and must take responsibility for that decision. If the technician is good, I think the benefits outweigh the risks, but that's my opinion. It's your body; it's your call.

## FORE-AFT ALIGNMENT

I have to admit that I never gave much thought to this dimension in the alignment calculus—until I had a problem with it. That should be a lesson to all skiers when it comes to alignment: if you think it's bunk, you probably don't have a problem.

A skier's balanced stance is predicated almost entirely on his being centered on his skis. A ski is designed to be worked from its designated center, and new shaped skis—more than ever—are most effectively used by a skier who doesn't weight only the shovel or mainly the tail but stands balanced in the middle and uses accurate edging movements.

Why wouldn't a skier be centered, since bindings virtually plant the boot exactly where it needs to be on the ski?

It's a matter of the gear in between the ski and the skier. The boot and binding both affect how the skier's stance balances front to back, and different boots and different bindings have different design features that can alter this balance.

### The Basics of Good Fore-Aft Alignment

The skier's neutral stance, the stance unaffected by the loads built in turning, should be tall and the skeletal frame should bear the body's own weight without having to expend much muscular effort. For example, a chair-sitting type of

Proper fore-aft alignment is generated by boot and binding to produce a tall, relaxed stance. BRIAN ELLING ON ED'S GARDEN, MT. BACHELOR

stance would require a lot of muscular effort to maintain. This tall stance should be *created* by the boot and binding.

A ski boot has a certain amount of high heel factor built into it, called *ramp angle,* and its upper boot also has a certain amount of forward lean to it. The ski boot starts the amount of leg bend and forward tip of the skier's stance, but the ski boot should hold the skier up, allowing her to place some weight against the tongue of the ski boot with her shin and meet resistance. It's this resistance in the boot tongue that helps the skier stack up her skeletal frame into a tall and relaxed stance.

A binding also has a bit of high heel factor—also referred to as ramp angle, or as *delta* by some technicians—that adds to the forward tipping of the skier's body when it's on the skis.

When a skier is in boots and bindings, she should still be standing tall and should be supported by the tongues of her ski boots. The skier should be able to relax into her boots and be propped up in a stance where the angle of the lower leg is parallel to the angle of her spine. Both should be tipping forward equally.

## When Fore-Aft Alignment Goes South

Boots and bindings can be combined to produce perfect fore-aft balance for a skier—but they often don't.

It's possible to combine a boot that has very upright, forward-lean characteristics with a binding of a fairly flat ramp angle and end up with an overly tall stance where the skier doesn't have enough forward lean in the lower leg. This skier will not feel centered on her skis; instead, she'll feel as if she's working off the tails of her skis. Oftentimes, this skier will not show a parallel relationship between her lower leg and her back; she'll exhibit more forward tipping in the upper body than in her lower legs in an attempt to get more forward on her skis.

It's also possible to combine a boot that has average to high amounts of forward lean with a

A boot and binding combine to allow too much forward lean in the lower leg. JAY "BAD EXAMPLE" GARRICK AT MONTANA SNOWBOWL

binding that has a lot of ramp angle to produce an overly bent, or squatty, stance in the lower body. The boot is tipped too far forward by the binding to hold the skier in a tall stance. The skier can receive support from the boot, but only by driving the lower leg farther forward, which produces that chair-sitting stance that's characterized by a forward leaning lower leg and an overly upright spine. This skier feels that she has to "get low" to make turns and her quadriceps tend to burn.

The slight forward lean of the spine should match that of the lower leg. Here, a fore-aft balance board tips forward to signal proper fore-aft balance. MT. BACHELOR SKI AND SPORT

## Finding Fore-Aft Balance

In an ideal world, a skier would have several perfectly fitting boots to choose from. And in this case, she would buy the boot that felt just a shade too upright for her skiing style while hanging out in the shop. But once she was on a binding with some ramp angle, all would be well.

Unfortunately, skiers are often lucky to find a boot that fits perfectly everywhere without any extra bootfitting. It would be a shame to have to pass on a great fitting boot simply because it was either too upright or leaned you too far forward. But you might consider it. If the boot feels extreme in its upright or forward-lean characteristic, it's probably going to limit your balance and performance. If it's only a little off from what feels like a balanced fore-aft stance to you, then don't worry. There are ways to manipulate your fore-aft balance in the binding after the fact, but this gets a little too technical for a lot of folks. Try to find good fore-aft balance in the shop, and if you need to, check out Fore-Aft Alignment: Project Delta in the Getting Techno section later in this book. For many skiers, and commonly for women, their anatomy and body shape can play a role in getting balanced fore and aft. See the Binding Placement section in Getting Techno.

# PART IV
# Getting Tough: Advanced Situations

Difficult and varying terrain is where expert skiers go to test their performance. Steeps, bumps, hard and icy terrain, powder, crud, and trees are where good execution of skiing skills counts—and where the fun and challenge of skiing can be found.

Even if you are skiing at an area not known for its advanced skiing, you can find ways to put your skills to the test. There may be a south-facing slope with a thick crust or a mild bump run that had sun the day before and is now bulletproof and fast. Tight trees on mild slopes can be tricky enough for an adrenaline rush, and a sleepy intermediate cruiser can be a rush with six inches of good powder.

The key to getting tough is learning to make it easy on yourself. BRIAN ELLING AT MONTANA SNOWBOWL

Extreme variations in terrain and snow conditions are the true allure of skiing—and these conditions can change daily, even hourly. This skiing smorgasbord is lost on the skier who can't handle the range of conditions and who finds skiing trees and crud a nightmare. Varied terrain and conditions are a sensory festival for a master, and a lot of work and little enjoyment for skiers who aren't masterful.

There is really no middle ground to performance in advanced situations. Either you can rip it up in them, or you get ripped up by them. Making the entire mountain your playground requires finesse, refined movements, and quick thinking, but burly musculature is not necessary. When skied properly, extreme terrain is no more physically taxing than an aggressive run down a steep groomed slope. This section is dedicated to making expert terrain that easy.

Skiers tend to have a primary, common problem when skiing each type of terrain or snow condition, along with a few secondary problems. In response to this common-problem pattern, I have developed a strategy for teaching in variable terrain that addresses the primary problems, and I've developed tactics that address the less common problems.

In this section, I will discuss the ideal performance in a given terrain or snow condition. I'll follow this discussion with an explanation of what usually happens to skiers in this terrain and why, including methods you can use to address these difficulties. Using a format similar to the Creating a Toolbox section, this section also includes helpful You Can See and You Can Feel exercises, drills, and troubleshooting guides.

Expert performance in tough terrain is not a matter of skiing any differently than you would on a groomed slope. It is about having full use of your basic skiing tools and knowing how to blend them. Many of us find ourselves dominant in certain skills and weak in others. The inability to tone down strong skills and strengthen weak ones is what prevents many skiers from becoming experts.

By this point in the book, you've got the right tools. It's time to learn how to use them like an expert.

# 14

# Carving

Carving on firm snow surfaces requires what racers call the *touch*. This touch is not a special trick and it's no different from the carving technique used on softer snow. Being able to carve on hard or icy snow requires the same skills essential to making a carved turn on groomed snow. But you must be precise in your use of these skills on hardpack and ice because hard surfaces provide less margin for error. This chapter is a primer for making powerful, carved turns—on groomed terrain, hardpack, and ice.

## THE IDEAL GOAL

To carve a turn is to ride a ski's arc through its natural radius without interruption or skidding. Any ski has a certain degree of sidecut, or shape. By simply tipping a ski on edge and standing on it you can make a purely carved turn by pressing the ski's sidecut into contact with the snow. Making your basic, carved turn is very simple; anyone can do it, and beginners often do it by accident.

It used to be that straight, or traditional, skis were a real trick to carve on because the size of the circle that the skis' sidecut was taken from was huge. This large-radius turn made the purely carved turn of the straight ski difficult in all but the biggest, fastest turns on wide open runs. A large part of carving skills used to revolve around how to tighten up this large-radius

turn by *working*, or bending, the ski throughout the turn.

Frankly, life's a lot easier for skiers who want to carve these days, as new ski design has brought the kind of increased shape that we discussed in the previous section. What we have to work with now is an arc shape taken from a smaller circle, which makes a carved turn more useful in recreational skiing: you don't have to travel at warp speeds in huge turns to carve.

Carving well lets you ride the arcs built into your skis.

A large part of carving is allowing a ski to do what it's designed to. CHRIS SMITH ON EAST HEALY, MT. BACHELOR

Many of the same skills we used on straight skis still apply to carving clean turns on firm snow, but much of the extra work of carving has been eliminated. For example, before the trick was to make sure that the outside ski kept bending throughout the turn so it didn't go straight and wander off the carving path. The way we used to do this was to progressively pressure the outside ski throughout the turn, slowly building extra pressure against it as the turn developed, then smoothly back off on that pressure to exit the turn. This kind of pressure control is still needed—just not to such extremes. New skis still have sidecut and camber, so they still need to be bent to carve. They just happen to be shorter and softer, so the job is easier.

Now carving is less about bending long, straight skis and more about rolling smoothly from one set of edges to another. The basic skills of edging movements, discussed earlier in this book, really pay off with shaped skis, as the simple motion of engaging the skis' edges can produce a carved turn. A skier can engage the skis' arc shape without much more than the weight of her body and begin to ride the circle that's built into the ski. More dynamic carving comes with higher speeds, greater edge angles, and the resulting greater buildup of force in the turn.

The precise pressuring and edging movements of carving come from smooth blending of basic skills. The entire toolbox gets mixed into the works, but with balance and constant motion being the keys to staying "hooked up," and continuing to carve through a clean turn on hard snow.

a. Both skis being engaged in a carved turn;

b. and c. center of mass moving up and across, shifting weight off of the outside ski;

d. center of mass has crossed over and drops to inside of the new turn; previous outside ski has rolled onto "little toe" edge and carves along course of new outside ski;

e. skier continues to increase edge angles while maintaining functional balance over both skis;

f. hip-angulated (long-leg/short-leg) stance helps balance most of the skier's weight over the outside ski, engaging it in a deep carve;

g. edge angles are greatest when the hips have moved farthest to the inside of the turn.

Note the way the skier's center of mass moves both vertically and laterally as he finishes one turn and enters another. Notice how the transfer of pressure from one ski to the other happens progressively.

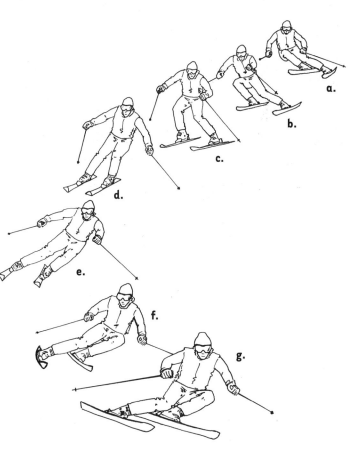

Skiing on ice is like driving a car on ice. You have to do everything slowly and gingerly so you don't interrupt the precarious grip your tires (or skis) have on the slick road; quick starts and stops and erratic changes of direction create problems. Imagine that you are driving a long, icy curve on the highway at 60 mph. To make the turn, you need to keep your speed constant, enter the turn smoothly and gently, hold it steady momentarily, then exit the turn carefully.

Carving clean, powerful turns on skis requires an aggressive and offensive attitude. But the goal is to be powerful without being abrupt, to be aggressive without being erratic. As Dave Mannetter, then a member of the Professional Ski Instructors of America (PSIA) National Demonstration Team, said, "Never surprise the ski."

This doesn't mean you should sit back and do nothing. You must use rhythmic, ongoing movements, as there is constant movement in any good turn. A skier who finds herself frozen at some point during her turn—even if only for an instant—will wonder why she's not performing the way she knows she can.

## PRIMARY PROBLEMS THAT CONFOUND POTENTIAL CARVERS

Skiers who have trouble skiing on ice—much less carving on ice—will also experience problems on hardpack and even on firm groomed snow. This generally happens for one of two main reasons, and these skiers tend to fall into two fundamental categories: the timid and the spastic. Timid and spastic skiers will never learn to carve until they strengthen some skills they probably already have but fail to use properly. Timid skiers fail to use their skills aggressively enough to carve, and spastic skiers do too much, too hard, and too fast.

Carving on hard surfaces requires aggressive edge engagement and pressure applied against the skis. Both of these ingredients rely on generating centrifugal force by carrying some speed

and following a round turn shape. Laying the ski on edge, bending it, and going fast are three things that timid skiers have trouble with. Spastic skiers, on the other hand, may have trouble edging and bending their skis in the smooth, progressive way that's required. To learn how to solve these problems, it will first be helpful to understand how edging, pressure, and force work together in the carved turn.

Edging in the carved turn is simple to understand: you need enough so you can bend the ski but not so much that you fall over. A flat or only slightly edged ski cannot be adequately bent to fully engage a powerful, carved arc because of the resistance it meets from the snow. Imagine a ski lying on a hard surface like a cement floor. When the ski is flat, its entire bottom surface meets the cement; when it is tipped on edge, only the shovel and tail of the ski makes contact with the cement. The more you lay a ski on edge, the more you can bend it because the waist of the ski doesn't come into contact with the snow as quickly as it would if it were flatter. Even though shaped skis put less emphasis on bending the ski into a tighter arc, you still need to get a ski on edge so that it can be fully engaged.

Edging the ski is a prerequisite for bending it so you can carve, but pressuring the ski is what does the work. This is not as easy as it sounds. Leg extension can increase pressure against your ski, which you saw earlier by making a bathroom scale read a greater weight by standing on the scale in a crouch and then standing up. In the bathroom scale analogy, the scale read a greater weight when you extended your legs, but for what duration can you maintain this higher reading? Not long. The amount of pressure you can exert on a ski by leg extension may be large, but it doesn't last. So while this might be enough to bend a ski, it's not enough to hold it in a smooth, progressive bend.

You need help to aggressively engage your skis' edges for the duration of a carved turn. The help you need is force, which you use to exert extra pressure against your ski and bolster the power you have already achieved through leg extension. You gain this extra force from components of the turn itself: speed, turn shape, and turn radius. What these elements add up to is centrifugal force, which pushes against the ski and helps you bend it properly. This is where carving becomes an expert skill because you are involved in a tricky, skill-balancing act: mixing turn size, turn shape, and speed, while at the same time making precise edging and pressuring movements. Speed, turn shape, and turn radius produce the force that you balance against—the force that allows you to edge your skis by moving your body mass toward the center of the turn without falling down. Force allows you to use your edging and pressuring skills at a higher level and ultimately allows you to carve.

## SOLVING THE PROBLEMS OF THE TIMID AND SPASTIC SKIER

The timid skier has all the skill components of a carved turn in his toolbox, but he's not performing them in an aggressive enough fashion. The spastic skier may overuse or lack any one or two carving skills, and it will be up to the individ-

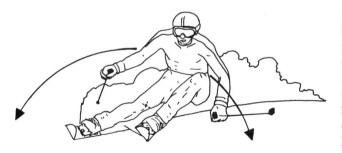

At a point of balance between falling to the snow and tipping over into the next turn, you find equilibrium. Don't "park" yourself at this point in the turn; you must continue moving through that point toward the next turn.

ual skier to determine which skill he needs to focus on.

Timid skiers have a hard time generating adequate edge angles, and instead they ski with their skis fairly flat on the snow. This fear of edging is revealed in a tall, upright stance and skidded turns that lack power. It may be obvious that the timid skier's problem is a lack of edge angle, but you can't simply correct this by adding more edge angle. Adding more edge angle without the ingredients of pressure and force results in awkward, precarious movements that put you out of balance and rarely result in a carved turn.

You increase your edge angle through greater body mass movement toward the inside of the turn, or, in other words, through greater lateral movement of the hips. Moving your center of mass toward the inside of the turn is the same as starting to fall down. Aggressive skiers generate the centrifugal force that allows them to find a moment of balance during the turn. Timid skiers may increase their edging via more body mass movement. However, they tend not to generate enough force to stay upright, and they find themselves on the snow.

How do you learn to generate force in a turn so you can increase your edge angle without falling down? This requires using several tools from your toolbox at once.

First, you need to be able to make the smooth, round turns described in Turn Size and Turn Shape (see pages 51–53). In the same way that a pile of letters slides across the dashboard of a car during a turn, force is similarly exerted against the skis. If a turn is quick and abrupt, short-lived force is exerted against the skis. Strive for smooth, continuous turning arcs without dead spots or traverses. This round turn will help produce a progressive buildup of force during the turn.

When you make the commitment of dropping your hips toward the inside of a turn, you need to know there will be something there to balance against. That something is the force that results from a smooth, round turn. To make this

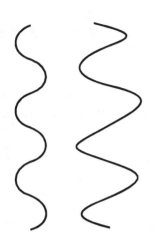

Round, continuously turning arcs are shown next to an abrupt, traversing line.

kind of turn, you need to utilize the skills described in chapter 4, The Footwork Blend. Steering and outside ski dominance will work together to keep your skis turning so force can continue to build. Keeping your skis turning with the above skills is crucial for a carved turn. Once your skis stop turning, so does the force buildup that lets you achieve a more aggressive edge angle.

Once you make the commitment to move your body mass to the inside of the turn, keep your skis turning, and find there is force to balance against, you need to learn how far you can continue to edge your skis: too far and you'll fall down; not far enough and the force will tip you over into the next turn. Here is where speed and pressure come into play. Speed is one element that determines how far you can move toward the inside of a turn. The faster you go in a given turn size, the farther you can drop your hips to the inside of the turn. This is like riding a bicycle: You turn at slow speeds by using the handlebars and leaning slightly; at high speeds you rely less on the handlebars and more on leaning the bike toward the inside of the turn. Judging how far you can drop your hips to the inside

of a turn is first a matter of trial and error—and then one of feel.

Pressure in the carved turn is what makes the turn click once you have put the other elements into place. With expert pressure control, you can manage the intricacies of entering and exiting turns, recovering from inaccurate body mass guesses, and negotiating variations in snow texture and consistency. The amount of centrifugal force acting against your skis is what makes dynamic skiing possible.

The mechanism for increasing pressure on the skis is leg extension; the mechanism for decreasing pressure is leg flexion. If you need to maximize pressure on the outside ski's edge to bite into very firm or icy snow, you extend the outside leg and flex the inside leg. There are times when it's preferable to maintain firmer contact between the inside ski and the snow; at those times less flexion of the inside leg and less extension of the outside leg would be appropriate. New ski design makes it possible to engage both the outside and inside skis in a carved turn, but how much pressure is required on one or the other is primarily dependent on the snow. As a general rule, softer snow necessitates more help from the inside ski; harder snow requires as much pressure generated along the edge as possible, meaning the use of primarily the outside ski with minimal weight transferred to the inside ski. However, many racers are experimenting with transferring more weight to the inside ski, even on ice, to generate a wide and powerful stance. There are infinite combinations for distributing pressure between both skis, and playing with as many as you can will only strengthen your skiing.

Mastering increases and decreases of pressure during carved turns in which centrifugal force is doing most of the work is mastering the touch. The key to making expert pressure-control movements is to make these movements smoothly and rhythmically. If added pressure is needed for the edge to bite into the snow, then that pressure should be added progressively up to the point where the turn is under control.

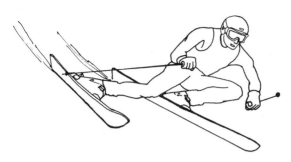

Extension of the outside leg and retraction of the inside leg can maximize pressure over the inside edge of the outside ski.

Less flexion (retraction) of the inside leg will keep weight more closely distributed between both skis for softer snow where flotation is required.

Then that pressure should be smoothly tapered off. In pressure control, as one ski's pressure is decreasing, the pressure on the other ski should be building. The skier should feel as though he is moving *with* the ski, never *against* it. These cycles of pressure increase and decrease give expert skiing its dancelike quality.

*You can feel*
**YOURSELF BEGINNING TO CARVE**

1. Carving a turn feels like hitting a good golf shot or a good forehand in tennis, because the tool does most of the work. You will feel your ski do the work of turning. You may even feel as if your outside leg is being turned by the ski as the ski engages the snow and arcs beneath you. A solid carve is like riding a bicycle at high speeds, because steering becomes less dominant. The bicyclist relies on leaning the bike to make it turn when going fast rather than on turning the handlebars.

2. Carving feels foot-pressure dominant, even though how you press with your feet is only part of your carving skill. Feet are sensitive to pressure changes. Because pressure is a large part of carving, your feet become the sensory centers of the carved turn. You will notice that the inside edge of the outside foot is bearing most of the load in a carved turn. Pressure is also felt along the outside edge of the inside foot, but usually to a lesser extent. This blend of pressure, from outside foot to inside foot, will vary depending on snow surface consistency or your style.

3. Carving involves your lower body in a kind of cyclic gravity game. Your legs feel as if gravity increases and then subsides during each turn, producing a rhythm of stress or force. You push back against these forces in order to remain upright, and the result is a carved turn. Sometimes these rhythms of centrifugal force feel like a swooping dance in which your partner is pushing you around or hanging on you, but doing so in a predictable, cyclical way from one turn to the next.

4. Linking carved turns requires a sense of rhythm and an ability to be in constant motion. This feels like using a stair-motion ex-

ercise machine, because one foot becomes pressure dominant at a time when the other releases its pressure. As one leg is extending, the other is retracting. If you can make your carved turns feel as if you're pedaling a stiff stair machine in a smooth and rhythmic way, you've probably got it.

*You can see*
## WHEN YOU HAVE CARVED A TURN

1. What you can most easily see in a carved turn is a clean arc drawn in the snow by your skis. There is no gray area with a carve: either your track looks like a single trench sliced in a smooth arc, or it doesn't. Look at your tracks and determine where the clean, carved line disappears. Pay attention to this phase in your turn to figure out what's going on. Check the troubleshooting section at the end of this chapter to see if you recognize the symptoms listed there.
2. What good carvers notice when they ski is the downslope snow surface. This skier is entering and exiting turns without long traverses, which means the skier is focusing downhill—not at the sides of the run. Being visually focused on your feet or on what's to your left or right can interrupt the commitment to the fall line that carving requires. Watch other skiers who carve well. You will notice their body movements are rhythmic and consistently smooth, but they will also be directed toward the next turn: traverses and the cessation of smooth body movement are rare.

## OTHER DRILLS

More drills that will help you learn to carve follow.

## Training Wheel Carves

These are best attempted on flat roads with little pitch. Starting with your skis parallel, gather speed, and then set one ski on edge. Keep your other ski flat for balance, like training wheels on a bike. Try to place enough weight on the edged ski so you bring the entire edge into firm contact with the snow. The edged ski will begin to turn. Ride this automatic turn as far as you can, then switch feet. Try to both increase the edge angle of your ski and vary the amount of pressure you put on it. Try to find a combination that produces a cleanly carved track.

## Railroad Carves

Perform these on a flat road that's not too steep. Skiing with your skis parallel, gather speed, and gently edge both skis in one direction. Try to make this edging movement primarily with your hips, but fine-tune your edging with knees and ankles. With this subtle edge angle, you will feel a gentle turn result—something like a floating shift to one side. Don't steer your feet, just rely on edging alone. Try the drill again, but increase the edge angle substantially. A more pronounced turn will result, so hang on. Your skis will arc along their prescribed sidecut radius and leave two carved tracks in the snow (if you are able to maintain your balance over them as they take you for this ride). When you run out of room, turn in the other direction. This represents a ski's big-easy carve—the one produced simply by engaging the ski's sidecut. Tighter carved turns are mutations of this arc and can be achieved with extra steering and by bending the ski farther.

## Railroad Carve Traverses

If you can make pure carved turns via the big-easy method described above, then you can try this next step in carving stronger, deeper trenches. A railroad carve traverse is performed the same as in the above drill but on a wide, groomed slope of moderate pitch. Remember to increase your edge by using mainly your hips. Aim your skis across the hill at a 45-degree angle and let them run. Adjust your edge angle until you feel your skis turning on their own, then increase the edge angle more so your skis carve pure arcs in the snow. Hold your position and let the skis take you on a long turn across the hill. You may turn enough to come to a stop, or you may have to stop before you reach the side of the run. Do this in the other direction. For variation, try the drill aiming more downhill and more across the hill.

## 1,000 Steps Extreme

Perform the basic 1,000 Steps drill (see pages 22 and 24) on a groomed slope of gentle to moderate pitch, but begin the drill with a railroad carve traverse. Once the carved traverse is started, begin aggressively stepping away from the outside ski. Each time the outside ski is picked up to catch the inside ski, concentrate on placing it back on the snow in a position that allows you to carve as you did at the beginning of the drill. The increased pressure exerted on the outside ski during the step will bend the outside ski. Try to maintain the carve as you apply pressure to the outside ski and resume the carve after stepping toward the inside ski.

## Chewing-Gum Carves

This is a mental imaging drill that enhances carving. Use a moderately pitched, groomed run and make high-speed medium to medium-large turns. Pretend you have stepped in gum with both skis. The gum is directly under each foot and is extremely tough stuff. At the beginning of a turn, begin pulling the inside ski off the snow. The tough gum will provide a lot of resistance, so the lifting occurs slowly and smoothly. Pull the inside ski about eight inches off the snow by the time you have reached the control phase of the turn; then begin to let the ski slowly return to the snow. The inside ski

should touch down just as you are exiting the turn. Because the gum is strong, the effort at the inside ski's highest point will require the most effort. In order to pull up against this resistance, your outside ski must push hardest at this point as well (for every action, an equal and opposite reaction). The goal is to increase and decrease pressure on the outside ski smoothly and progressively, and combine that with the balanced position required to lift the inside ski.

## Lay-Down Carves

You may have seen snowboarders who can lay their bodies out toward the snow when they carve a high-speed turn. You also may have seen boarders fall on their sides during one of these radical turns. They fell because they leaned too far for their speed, turn radius, and turn shape. A snowboarder falls because of an incorrect guess at how much lean is needed, but he gains valuable information in the process: that was too far. Ski on a wide, groomed run without obstacles and try to intentionally lay over too far. If you want, see how far over you can lean your body, increasing your edge angle to a point that causes a fall. Be careful! Then see how close you can come to that point of no return without falling. Try to maintain a proper stance and appropriate movement patterns. Increased edge angle is crucial to carving, but learning how to manage speed, turn size and shape, and force once that ski is on edge is just as important. This drill helps you put them all together.

## TROUBLESHOOTING THE ELUSIVE CARVE

One of the most common problems skiers face, even after working through the instructions above, is a carved turn that isn't quite there. You may be able to perform all the integrated movements of the carved turn but fail to produce a strong, aggressive carve. One symptom of the problem might be a less-defined track in the snow and a ski that breaks loose into a skid during parts of a turn. You may also experience unwanted skidding on icy snow. The foremost element of a strong, carved turn is adequate edge angle, but you must also know how to achieve that edge angle to maximize its power.

Moving your center of mass toward the inside of the turn is just the beginning in learning to increase edging in high-level skiing. Knowing how to position your hips and upper body can make all the difference between a weak carved turn and a powerful one. If you want to learn more about strengthening a carved turn, look ahead to the sections on hip angulation and counter-rotation and the Pelvic Tilt and the Hollow Back section, all in Getting Techno.

Another problem many skiers have with carving involves their outside ski during the control phase of the turn. In becoming more aggressive, skiers often move their body mass too far to the inside of the turn, so that the outside ski loses edge grip. To prevent a fall, they must step more onto the inside ski momentarily and reset their outside ski to regain balance. This is also commonly called *blowing out* the outside ski and will become more pronounced for skiers on icy snow.

The turn begins strongly with all the carve components working together to achieve a balance point in the turn. But once the turn progresses farther and approaches the middle where the most aggressive pressuring and edging happens, something goes wrong. Either the skier made an incorrect guess as to how far she should lean to the inside of the turn, or some ingredients of the carved turn faded prematurely. If you fail to continue pressuring and steering your outside ski progressively throughout the turn, your ski can stop turning and track in a straight line. This kills the force you are balancing against and you fall to the inside of the turn. Generally, this loss of balance during the turn is created by an unexpected change in centrifugal force. A related problem involves stance. Maintaining proper body alignment during the aggressive carve will help you make minor balancing adjustments if the force in the turn fluctuates unexpectedly. Leaning your entire body toward the inside of the turn makes it difficult to adjust your balance, but a hip-angulated stance gives you the ability to modify your center of balance easily. You can read more about this in Getting Techno.

Skiers who notice their outside ski tracking away from them as they start a new turn should pay attention to what needs to happen at turn initiation. Increased edging that is not accompanied by adequate pressure to bend the ski causes a ski to run in a straight line. One of the basic rules about carving is *commitment*. When you decide to increase your edge angle, you must be ready to steer and pressure your ski the small amount required to keep the ski turning. This allows force to build in the turn. Without a buildup of force, the ski will not engage properly and can track in a straight line. You may be forgetting basics such as foot steering and pressure control, using them too late, or not using them aggressively enough. It doesn't take much

Allowing the head and upper body to lean toward the hill, or toward the inside of the turn, can cause pressure to be transferred away from the outside ski, causing it to lose edge grip, or blow out.

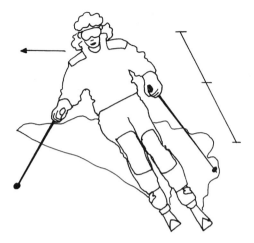

An inclined, or banked, body position can predispose a skier to leaning too far to the inside of the turn and blowing out the outside ski.

A more hip-angulated stance with an upright torso keeps proper balance over the skis.

New carving skis stay "hooked up" so well that skiers can generate enough force to remain in balance even during the deepest moves to the inside of the turn. CHRIS SMITH ON EAST HEALY, MT. BACHELOR

with shaped skis, but you can't forget about these skills altogether.

An additional cause of your outside ski tracking away at the start of a new turn can be poor fore-aft pressure control. At the start of any turn, you must be centered over the balls and arches of your feet. A ski's shovel is responsible for entering a turn, and a little added pressure there will help guide it smoothly into its arc. Skiers who find themselves slightly on their heels at the end of the previous turn must get forward so that their body weight is centered over the arch prior to the start of the next turn. Skiers having trouble with this should look at the diagonal crossover information in the upcoming section, Getting Techno.

Another common problem in carving comes toward the end of each turn. As you finish a turn, the outside ski's tail breaks loose, causing a momentary loss of edge control and an interruption in your rhythm. This problem is very apparent on slick snow. The most common belief is that tail washout is caused by dull edges, but this is often not the case: razor-sharp edges don't help skiers who have a chronic problem with their ski tails breaking loose.

The primary reason for tails breaking loose is the skier's timing and turn shape. Many skiers do little during a turn except gain speed, which they attempt to control late in the turn phase. This puts undue stress on the tail of the outside ski at a time when the body is not in the best position to deal with it, and the tail's edge grip gives out. Skiers can alleviate this problem by engaging their edges and applying pressure earlier in the turn. This decreases the need to slam on the brakes toward the end of the turn. These skiers should also try to slow themselves down by making round turn shapes and exiting the turn a little sooner, as explained under Arc Locus in Getting Techno, pages 214–15.

# 15

# Powder

Skiing powder is the Holy Grail of skiing. But for most skiers, the allure of powder is a myth. Even solid intermediate and advanced skiers who can make it down almost anything on the mountain sometimes believe the true enjoyment of powder belongs to somebody else—to the skiers in the magazines or in the movies. They have never had the experience of skiing powder well; they wonder what all the fuss is about and figure that powder is more hard work than the fun of cruising the groomed.

Any skier who feels that skiing powder is anything less than a religious experience is simply not skiing it well. Period. Anything less than peak performance in powder is simply extra work with little payoff in the way of fun. So if you secretly dread powder mornings and find yourself searching out groomed runs on a powder day, don't despair: you're not weird.

But you don't have to remain a closet powder-hater. Any skier who has mastered the fundamental skills in this book can be an expert powder skier if she learns how to blend and manipulate her skiing tools. Read on.

## THE IDEAL GOAL

To master powder, you need to think of it as a fluid, not a solid. Powder from one storm can be light and dry, while another storm will dump heavy, wet powder that acts less like a fluid. By *fluidity* I mean that powder will support weight

the same way water does. Swimming is not much fun for people who sink. Skiing powder is the same. It is not much fun if your feet are stuck way down, deep in the snow. Learning to float on snow is the key to powder skiing.

The fluidity of powder is its magic. On groomed snow, you are fully aware that you are in contact with the earth: the snow feels safe and solid. On powder, you lose that safe feeling. You are no longer in contact with terra firma, and the sensation is like flying. But the fluidity that makes powder an ethereal experience is also what makes it problematic.

Most skiers who hate powder hate it because it makes turning difficult for them. A skier who used to feel like an expert feels like a gaper when his turns don't come where and when he wants them to. This is a frustrating experience for an accomplished skier and can result in mental anguish. However, good skiers who have trouble in powder usually don't give up: they try harder. Believe it or not, this is the wrong approach.

Some good skiers have trouble in powder because they have a skill repertoire that is effective in firm snow. But firm snow involves a different tool blend than powder does. No matter how hard a firm-snow expert tries in powder, he's fighting a losing battle. He's simply focusing on the wrong skills. The advanced skier has the right skills for the deep stuff. It's just a matter of learning how to use them differently.

Approaching powder as a fluid unlocks a third dimension: depth. You'll find it addicting. GREG RUBIN IN SIXTY-NINER BOWL, MT. BACHELOR

## PRIMARY PROBLEMS THAT CONFOUND POTENTIAL POWDER SKIERS

The elements of skiing powder look pretty rosy on paper, but they fall apart rapidly on snow. While there are hundreds of ways that skiers end up falling on their heads in powder, there is usually a common cause: attempting to ski powder as if it were firm snow.

The first thing skiers notice about powder is getting bogged down in it. It feels like mud, hampering smooth and effective movements of the feet, legs, and skis. This resistance can make skiing more physically taxing and can prevent a good skier from making effective turns. Skiing powder incorrectly makes the snow feel like cement, but skiing it well can make it feel like feathers.

The key is to plane on top of the snow the way a water-skier does on water. While a water-skier waits for the boat to go, he feels awkward and immobilized. Once the boat begins to pull, the awkwardness he felt in the water begins to subside. As the boat pulls him faster, he begins to rise up out of the water until he has reached such a speed that he skims along the water's surface, planing on top of the fluid rather than plowing through it. Ineffective powder skiers fail to float on top of the snow and remain bogged down in the deep snow the same way a water-skier might plow through the water behind an underpowered boat.

Another result of skiing powder as if it were groomed snow is the loss of your centered stance. It is easier to find the fore-aft center of your ski on firm snow by shifting your center of mass forward and backward, because hard snow doesn't give way. Powder does not provide the same stable platform, and a skier whose balance is off a little will suffer. If you tend to pressure the shovels of your skis on groomed snow, you will immediately discover that a similar stance on powder results in a face plant. If you prefer to ski slightly on your tails, you will find your skis act like a rudder in powder—causing a loss of ski control because only the tails are being used. Although it is more difficult to do in powder, it is essential to find your skis' center of effort and use the entire ski from tip to tail.

Ineffective powder skiers also tend to have difficulty managing both skis when the snow gets deep. Skis can cross or track away from each other, with one diving to the bottom of the snow and the other climbing to the top. This is nearly always caused by applying pressure to the outside ski dominantly, just as you would on firm snow. These independent ski behaviors can result in a fall or cause you to lose control.

The advanced skier will often try to bend the outside ski rapidly, just as she would on firm snow. Bending your ski into a tighter arc is what you do in a carved turn. However, when carving on firm snow, there is a solid surface to push

In powder, you should be able to maintain a balanced stance, gaining flotation in the soft snow not by leaning back but by achieving necessary speed and using a ski that will allow you to float.

against, and you receive immediate feedback from your skis to let you know if you applied enough pressure, too little, or too much. If you jump into deep powder and try to work your ski in the same aggressive fashion, you will have little success. Powder does not offer the same resistance and will not let your ski respond with a carved turn quite as easily. There is a way to find the proper bend in your skis and make a carved turn in powder, but the aggressive skier of firm snow won't find it easily.

## SOLVING THE PROBLEMS OF THE INEFFECTIVE POWDER SKIER

Skis that burrow along at the bottom of whatever new snow has fallen don't tend to turn as well as if they cruised higher toward the surface. As your ski dives deeper into the new snow, it encounters more firmly packed snow. If your ski stays in that tightly packed snow, it will be trickier for you to ski. As the saying goes, you've got to rise above it all.

We've heard skiers talk about Sierra Cement: the wet, heavy, dense powder that's tough to ski well. We've also heard fans of Utah skiing rave about the snow's dryness and low density. Utah skiers are often skiing on the firm groomed snow from the day before, and the fresh fluff simply lofts around their knees more for decoration than anything else. Light powder is simply easier to ski—and this is information you should make use of.

You can make whatever powder you're skiing in feel a little lighter by getting your skis to ride higher in the new snow where it's less dense. How do you improve your flotation in powder? This requires two things: surface area and planing speed.

Let's return to the water-skier. Improving flotation in powder is similar to learning to get up in waterskiing. Beginner water-skiers tend to learn first how to get up behind a boat on two skis rather than one, because two skis provide more surface area and it's twice as easy to plane on top of the water that way. In snow skiing, you always have two skis of a determined surface area. But you can maximize that surface area by using both skis to create a platform. To create a perfect platform, you must stand on both skis with equal weight. This allows both skis to buoy you to their fullest capacity. If you weight one ski more than the other, that ski will dive deeper into the snow and the other ski will climb toward the surface, causing stance problems that negatively affect flotation. Firm snow skiers are used to being aggressively outside ski dominant, which does not work in powder. Remember: to start, use equal weight for the left and the right.

The other ingredient for improving flotation in powder is speed. A slow, underpowered ski boat makes it difficult for a water-skier to get planing on top of the water; going slow through powder results in the same agonizing plow. As the speed you travel through fluid increases, so does the number of fluid particles passing under your skis. This amounts to pressure, and as your speed increases in powder, the pressure exerted by the snow against your skis also increases. This increased pressure pushes your skis up toward the surface of the powder; the faster you go, the higher your skis will ride in the powder.

This second ingredient in improving flotation is the real problem for many skiers. Skiing powder is tough enough, and increasing your speed is probably not the first thing on your mind. But it should be. Ineffective powder skiers have trouble in the deep stuff because they're not planing on it: they're plowing through it. If you use equal weighting between your feet and increase your speed a little, you will see immediate improvement. (OK, you need to know how to control this new speed, but that information is coming.)

Surface area plays a major role in floating through powder. If you increase your skis' surface area, you increase your flotation in powder. Well, it takes money, but you can do it. Surface area is the product of an object's length multiplied by its width. You can get a longer pair of skis, a wider pair, or a longer and wider pair to increase your skis' surface area. This is not to say you can't plane on skinny skis. You can, but you must ski at a higher speed to achieve the same flotation you could get from a wider ski of the same length.

Today's shaped skis are available in several different widths, depending on the kind of skiing you want to do with them. The widest skis, still called fat skis, generate the greatest surface area, even at shorter lengths. All-mountain skis, often referred to as mid-fats, offer the next level of surface area for flotation in powder. These two types of skis will offer skiers the most margin for error in skiing powder, but just about any shaped ski out there will ski better in powder than your traditional skis, even at a shorter length: the wider tip and tail produce more surface area than you can find with straight skis.

Once you have mastered the methods for planing on powder, you must find a centered stance on your skis. We've already discussed the need for a laterally centered stance, so neither

ski dives or climbs in the snow. But the need for a functional fore-aft centered stance is just as important. A ski is designed to be used in its entirety, from tip to tail. There is no need to aggressively pressure the shovel or tail to make a ski turn, since modern ski design allows you to effectively work a ski from its center. The expert powder skier needs full use of her skis, and she needs to be properly centered—standing tall, in the middle of the ski.

There is a common misconception that to ski powder, you need to increase the pressure on your tails and assume a leaned-back stance. This is not true, but the rumor's widespread presence is understandable. Most skiers who have trouble in powder are not achieving adequate flotation by the means described above—and they are crashing like there's no tomorrow. They invariably discover that of all the crashes they take in powder, the Face Plant Grande is the least desirable. The way they can avoid the face plant is to simply lean back on their skis. They're still plowing along, but they're not getting pitched over the front of their skis. And they are even able to force their skis into a kind of turn, since their ski tips are close to the surface and they can lever them to the right or left.

If this sounds like your powder style, you need to stand up straight, pick up some speed, and wait a couple of seconds. Your ski tips should rise toward the surface of the snow, due to their surface area and your speed. You may apply slight heel pressure to coax your ski tips closer to the surface, but this does not mean you should lean back with your calves against the backs of your boots. Having your ski tips reach the surface is not a requirement, but it will indicate that you have achieved adequate flotation. In fact, in light, deep snow you may never see your ski tips: you may be at floating speed, but in this kind of snow your skis will never ride high enough to be seen.

Once you've learned to float in powder and have found your centered stance, you need to start managing both skis so you can start turning like an expert. If you try to ski powder the way you ski firm snow, your skis can diverge into the splits, cross each other, or deviate vertically from each other. To avoid this, you must tone down your outside ski dominance dramatically.

The movements that create outside ski dominance are called independent leg movements because each leg is doing something different than the other. This is how you achieved the footwork blend—with one ski pressuring and edging and the other steering. This worked on smooth, firm snow. You now need to manipulate the footwork blend so you can use it in powder.

Instead of a strict division of labor between the inside and outside skis, powder requires each leg to do both jobs. You need to maintain a good platform in order to maximize your surface area and improve flotation, so you can't let your outside ski simply push while the inside ski twists. Turning in powder requires the same blend of edging and pressure with steering that we use in firm snow, but you have to implement those skills with each foot.

When skiing powder, I think of my legs, feet, and skis as Siamese twins: they're not

As powder gets deeper, feet and legs must make simultaneous movements to maximize flotation. Note that there is less long-leg/short-leg positioning and reduced hip angle.

locked together, but they do everything just about the same. These mirrorlike actions are called simultaneous leg movements. Both skis need to be pressured similarly, edged similarly, and steered similarly. There will never be an equal match between the outside and inside skis because the outside ski will always bear more force during a turn. But in comparison to the footwork blend used on firm snow, we might as well consider our feet twins in powder.

The skier who can float, stay centered, and manage both skis simultaneously needs to learn how to make a carved turn through powder. Carving means using the ski's design to make a nonskidded turn. On firm snow this results in a thin, defined track in the snow. When carving in powder, you bend your skis so they follow their designed arc without having to be overly steered. You won't see a well-defined track, but your skis' performance will be the same. Doing this is fairly simple. First, let's review the elements of a carved turn for firm snow.

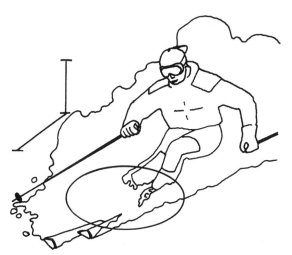

In only a few inches of powder, or using a fat ski at high speed, you can still utilize an outside ski-dominant turn.

All the things that happen on hard snow when you make a carved turn must happen on powder, but there are two primary differences. First, you need to maintain the most effective platform you can with your two feet so you will continue planing through the snow. Second, you must attempt to bend both skis into tighter carving arcs in a different way than you would on firm snow because powder does not offer the same amount of resistance. These are finesse tools that require practice to develop.

Learning to move both feet simultaneously in order to maximize your platform and prevent your skis from going in unexpected directions can be tricky for skiers who are used to being outside ski dominant. Your outside ski and outside leg bear most of the load in a turn because the centrifugal force you develop by turning tries to throw you to the outside. You typically resist this force by balancing on your outside ski in just the same way you would resist someone trying to push you off a cliff from the side. In order to increase pressure on your inside ski, so your platform can be maintained, you must perform a subtle trick that feels a little strange. You must apply muscular pressure to your inside ski so it doesn't go unweighted and climb toward the surface. Use a little muscle to push on your inside ski in powder, since leaning on the inside ski can cause you to adopt an out-of-balance stance.

Once you are able to maintain a platform, you are ready to begin bending both skis into tighter arcs. It is impossible to pressure your skis in powder the same way you do on firm snow. But at planing speed, powder begins to feel firm—just as water feels solid when a water-skier is skimming along its surface. Not only does the snow or water *feel* firm, but it acts on skis as though it *is* firm, and you can press against it and bend your skis to carve. However, there are limits to the firmness, or surface tension, that buoys you. Rapid, spastic pressuring movements that might work on firm snow will break powder's surface tension. Smooth, progressive pressuring movements allow you to bend your skis into carved turns without rupturing the limits of the snow's resistance.

Modern fat skis are allowing skiers to stand hard against the outside ski, because the extreme surface area resists "augering" (burying the tip) in when the ski is pressed. This has brought on a new school of powder skiing style that looks more like skiing on groomed snow. However, powder skiers need to know the ba-

The right form for firmer snow: weight distributed over the outside ski, hips shifted to inside of turn.

In powder, you apply muscular pressure to the inside ski to maintain a platform for flotation.

sics before they can open it up like the rock stars, so read on.

Any skier can perform smooth, progressive pressuring movements if he knows which body parts to move and what those movements should feel like. Nearly all pressure-control movements in powder come from simultaneous leg extension and flexion. The motion is like using a jump rope: both legs extend to push and then retract to jump. *In powder this push and jump happen subtly.* A good way to visualize proper leg movements in powder is to first imagine jumping rope on a sidewalk. Then imagine jumping rope on *thin ice.*

On ice you would not jump as high into the air; you would push off smoothly and try to cushion your landing by flexing both legs. Now imagine jumping a rope as thin as a hair, on ice, wearing ski boots. Becoming airborne is virtually unnecessary, and your ankles, knees, and hips handle all extension and flexion movements.

This is the way to move in order to bend your skis and carve in powder. Approach the snow as gingerly as you would approach thin ice, and enough pressure to bend your skis will build beneath them. It takes patience to slow your movements down and allow your skis to bend. But knowing how much you can pressure your skis and at what rate is the mark of a master.

Although you need to maintain a certain velocity in powder, speed control is necessary here as well. Speed control primarily comes with turning and bending your skis. The tighter you bend them, the sharper the skis turn, and the more you will slow down. It's important to control your speed by turning; in powder it's difficult to perform a hockey stop or wedge without tripping and going over the handlebars. In deep powder over your knees, the flexing movements of your legs during turns can drop you farther into the snow and produce drag. In some circumstances, you can purposefully flex deeper into the snow as you are turning or aim for deep pockets of snow in order to slow yourself down.

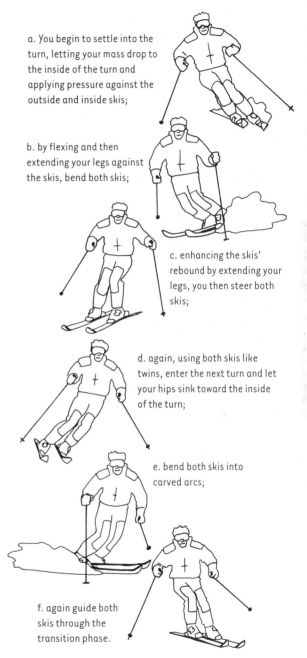

a. You begin to settle into the turn, letting your mass drop to the inside of the turn and applying pressure against the outside and inside skis;

b. by flexing and then extending your legs against the skis, bend both skis;

c. enhancing the skis' rebound by extending your legs, you then steer both skis;

d. again, using both skis like twins, enter the next turn and let your hips sink toward the inside of the turn;

e. bend both skis into carved arcs;

f. again guide both skis through the transition phase.

Short-radius turns on firm snow are a good visual representation of effective powder skiing if both skis are being pressured, as they are here. Lower body flexion and extension is subtle in the illustration. More may be needed in deep snow.

*You can feel*
## WHEN YOU'RE SKIING POWDER PROPERLY

1. In order to reach speeds adequate for floating in powder, you must point your skis down the hill and keep them pointed that way. Depending on the run's steepness and the snow's consistency, you may hardly turn at all—making slinky little turns down the fall line in order to maintain an appropriate speed. Many people have trouble floating in powder because they don't have the patience to reach an adequate speed. Skiers must point their skis down the hill, then wait until they feel themselves "hydroplane" up from the bottom of the new snow.

2. You can feel a fore-aft centered stance once you're floating in powder when you notice that your skis feel like a sluggish spring. You should be able to gently bounce up and down on your skis while skiing in a straight line, feeling the rebound that's coming from the flex of the skis and the snow pressure beneath your feet. If you lean slightly forward or backward you won't feel a springlike sensation because you're not using the entire ski.

3. Learning to use both feet and skis in unison can feel as awkward as trying to write with the opposite hand. When you begin to make simultaneous leg movements properly, you may notice a kind of muscular deliberateness of the inside leg—like muscular concentration. Some skiers will feel a slight tension in the muscles of their inner quadriceps and hip flexors on the inside ski's side. (These are the muscles at work when you try to close your knees and provide resistance by placing your hands between them and pulling them apart.) Duplicating this feeling of slight muscular contraction may help coax the inside ski to follow the movements of the outside ski more accurately.

4. Learning to bend both skis in powder so they

carve has everything to do with feeling your way through the phases of a turn. Let's say that in skiing powder there are four phases in every turn: the entry, the control phase, the exit, and the transition. For every phase there is a particular feel that goes with it. At the entry, you begin sinking deeper into the snow as your legs flex and prepare to bend your skis. In the control phase, you have reached the position of greatest flexion and have fully bent both skis by loading them progressively. As you exit, your skis begin unbending and release energy as you begin returning to a tall stance. In the transition, you return to a tall, centered stance and allow your skis to float toward the snow's surface momentarily before entering the new turn (see illustration, opposite). From start to finish it feels like this: sinking, loading, rising, floating. This sequence of sensations will repeat for every turn in powder.

*You can see*
## WHEN YOU'RE SKIING POWDER EFFECTIVELY

1. In my opinion, skiing powder is more kinesthetic than visual. But there are a few basic things about functional powder skiing that can be seen. One visible sign of proper powder technique is being able to watch the snow level rise and fall along the side of your boot or pant leg as you vary your speed. Go as slowly as possible through the new snow and note where the upper surface of the powder meets your leg. Steadily increase your speed in a safe place and watch that level drop as you begin planing higher in the new snow. You may see a change ranging from a couple inches to more than a foot, depending on the snow's consistency.

2. You can see yourself achieving a functional stance while skiing powder by looking for

a. The arrow indicates that the skier is descending in the snow to load and bend the skis; the hand is sunk deep to plant the pole, aiding that downward movement.

b. The arrow indicates the skier is rising with the rebound of the skis and body elongation; the hand is rising into a pole swing to enhance this rising movement.

c. At the top of the skier's upward movement the skis are being guided toward a new turn; the hand continues swinging.

d. and e. The skier begins sinking into the next turn and the hand-pole movements also start their downward plant; the skis bend progressively as the skier settles against them.

f. The skier's movement is upward with hand and body mass, retracting legs to further free the skis for steering movements at the transition between turns.

Because poling movements in powder are just extensions of what the body is doing to bend and guide the skis, all components of a powder turn sequence are shown.

two things: your hands and your feet. Maintaining visual contact with your hands out the corners of your eyes while skiing indicates that you most likely are keeping your hands and arms in position in front of your hips, which helps prevent a backseat stance. Being able to glance down and see the front third of your ski boots while skiing in a few inches of powder is a sign that you're standing tall and centered (leaning back would obstruct your view of your boots).

3. After making turns in a place where you can inspect your tracks, either from the chairlift or from a vantage point on the run, look at the tracks you left in the snow. There should be only one thick track through the snow, not two skinny ones. One main track indicates that you are moving your feet and legs simultaneously and blending skills evenly between them. Seeing two separate tracks is a sign that you are still using your skis independently and may be too outside ski domi-

nant. In denser snow two tracks may show up at the transition between turns, but the control phase of the turn should be marked by one unified arc in the snow.

4. In order to check that you are properly bending your skis in order to carve turns through powder, inspect a series of turns from a vantage point that allows you to discern the depth of your tracks (a chairlift tends to work best). First note your tracks' shape. They should be consistently round, which indicates your turns happen progressively and not abruptly, and they should be constantly turning without any straight sections. The transition between turns should not appear as a traverse, but simply as the intersection of two similar arcs in the snow. Most importantly, look at where the tracks are deepest and most shallow. The deepest part of the track should coincide with where the turn's control phase occurred; this is where your skis should be at their greatest bend and pressure. The most shallow portion of the track comes at the transition between turns, where you should achieve the most float through ski rebound and returning to a tall stance between turns.

## OTHER DRILLS

The drills below will help you rip it up in powder.

### Bounce Traverses

On an untracked section of a slope of moderate pitch, traverse across the run in a tall, centered stance and bounce gently on both feet as if you were jumping rope. Start at a slow speed and note that your bouncing does not happen easily. Gradually increase your speed during the traverse and continue to bounce at the same pace and intensity. As your speed increases and your skis begin to plane in the soft snow, bounc-

ing should become easier. Increase your speed in your traverses until your skis feel springy underfoot and give you a few inches of vertical bounce with little effort.

### Bounce Traverse Variations

The bounce traverses described above will reinforce your need for the minimum speed necessary for functional powder skiing, but they also encourage a fore-aft centered stance because gentle bouncing tends to place you in a position where you balance over your skis' sweet spots. Vary this drill by shifting your balance laterally as well as forward and backward to find your functional platform for flotation in powder. Proper lateral weight distribution feels as though the snow is pressing against the bottoms of both feet with an equal amount of pressure. Remember, however, that some muscular pressure must be exerted on the inside ski to create your platform during turns. Try moving your center of mass forward as you continue the drill until you reach the point where you almost bury your tips and crash. Then shift your mass backward gradually until your ability to bounce effectively is compromised. The two extremes you find here should not be exceeded when skiing powder.

### Bounce Straight Run to J-Turn

The basic Bounce Traverse drill is effective for honing powder technique because it emphasizes achieving flotation while maintaining a functional stance. It also introduces the basic lower leg movements needed for bending your skis into carved turns. It's important when performing this next drill to bounce by smoothly extending and flexing your legs while preserving an upright torso. This is a relaxed, easygoing movement that should not become tiring or alter your balanced stance.

Begin the drill in a straight run down the hill and gradually add the rhythmic bounce. When you achieve a speed adequate for good flotation and create a good platform, continue bouncing and make a turn in one direction until you come to a stop. Remember to keep bouncing gently during the J-turn. Begin again, following the same sequence of actions, but turn in the opposite direction. During the turn pay attention to the way your skis bend during the weighting phase of each bounce and how they float toward the surface afterward. This bend and float is the bread-and-butter combination of good powder skiing, which you can build upon. Note that the bend of your skis and resulting rebound becomes more labor intensive and ineffective as you slow down and come to a stop. This is a reminder that adequate speed plays an important role in skiing powder.

## Straight Run, Half-Turn, Repeat

The straight run is a necessary part of any successful venture into powder snow. This is because every run must start with the first turn, and the first turn is always the hardest. In powder, it is the hardest of all. Skiers usually jump into making turns too quickly after pushing off, and they have not built enough speed for good flotation. Always begin your entry into powder with a small, straight run that will lead to your first turn. Skiing powder fluidly has been compared to the effortless motion of a pendulum—but even a pendulum needs a push to get it started. This drill helps give you that push.

Begin with a straight run down the hill through untracked powder to achieve floating speed and a functional platform, then initiate the entry phase of the powder turn by beginning to flex your lower body at the knees and ankles, and at the same time drop your hips slightly toward the center of the turn. This sets the sinking-loading-rising-floating sequence in motion and places you in a position to begin pressing your skis into a tighter arc. Because you've only dropped your hips slightly to the side, this will be a shallow turn (essentially, a

half-turn) just large enough to set things in motion for your first real turn in the other direction.

## The Deviant

It is of utmost importance to maintain adequate speed while turning in order to continue planing in powder. The primary way to speed up or slow down while preserving the rhythm of your turns is to change the degree to which you deviate from the fall line on each turn. For example, you can maintain the same turning cadence but slow down if you really bend the skis and make them arc more tightly to cross the fall line in a braking fashion. Conversely, you can speed up by bending the skis less and snaking along the fall line without deviating from it quite so much.

In this drill, progressively tighten the radius of each turn by bending the skis more to cause a reduction in speed. When your speed drops to a point where flotation is compromised, begin loosening your turns by deviating less from the fall line. Do this incrementally until your speed has reached a point where slowing back down is a good idea. Repeat this sequence a couple times in varying snow to become more familiar with how to find your ideal speed for a given turn rhythm, snow depth, and slope.

## The Extremist

Skiing powder is about finding the right combination of speed and movement patterns for a given consistency of snow on a particular slope. No run ever uses exactly the same blend of these elements, which is part of the reason why skiing powder is such a rewarding challenge. However, mastering powder requires being able to make minor adjustments in technique so you can tackle varying situations. This drill helps increase your skills' flexibility.

In essence, you are exploring the extremes of your powder tools' performance range. For example, see how slow you can ski effectively through powder, then see how fast you can ski the same snow on the same slope. Change your stance during the run, first moving a little forward, then backward. Experiment with how much and how little outside ski dominance you can use. Try to get your skis to bend into carved turns with very subtle pressuring movements, then play with explosive extension and retraction that bounces you completely out of the snow. In testing the limits of your tools, you will discover their most effective level of use. Use only enough energy to get the job done—using any extra is a waste.

## TROUBLESHOOTING POWDER PROBLEMS

The number of ways skiers can have trouble in powder is infinite. However, there are a few common problems. First, you should understand that the techniques for tool blending described above are only models for effective powder skiing. Expert skiers continually make adjustments to traditional methods, so you should use the information as a starting point rather than an end unto itself. The goal in powder is to ski it well enough so you enjoy the snow. If you're doing that, you're succeeding.

If you are still cursing the powder for ruining your day on the slopes and you don't know what to do about it, then everything I've discussed so far has failed for you. There are a few more tricks you can try before throwing in the towel.

If the essential step of floating through fluid powder just will not come, and you're still moving along in plow mode, there is definitely something wrong. But the cause may have nothing to do with your technique. One reason skiers have a hard time reaching a floating speed through the powder is wax. Riding on skis that are lacking wax, or are waxed incorrectly, can prevent you from traveling fast enough to plane on powder.

The issue of wax is pretty basic: no wax, no speed, no fun in powder. While you probably are not suffering from a complete lack of wax, you might be having trouble because your skis are waxed poorly. The wax on your skis may be just wrong enough for the snow temperature to cause increased drag. While this amount of friction is not really slowing you down and preventing you from reaching planing speed, it can cause your body mass to shift slightly forward as though you were tripping over your slowed skis. This shift in fore-aft balance initially causes your skis to dive toward the bottom of the new snow. Once you realize this problem, you compensate by leaning back. You have now assumed a stance that prevents you from making functional movements for expert-level powder skiing.

I carry in my coat pocket a couple waxes for different temperatures. Draw circles or Xs on the base of your ski with the wax, just as if it were a crayon. A couple applications will get you through the day, but be sure to hot wax the next time you go out.

If you are properly waxed, you follow all the basic steps for achieving flotation, and you still can't get your skis to ride a little higher in the powder, you may need skis with more surface area. If this is your situation, demo a pair of fat skis the next time you ski powder. You may not want to make a fat ski your only ski, but a demo session on them will serve as a controlled experiment to find out if surface area is your problem. Do the drills in this chapter and try to blend your basic skiing skills while skiing on the fat skis as outlined earlier in this chapter in Solving the Problems of the Ineffective Powder Skier. You should notice an instant difference in the amount of flotation you experience. Achieving immediate flotation will identify surface area as your primary problem. You will then need to decide whether you want to go all the way to a fat ski or just to a ski with greater surface area than the one you were riding on before.

Skiers who can't achieve flotation in a balanced stance and must lever their skis toward the surface by leaning backward (even on wider skis) can look at two possible solutions. One reason your skis are burrowing deep into the powder could be binding placement. If the technician who mounted your skis placed your bindings farther forward than they should be, you will always be at a mechanical disadvantage in powder. The added pressure on the fronts of your skis will make them dive. Some women prefer mounting their skis forward for improved performance on groomed slopes: this may be fine on firm surfaces, but it's the end of good powder skiing when it's deep. A better way to manipulate binding placement is with bindings that offer fore-aft adjustment range. This way a skier can set them forward for carving and move them to the center or even a little back of center for skiing the deep stuff.

Another reason skis dive in powder—even fairly wide all-mountain skis—is the overall forward lean in the skier's lower leg is too great. Too much combined ramp in the boot and binding, along with too much forward lean in the boot, can cause an overly flexed stance and shift a skier's center of mass too far forward. This skier will find that he has to squat and lean back to get the tips to float in powder—and he'll feel his calf against the back of the boot and his quadriceps muscles will be screaming for mercy (see Fore-Aft Alignment in the Getting Techno section, pages 211–14).

Finally, inspect your boots. Sometimes skiing in a boot that is too stiff in its flex can negatively affect your flotation in powder. A ski will seek the surface in powder if there's nothing restraining it, but an overly stiff-flexing boot can prevent your ski from floating. A softer-flexing ski boot will let your ski float, since the boot gives way at the ankle and allows the skier to remain in a tall, balanced stance. Try loosening the upper buckles just a little bit and see if your flotation in the powder improves. If it does, it's an indication that you may want to have a boot-

Many equipment-related problems can cause a ski to dive in powder.

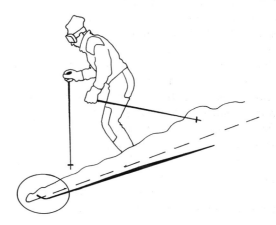

Making some changes to boots or bindings will often solve the problems that kept skis from floating in powder.

fitter soften your boot's flex or start looking for a new, less stiff boot.

For the skier who can float in powder but can't manage to control both skis in order to use them simultaneously, there are only a few things to try.

If your left and right skis tend to go their separate ways all the time in powder, there is a chance your alignment is not symmetrical. No matter how hard you try to move your legs and feet as if they were twins to maintain a good platform, you'll meet with little success if your left and right sides are aligned differently. To be sure your skis are really doing what you tell them to do, review the material on alignment in You *Can* Blame It on Your Gear! Sometimes. Pay close attention to the information on leg length.

If you experience an inability to manage both skis in powder only on occasion, your trouble could be caused by snow packed between your boot and binding. After any crash in powder, take the time to dig out a small platform for your ski to sit on before stepping back in, and be sure to clean off the bottom of your boot. Any snow packed beneath the toe or heel creates a completely different ramp angle for that foot, which can affect your skiing.

If you still have trouble controlling both skis in powder, there's a chance that you simply are not flexing and extending your lower body enough. Working both skis together requires muscular effort, primarily in applying pressure to the inside ski to keep it from rising toward the surface and away from the outside ski. This isn't a lot of work, and it won't give you a workout or make you sore—but it doesn't happen by itself.

Some skiers can go fast enough to float in powder and can control both skis to maintain a functional platform, but they have a hard time carving a turn. Bending both skis smoothly to carve a turn in powder can be tricky. Skiers who have trouble with this often resort to pure steering through turns, or they may even use a slight wedge. Trying to steer a turn or use a wedge to initiate a turn in powder results in a ski that is turned across the fall line while the skier's body remains in a tall stance. While this maneuver works fine on firm snow where skis can skid, a ski that is positioned overly sideways at the start of a turn in powder tends to trip the skier.

This is why experts bend their skis to make them turn in powder. This way, their skis can continue to slice through the snow rather than push sideways against it. Skiers who have trouble with bending both skis usually do too much or too little, or move too fast or too slow. The basic pressuring movements used to flex the skis into tighter arcs are not complicated, but they do require a soft touch and a sense of timing. It's like learning to do the three-step approach to a dive from a springboard into the pool: Get it right and you really fly; mess it up just a little and you get a poor bounce and little control.

Your difficulty in bending your skis into a carved turn in powder may be connected to your skis. A ski that is too stiff—either by design or because it's too long for your body weight—will never bend easily in powder. Extra effort will always be required for the too-stiff ski, and your extension and flexion movements will become exaggerated. One way you could test this is to load a backpack with 20 or 30 pounds and then ski a slope you've just had trouble with. The pack may throw off your technique, but it will give you a few extra pounds with which to bend your skis. Another way is to demo something softer; a softer-flexing ski makes skiing powder almost effortless, since it takes less effort to bend your skis.

Aside from these primary problems, there are a few secondary issues regarding powder technique. These include hand position and pole use, turn size, and difficult first turns.

My philosophy is that the best skiing is done with just about everything but your hands. The best thing you can do with them is keep them in a balanced, ready-to-pole position. However, there are a few things you can do with your arms, hands, and poles to enhance the powder experience.

Strive to keep them in front of your hips and held away from your body, as though you were hugging a barrel. Keeping your hands forward helps prevent you from leaning back, and holding them slightly out to the side provides the kind of balance a tight-rope walker gets from his pole. The drag of your pole tips over the surface of the powder will also send you information

Wider skis generate more surface area and allow skiers to stay on top of powder; at faster speeds, this enables a skier to make a large turn more effectively than in the past. MARK ELLING IN THE NOTCH, MT. BACHELOR

about the location of that surface and its texture or consistency.

Poling movements in powder should mimic the smooth, pressuring movements of the lower body that produce the sinking, loading, rising, and floating phases of each turn. Think of the poling movement as an extension of that sinking-then-floating cycle. Your poling action may therefore have a greater range of motion in powder than on groomed snow: the pole plant will usually drive deeper, and the pole swing will bring the hand higher than it does on firm snow. Slight exaggeration of these extremes in powder can even help bend and float your skis, but too much arm movement can have a negative effect on your balance.

When troubleshooting powder, look at some of the fundamental rules of turn shape and size. A continuously arcing turn that has no flat spots is the ideal shape for allowing useful force to build. This constantly turning arc is important for carved turns on firm snow. Without this arc, you cannot generate enough force to carve turns.

Turn size also can affect your enjoyment of powder skiing, depending on the width of the skis you're riding. Try to remember the last ski film you saw and recall how the skier skied powder versus how the snowboarder rode powder. Which athlete was better able to vary the size of her turns in powder? If the ski film was from the 1980s or 1990s, there's no doubt that the snowboarder was more versatile in deep snow. Modern ski films would show skiers making all kinds of turns in deep powder, for changes in style have been driven by new equipment.

It used to be the case that it was difficult to make anything other than small- or medium-radius turns in powder because you had to manage two skis as a unit, moving them simultaneously to maintain a functional platform for flotation while trying to bend them for each turn. You can do this most effectively by generating a cycle of pressure and release in which you bend the skis deep in the snow and then

guide them toward the next turn as they float higher. This cycle of flexion and extension—or sink and float, bend and rebound, or whatever you decide to call it—tends to work best when you make a smaller turn.

With the kind of fat skis available today, a skier can generate enough flotation to navigate powder with all his weight over the outside ski, if he wants, as long as the skier is moving fast enough. What this has done to powder skiing is open it up to the kinds of variation in turn size that mark the snowboarder's powder style. But the key to this kind of powder skiing is still surface area and speed. A fat ski may generate enough surface area so a skier can stand hard against one ski, but this skier needs to be moving fast. This allows for Super-G-sized turns in powder, which can be a lot of fun. But remember that the trees come up fast and tend not to move.

You will discover that narrower shaped skis still work best in powder if a skier uses smaller turns: narrower skis can be pushed down into the snow and bent into a carved turn. Wider skis cannot be pushed as deep into the snow and tend to plane on top of the snow and make larger turns. Skiers thinking about fat skis should realize that this difference exists. Fat skis have a lot of surface area and will jump up on a plane and take off in powder. This is what those powder Super-G rock stars want, and they'll buy the fat ski as long as they can to get that kind of high-velocity planing. A lot of skiers are choosing fat skis in shorter lengths so they can get them down into the powder a bit, where they can be slowed down and bent into tighter turns. Be sure you know what kind of skiing you want to do before you choose the longest, fattest ski out there.

Last, as described above in the Straight Run, Half-Turn, Repeat drill, a perplexing inability to start the first turn in powder haunts many skiers. This problem is generally not caused by any physical skill deficiency but rather by a mental block that some skiers develop. They simply psych themselves out of being able to make a good first turn, which limits their entire run. Rather than delve into the tortured psyche of the troubled powder skier, I will offer a few tactical tricks for getting that first turn started.

Try entering the powder field on a traverse to gather speed. When you've achieved adequate flotation, add a small hook to the traverse by turning slightly up the hill, then immediately make your next turn in the other direction. With the hook as your first turn, your second one should come more easily. You can also try hopping or bouncing gently with both feet during your initial straight run and continue to do so for the first three turns. The bouncing will help you bend your skis simultaneously, and the rebound you get will help you guide your skis a little farther into each turn. Similarly, you can try "pedaling" gently through your turns to achieve the same benefits as bouncing with both feet. But be careful not to transfer too much weight from foot to foot, because your skis will diverge. Finally, if you struggle with a stubborn first turn in powder, relax. Being mellow in mind and movement is the underlying key to being able to perform properly. Take a deep breath and chill: slowing everything down will help.

# Crud

Crud. The word alone conjures up images of pain and frustration for most skiers. It sounds like what it is: ugly, nasty stuff. But what exactly is crud? Skiers have a lot of ways to describe funky snow conditions: *glop, boilerplate, crust, windpack, slush, mung, cake, slab,* and *poo,* to name just a few. Crud is the general term that I'll use to cover all these conditions. It is not one particular kind of snow; rather, crud is many different kinds of snow, and trying to ski it only one way will never work.

The first step in learning how to ski crud well is understanding where it comes from, where it's going, and what happens to it along the way. Crud begins as fresh powder. At most ski areas, powder does not last very long. Skiers and snowboarders race to their favorite spots for first tracks—and second and third tracks. Some runs are so well traveled that skiers pack this new snow into packed powder. These runs will likely be machine-groomed within a few days. But on runs where neither skiers nor groomers pack the snow down flat, crud is born.

Crud is transition snow; it starts as chopped-up powder, and it eventually will become smooth firm snow, turn into bumps, or become covered by the next snowfall. And crud is variable; it changes with time, temperature, sun, altitude, and moisture. Each of these factors alters the way you ski crud of a particular flavor, and the name of the crud-skiing game is flexibility. Crud is difficult to ski because it isn't powder, but it's not firm snow either. You can't

use only firm-snow or powder techniques to ski crud. You have to blend your basic skiing tools.

But this method of combining the techniques you use on firm snow and on powder is not enough, because crud is always changing. You must learn to read the snow by both sight and feel to judge how to blend your skills effectively. Crud can pass through many phases on its way to becoming firm snow. Identifying a few types of crud and how each forms will help you understand the techniques covered in this chapter.

Newly fallen powder tends to fluff back into a skier's tracks, leaving plenty of snow for the next skier. Tracked-up, wet powder, however, can be a crud situation because skiers' tracks remain entrenched in the run. This results in two kinds of surfaces: the dense powder surrounding the tracks and the firmly packed snow of the track itself.

Another common crud situation is tracked powder that gets warmed by the sun or by rising air temperatures. As the powder is warmed, it begins to settle and becomes denser and wetter. This density makes it difficult to make steering movements or last-minute corrections with your skis once they enter the snow. The added water in the snow also makes skis feel grabby or slow.

A particularly nasty variety of crud is a fairly wet snow that has frozen solid (or semisolid) overnight; this is sometimes called *coral reef.* This surface is unpredictable. It can be rock-hard and full of ruts that don't give way to your

Sometimes crud looks ugly, and sometimes you look ugly in crud. Remember, skis are easy to turn when they're in the air. SETH WARNER ON WEST RIDGE, MT. BACHELOR

skis, or it can be in a semisolid state that gives way just enough for your skis to become locked in whichever direction they are pointing.

Another type of crud contains crust layers. Crust at or near the surface can wreak havoc on an unsuspecting skier. Some crust is unbreakable, and you can ski it like firm snow. Breakable crust is insidious, because your skis break through into softer snow beneath and often become locked into place. The crust's breakability can also vary from day to day and from slope to slope, making it difficult to anticipate how much force will break you through the crust.

## THE IDEAL GOAL

In a perfect world, an expert skier would ski crud with a mixture of powder and firm-snow technique. The mix would depend on whether the crud was more like powder or firm snow, and the skier would alter her technique as the snow became softer or harder. But crud skiing is not as simple as this. There are additional factors you need to know about.

Three basic characteristics make crud a different animal from powder or firm snow: dense consistency, crust layers and surfaces of variable penetrability, and an irregular surface. These elements can produce the following troublesome conditions: your ski cannot be steered once it sinks into the snow; you have difficulty bending your ski into a carved turn; your skis behave unpredictably due to the irregular surface.

You need to overcome the snow's resistance by freeing your skis from its grip. You need to bend your skis regardless of the snow's penetrability, and you have to maintain a balanced stance to deal with the sudden changes of an irregular surface.

Good crud skiers can launch themselves up and out of the stubborn snow or at least closer to the surface where it is less dense. Freeing your skis from the crud's grip will allow you to steer both skis through a turn's transition phase, just

as you would in powder. To accomplish this vertical escape from crud so you can turn, you must combine your skis' rebound from the snow with leg flexion and extension to "jump" your skis (either gently or explosively) out of the crud, or at least closer to the surface.

To get this rebound out of your skis, they must be bent into a carved turn. The method of bending your skis is similar to the method used in skiing powder, but the snow may not be as cooperative. Crud can set like concrete, be covered with a breakable crust, or be wet and dense. These qualities make bending your skis into controlled arcs very difficult. To ski crud well, you may need to use explosive movements to literally bust deep enough into the snow so your skis have room to bend. In other situations, you will need to pressure your skis gently to coax a bend out of them without breaking too deeply into the crusty snow. In addition to freeing your skis at turn initiation and bending them, you must maintain a functional stance to

In very nasty crud, you may need to explode up and out of the snow to clear the skis from the crud, ensuring easy steering to initiate the next turn.

balance yourself as the snow becomes harder, softer, faster, slower, smoother, or rougher. Skiing crud is like sailing in a stormy sea: you are more likely to be swept overboard if you aren't focused on your balanced stance.

## COMMON CRUD PROBLEMS THAT DRIVE SKIERS INSANE

Let's look at what happens when you ski crud the way you ski firm, groomed snow, and then at what happens when you ski it the way you ski powder.

A groomed-snow expert charges into a sea of crud with two disadvantages. She will be using a fair amount of outside ski dominance to engage her outside ski, and she will try to make smooth transitions between turns by shifting her hips across her skis and toward the center of the new turn. What happens when she pushes hard against her outside ski is the same thing that happens in powder, but worse. Her skis will split, and the outside ski will drive deep into the crud while the inside ski floats on a semifirm surface and becomes squirrelly. The ski that dives deep into denser snow becomes stuck and locked in. The ski that floats to the surface will find snow that is fast and soft enough to dent but not soft enough to steer through. Excessive outside ski dominance in crud often results in your two skis heading on irreversible tracks to different destinations.

Skiing crud as if it were powder is, in most situations, a better bet than trying to ski it as if it were firm snow. Using a powder technique, however, still leaves room for failure. Skiing crud powder-style means using your feet like twins and using a lower body cycle of flexion and extension, or gentle bouncing. But this tool blend is usually too weak for crud.

Using simultaneous foot and leg movements prevents your skis from going their separate ways. But with this technique, both your skis will ride on the surface of the crud. This flotation is exactly what you want in powder, but it causes problems in crud. The gentle, rhythmic flexion and extension movements used in powder are usually not strong enough for crud, where you need to drive your skis deep into the snow to bend them. When you use a powder technique, your skis run along the crud surface and get pushed around by the ruts and tracks there. Your skis are never fully bent into a solid, carved turn. When you are too gentle in crud, you only partially engage and bend your skis, which is inadequate for completing turns and controlling speed. Remember that crud, like powder, is difficult to steer in. In crud you can't skid your tails sideways at the finish of the turn in order to slow down, so you end up bending the skis and carving them through the crud; no bend, no turn, no speed control, no style points.

In crud, many skiers find their skis do not respond to the instructions their brains and bodies send them. Dense snow and breakable crust can act like glue that sticks to your skis and fixes them wherever you place them. Once your skis are stuck, it is difficult to make the kinds of corrections you might regularly make on groomed snow or forgiving powder. The section below offers solutions.

## SOLVING THE PROBLEMS OF THE FRUSTRATED CRUD SKIER

In the world of all-mountain skiing, crud may be the most physically taxing terrain—even when skied properly. Even experts get beaten by crud. Some skiers make skiing horrendous crud look pretty, but those same skiers can look downright ugly in another kind of nasty crud. Some skiers even seek out crud for the challenge they can't find anywhere else on their home mountain. Remember to give yourself a break in your battle against crud. Many skiers never totally master this condition. The goal is to shoot for more wins than losses.

To begin mastering crud, start thinking of every turn as an experiment. Because there are many ways to ski crud, there is no way to know which tool blend will work without getting out there and testing it. With each turn, you gain more information about the snow's consistency and which tactics bring success. This is how the experts do it: by jumping in and going for it but altering their technique as they make it down the hill. If you're really good, you'll get it right in three turns. However, some skiers use half the run to figure out what works. To explore how to conduct this crud experiment, I'll review your first turn sequence.

At the top of the run, look at the snow. Does it look relatively smooth or very chopped up? Does it look wet or dry? Do other skiers below look as if they're having a particular kind of trouble? Get a feel for the snow's consistency before setting off. If you didn't gain this by approaching the top of the run, traverse into the crud a bit before starting your run.

The clues you gather from the snow's look and feel can help determine the starting place for your tool blend. If the snow looks rock-hard and rutted, carrying a lot of speed would not be wise—it's not necessary to achieve flotation, and speed could prove dangerous. If the new snow looks rough and feels crusted, you might begin with plenty of lower body pressuring movements to bust through the crud and rebound your skis up and out of the snow for the start of the next turn. The visual and kinesthetic clues you collect help you decide where to start, but you won't know for sure which tools you'll need until you start skiing.

I begin with a short, straight run, just as I do in powder. During this run I can learn how dense the snow is, whether it's crusty, and what the surface feels like. And I can find this out without having to worry immediately about making a turn. Granted, I have to turn soon so I don't build up too much speed. But I've probably gained enough information about the snow within the first few seconds to make my first turn count.

Take note of the snow's depth on this short, straight run. If the crud is only a few inches thick, you may be able to ski it as if it were groomed snow: power up over the outside ski and start motoring through the stuff. There are times when crud does nothing but add new texture to the snow's surface, and you can pretend it's not there at all. It's easy to identify those situations, because skiing the way you would on groomed snow actually works! If the crud is deep (say, 5 inches to a few feet), you'll have to use your legs and feet simultaneously to create flotation and prevent your skis from taking different routes.

You should determine how dense the snow is on your short run. If it feels like cement and holds each ski in its own private track, you can anticipate getting some rebound out of your skis and using your lower body to guide your skis up and out of the goop to initiate a new turn. If the snow seems to allow your skis some freedom of movement, even when they are down deep in the crud, then such drastic bend-and-leap tactics won't be necessary.

Your straight run should clue you in to the crust's breakability. If it breaks easily as you move over it, then you can ski with lower-body movements similar to those you use in powder. If it breaks unpredictably or only under your full weight, it will be necessary to use aggressive pressuring movements of your legs to ensure the crust breaks when and where you want it to. Any crust that doesn't break at all or breaks only under severe stress should be skied gingerly. Unbroken crust is as good as groomed snow, so make it easy on yourself and stay on top of it.

You will find that the width of the skis you're riding on will affect how deeply you penetrate in the snow. Skinnier skis drive deeper into the snow. Depending on body weight and ski surface area, some skiers will do better in a particular crud than others. Roll the dice . . . if it's your turn to hack now, maybe the next crud day will be made for you and your skis.

When the time comes for you to make that first turn, you will need to free your skis momentarily and guide them toward the turn. Because you've done only a brief, straight run and

In variably breakable crusts or extremely dense snows, it may be necessary to use both the skis' rebound and hyperextension and retraction. The purpose is twofold: free the skis from the tricky snow for ease of turn initiation, and load them for a crust-busting landing that will allow you to set your skis deep into the snow to bend them into a carved turn.

On a crust that breaks rarely or only when under stress, you can ski with less vertical range of motion, moving gingerly so as not to break through.

have not driven your skis deep into the snow, there will be no need to make any exaggerated movements to get your skis out of the crud; they should be riding fairly close to the surface. I often pump my skis during this initial straight run by gently bouncing on them. This helps me determine what the surface penetrability is like and generates a small amount of rebound each time I bend my skis. I use this rebound to allow me to steer both skis slightly across the fall line before I let them make full contact with the crud.

As you begin to drive your skis into the crud, you need to decide how much or how little outside ski dominance to use and how much force to apply to your skis through leg extension. If the crud is not deep and is relatively firm, you can utilize quite a bit of outside ski dominance. As crud becomes deeper and softer, you must use simultaneous, equal-footed movements to gain flotation and prevent your skis from taking off in different directions.

At the same time, you will be deciding how hard to push against the snow as your skis come into contact with the crud. This pressure can range from a gentle press, such as you might use in light powder, to an extremely aggressive punch to drive your skis deep into the crusty snow. The goal is to make your skis bend.

In powder, you rely on your skis' flex, the resulting rebound, and flexion and extension movements to generate vertical body mass movement, or bouncing. Crud requires extra effort, and the gentle bouncing you use in powder often isn't enough. In addition to the rebound you get from bending your skis, you also need to use extra leg flexion and extension to get the job done. This is a crud skier's secret weapon: the aggressive punch that busts through crust layers and overbends a ski to produce extra rebound. This is what counts in nasty crud that resists normal attempts to bend your skis and/or requires you to completely free your skis from the snow to start a new turn.

To work reliably, busting through the crud and bending your skis involves some other tricks. One tool is simultaneous foot steering

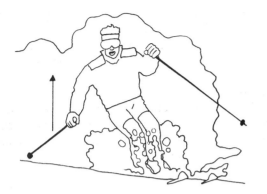

This is the top of a skier's range of vertical movement or elongation in powder.

This is the top of a skier's range of vertical movement or elongation in tricky crud; begin retracting your legs before you reach this full extension in order to more quickly clear your skis from the snow.

during the pressuring phase of the turn. In crud, skis can wander off in undesired directions— even as they are being bent into an arc that should produce a nicely carved turn. By steering both feet while your legs are pressuring the skis, you can overcome your skis' tendency to deviate from their course.

How you use your ankles—whether they're loose or tight—can make a world of difference in crud conditions. You can feel the difference between loose and tight ankles in the following exercise. Sit in a chair and hold one foot off the floor; shake it as if something were stuck to the bottom of your shoe. Relax all the muscles in your shin and around your ankle. Your foot is loose and begins to flop around. Now tighten your ankle by flexing your foot toward the shin. Hold it there and don't allow any movement of your foot as you again try to shake something off the bottom of your shoe. Skiing crud with overly relaxed ankles will make your skis un-manageable, as if they had minds of their own. Maintaining a flexed foot that restricts ankle movement while skiing crud enables you to get the desired response out of your skis.

It pays to look for shortcuts when you bend your skis into a carved turn, whether you use a gentle press or an aggressive punch. In the variable textures of crud, there will be some spots of snow that are particularly nasty and others that aren't so bad. Try to ski through the easier patches of crud. You will know what those are once you've sampled the slope. Look for features in the snow that allow for easier turn initiation and speed control. Perhaps there is a hump in the snow ahead that you could use as a jump to unweight your skis and make the start of the next turn easier. Crud with fewer tracks or softer patches offers a better spot for pressuring and bending your skis, since there are fewer obstacles for achieving a carved arc there. Look for a path through crud that maximizes the best snow and minimizes the amount of effort you must expend.

Balance comes into play as you pressure your skis. You should be able to instantly alter the pressure on your tips or tails. It pays to enter the first turn with as centered a stance as possible, but you may need to change this stance slightly during the turn. For example, you may have to use additional heel pressure during the control phase of the turn when your skis are being bent. Without this added heel pressure, your ski tips may burrow deeper into the snow—with little chance of your seeing them again. It's possible

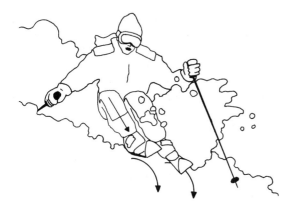

Anticipating the carved line skis should take and guiding the feet (with ankles held rigidly) along that arc will tend to ensure that the skis do continue to carve along that line. Here, the skier continues to maintain inside ski pressure while guiding both feet.

to increase tail pressure on your skis without shifting your entire body mass backward. Increase your ankle flex the same way you would if you were walking on your heels across a wet floor. This move helps your ski tips float to the surface of the crud but preserves your overall balance.

The other major part of the balance game in crud involves the way you set your skis on edge as you pressure them into a tighter arc. There are two main methods you can use to tip your skis over. One is by leaning your entire body to the side or toward the middle of the turn, called *banking* or *inclination*. The other is by letting your hips move toward the turn's center while your upper body remains upright, called *hip angulation*. Instructors and coaches generally agree that hip angulation is a more effective way to ski because it provides better edge hold and better balance. In crud and powder, many skiers exhibit poor hip angulation and develop a habit of banking turns. This is partly because their loss of edge grip is less noticeable in softer snow conditions, and also due to the need to pressure the inside ski in softer snows. Many skiers lean onto the inside ski to generate pressure, rather

than pressing on it muscularly, and they end up banking. Banking places your upper body inside your hips rather than above them, which means you are much more likely to fall if you encounter difficult snow or need to recover from a mistake.

Once you have entered your first turn in crud and produced adequate bend in your skis, you are on the verge of using the energy that will be released from your decambered skis. In crud, as in powder, you assume a body position of greatest flexion at the point where your skis have the greatest bend. You now have two loaded springs working for you: the leaf spring of your bent ski; and the energy stored in your leg and torso muscles, which want to elongate and return to a tall, energy-efficient stance. Once you've bent your skis to such a point, there's nothing you can do to keep them there. They will spring back to their normal state, and you may as well go with the flow.

In powder, elongating your body and standing back up when your skis are snapping back to their flat state produces the energy that propels you toward the surface. In crud, you often need to enhance this vertical movement to propel yourself higher or completely out of the snow and into the air, where steering movements can be made without interference from the snow. You need more active lower-body elongation to launch yourself. In powder, you merely allow your body to return to a tall stance; in crud, you get there in double-time by quickly moving from a flexed position to a tall one, using explosive extension and then retraction of your legs. This rapid return to a tall stance may come slightly faster than it would in powder, or it may be very aggressive—like a jack-in-the-box. The pace of this return to a tall stance is determined by the crud's nastiness. The tougher the snow is to turn in, the more aggressive your elongating movement needs to be.

This move is referred to as *up-unweighting*. Your extension results in a reduction of pressure on your skis, or unweighting, and the term describes both the method and the result. You

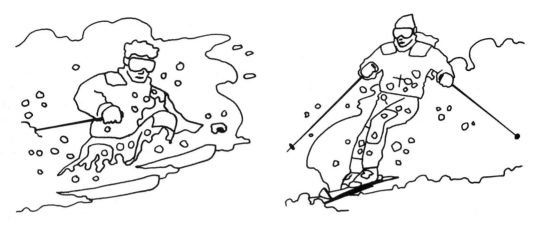

You must get from a loaded stance at turn finish *(left)* to an elongated stance at turn initiation *(right)*, but the quickness of that return to a tall stance depends on the snow. The nastier it is, the more intense that movement will have to be.

need the least up-unweighting on firm, smooth snow because the surface is predictable and offers little resistance to your steering movements. You need a moderate amount of up-unweighting in powder because the snow provides some resistance to steering movements. You need the most up-unweighting in nasty crud because the snow is both difficult to steer in and has hazards that make turn initiation difficult.

Remember: the reason for using elongation to up-unweight is so you can free your skis from

the crud and steer them toward the next turn. In the worst crud, you need to get your skis completely out of the snow to initiate the next turn. This requires a sudden stop to the aggressive extension of the legs followed by a quick retraction. By stopping leg extension after it has been started, your body mass can continue to rise and allow you to retract your legs and pull your skis out of the crud. At this transition between turns in crud, it is crucial that you are able to steer both skis simultaneously, like twins, to their next point of contact with the snow.

Foot and leg steering are important between turns in crud, as the skis are often momentarily freed from dense snow.

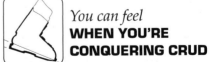

*You can feel*
**WHEN YOU'RE CONQUERING CRUD**

1. When you begin using the tactics in this chapter, you will feel as if you are doing too much work. This is a good sign, at least initially. In the beginning, skiing crud successfully will require extra effort compared to skiing groomed snow or light powder—but it will get easier. Your initial trials in crud

may feel awkward. But with practice, your movements will become more effective and energy efficient. It's more physically demanding to ski crud than be defeated by it—but it's also more fun.

2. In crud, you'll always feel worse than you look to other skiers. When you look back up the run to see your tracks, you might be surprised to see how good they look. It often feels as if you are chopping chunks out of the slope with your skis, the way you whack at a tree to chop it down—and sometimes you actually *are* chopping your turns out of the run. You should continually strive to reduce the amount of energy you are expending. On each consecutive turn, try to do less with your body until you reach a point where you receive unsatisfac-

tory results; then return to a skills blend that was both successful and as energy efficient as possible.

3. The well-executed turn in crud will never feel perfect, because crud is far from ideal snow. Adjust your perspective when it comes to turning in crud. Think in relative terms: "That first turn felt terrible, but the next one felt better." Try to make each new turn feel a little better than the one before by making subtle changes in your skills blend. By the end of the run, your turns might feel pretty good. Remember that the snow may change as you go, which can make things easier or more difficult. Skiing crud is like making a tough bunker shot in golf. Nobody expects it to look pretty, so the pressure's off. Experiment!

Stiff, wind-affected snow can prove treacherous, even when it looks great. Don't be afraid to use a wide, defensive stance and get ready to do battle. RUSS T. MERRITT ON THE MORAINE WITH THE SUMMIT IN THE BACKGROUND, MT. BACHELOR

4. Rarely does skiing crud feel tentative or defensive. A good crud skier takes control of the snow and skis it offensively. A skier on dense crud covered with a breakable crust would ski at the aggressive end of the spectrum: you might say he is attacking the crud and beating it into submission. Sneaking along the top of the crust without breaking through is on the subtle end of the spectrum. Conquering crud requires a take-charge attitude and flexible tactics.

 *You can see*
## WHEN YOU'RE CONQUERING CRUD

1. The best way to see your improvement in crud is to inspect your tracks every six or seven turns. Look for a unified, crescent-shaped arc with a fat middle section and tapered ends. Between turns, the snow should look less disturbed, possibly even untouched. This indicates that your skis are not being deflected by the crud and you are unweighting your skis to aid in steering at each turn initiation.

2. You will often see your ski tips when skiing crud, either because you are unweighting for the start of the new turn or because your skis are flexing enough during the control phase of the turn so they follow a tighter arc to the surface. When skiing crusty crud, it's common for the mid- to aft portion of your ski to break through the crust while the tip and/or shovel of the ski remains visible at the surface.

3. When you watch good crud skiers, you may see them use a wider range of overall body movement than they might on groomed snow or in powder. They will use more flexion to load their skis and begin bending them, with more extension to finish bending the skis and propel themselves higher in the snow to ease turn initiation. Good crud skiers make skiing crud look fun because of the dynamic nature of their movements.

4. You'll know you're conquering crud when you find yourself watching for bumps, tracks, soft spots, and obstacles ahead of you and skiing your line down the slope accordingly. In crud, you can mix up small, medium, and large turns in order to string together the best snow conditions on the run.

## OTHER DRILLS

More drills that will help you conquer crud are below.

### Marked-Time Traverses

Skiing crud requires you to utilize both independent and simultaneous movements of your legs; this drill helps break the skill down to its essential roots. While making a traverse across a groomed slope, begin by simply picking up one ski and then the other in a series of marked-time steps. This isolates the basic movement required to transfer weight from one ski to the next. Try making the movement crud-specific by shifting the weight completely from one to the other without lifting the ski off the snow. Try to maintain a quiet upper body and make your weight switch through flexion and extension of your legs.

### Continuum Traverses, Continuum Turns

You need to fine-tune your lateral weight-transfer skills for more subtle weight shifts rather than complete weight transfers. Building on the Marked-Time Traverses drill, continue to do traverses across the groomed slope but now try to achieve specific weight-bearing combinations between the inside and outside skis. For example, as you traverse, try to weight the inside ski with 20 percent of your body weight while the outside ski bears the remaining 80 percent. Then switch 80 percent of your weight to the inside ski and 20 percent to the outside. Experiment with more equal and more differential weight combinations. This hones your ability to weight your inside ski incrementally in variable snow.

## Fore-Aft Leapers

In addition to the way you vary pressure on your inside and outside skis, crud also requires precise fore-aft pressure adjustments to manage difficult and changing snow conditions. This exercise focuses on adjusting the amount of pressure on the shovels or tails of your skis. To begin, make jump turns on steep, groomed terrain, making sure to keep the tips and tails of your skis about the same distance off the snow. Then, try making jump turns while leaving the tips of your skis in contact with the snow. Then make jump turns keeping the tails of your skis in contact with the snow. Try to perform the jump turns with smooth movements, since controlled lower-body flexion and extension are a large part of skiing crud well.

In this jump turn, tips and tails are about the same distance off the snow.

## Extreme Speed

To understand how speed can affect your performance in crud, try skiing ten turns through crud as slowly as possible. Note how you must change your movements to cope. Then experiment with the opposite extreme and ski through the crud as fast as you safely can. Speed variance can alter the amount of outside ski dominance you can get away with and the amount of lower body flexion and extension needed to bust into stiff crud, as well as fore-aft pressure distribution. For certain crud conditions, your velocity may need to change to maximize your performance.

## To Pop or Not to Pop

Skiing crud often requires you to free your skis from the crud so they can be steered toward a new turn. This requires using lower body flexion and extension to launch yourself upward through the crud. This vertical movement results in an up-unweighting of your skis, and is often referred to as a *pop*. There are times when it's necessary to pop like crazy and others where using that much energy is a waste. Experiment with your unweighting range by skiing some crud using wild flexion and extension and see how high out of the snow you can get your skis. Then ski the exact same crud using zero unweighting. Attempt to find the right amount of unweighting to get the job done without wasting energy.

## Crossover, Pop

Simply because you use a little unweighting to start a turn in nasty crud conditions doesn't mean you can forget about the edge-change movement required to start any new turn. Just as you do on groomed snow, you need to redirect your center of mass from the middle of one turn toward the center of the next—in effect, crossing your hips from one side of the skis to the other. Perform the To Pop or Not to Pop drill, but pay attention to the lateral hip movement of the crossover, whether you are airborne or not.

## TROUBLESHOOTING CRUD

It's difficult to troubleshoot the problems you experience while skiing crud because of the variable nature of the conditions and the techniques. Most skiers have trouble in crud because they're not willing to experiment with many different tool blends. It takes time to figure out what works in crud. However, I can offer the tool blends that work for me in most crud situations. Use these as guidelines for easy access into crud. You will be better off learning to read the snow yourself, but these guidelines will help the thoroughly impatient skier.

### High Speed, High Outside Ski Dominance

There are times when you want to go fast. Using the inside ski aggressively at very high speeds tends to trip you up, so stand hard against the outside ski and increase your speed until you're planing on it alone. At this speed your outside ski should power through almost anything.

### Groomed Style with Inside Assistance

Many types of crud are softer than they look and not as deep as you might think. Try skiing crud as if it were groomed snow, but keep enough pressure on the inside ski to prevent it from taking a different line than the outside ski.

### Initiation Insurance

Some crud is hard and irregular enough that it would hurt you if you fell. In these instances,

I'm less worried about making a perfect turn than I am about simply starting a turn. Falls that occur at turn initiation happen when you are standing tall, which is a vulnerable position. If I don't want this to happen, I make sure my skis aren't even close to the problematic snow by using enough unweighting to ensure I can at least start the turn without trouble.

### The One-Two Punch

If crud is crusty or dense enough that I need to bust my skis down into the snow with heavy-duty flexion and extension, then it's probably funky enough that I need to use both skis like twins. Use both skis to enter and exit the snow aggressively.

### Blame It on Your Gear!

If I'm having trouble after I've gone through all the tips in this chapter, then something is really wrong. For most skiers, that something is their gear. Skis are by far the most common culprits, because many skis are not designed for use in crud. The typical carving ski is designed to be used on smooth, firm surfaces and is not at home in soft, irregular crud. Most all-mountain, or mid-fat, skis are built to encounter variable terrain and will therefore make your life easier in crud. Many of the new generation of fat skis rule in junky snow, as long as they are stiff enough to handle the *chunder*—stiff, gnarly conditions—at speed.

It is difficult to predict exactly what specific problems you will have with a particular type of ski, but it's easy for you to demo other kinds of skis through a ski shop. My suggestion for any skier who continues to have difficulty in crud, even after trying all the drills in this chapter, is to try riding on some different boards.

# Bumps

Because moguls are prevalent at most ski areas, many skiers have the chance to do battle with them. A large percentage of skiers probably list skiing bumps at the top of their problem list, and being able to ski bumps well can indeed be a matter of survival. If you can't handle the bumps, you may have few skiing options at some ski areas. If you have to avoid bump runs, just getting to where you need to be for lunch can be a major challenge.

The good news is bump skiing is one of the easiest advanced skiing situations to excel at if you approach the learning process in an effective way. It's also one of the few advanced skiing situations that allows you to break into expert performance incrementally and at slower speeds. In fact, it's best to learn how to ski bumps by first performing new movements slowly before increasing your speed in the bumps. Bump skiing also involves the least amount of decision making and skill blending of all the advanced skiing situations covered in this book—in part because the bumps themselves do most of the work for you. Like racing gates, moguls dictate where, when, and how you turn. And while this may be exactly what some skiers loathe, it can be to your advantage.

## THE IDEAL GOAL

When it comes to bumps, the goal for too many skiers is to simply make it down alive or with-

out major injury. This humble goal shortchanges skiers, because everybody can learn to ski bumps like an expert. And contrary to popular opinion, it doesn't take muscle or young knees to improve in bumps if you can perform some basic movements that form the foundation of expert bump skiing.

The expert skier strives to ski a single, continuous line through a mogul field without drastic fluctuations in speed or direction. We've all watched skiers who do this well, and it's impressive to watch a skier do a hundred turns in a row without faltering when we're struggling to link three or four turns together. One of the remarkable elements of expert bump skiing is a skier's ability to ski through bumps without deviating from his course and with flowing movements that enable him to maintain a quiet upper body and get away with what seems to be a minimal expenditure of energy. These are some of the ingredients of expert bump skiing: following a continuous line downslope, maintaining a consistent speed, and using smooth movements that preserve balance and conserve energy.

A factor inherent in the goals listed above is *speed control*. While controlling your speed is not as glamorous a goal as being able to rip straight down the fall line, it is speed control that will allow you to reach the more exciting goals in bump skiing. No matter how fast bump specialists travel, none of them exceed a speed they can handle. Each expert bump skier has a speed threshold in the bumps. It's important for every skier to understand and respect that limit. Expert bump skiers are able to slow down at any moment during a bump run, though they may choose not to. Being unable to slow down at will indicates you are not skiing the bumps as well as you could and, possibly, that you are out of control.

Bump skiing that sends snow flying with every turn and keeps the legs blazing like pistons is the kind of dynamic performance advanced skiers strive for. This goal is attainable over time with a lot of practice at slower speeds. Your bump skiing journey starts with the basics,

Controlling your speed in bumps is the key to good mogul skiing. Use the front side of each bump as a place to slow down. CHRIS SMITH ON CANYON, MT. BACHELOR

but the beauty of this method is that it won't prevent you from taking it to extremes. Instead, it will lead you directly there.

## COMMON PROBLEMS THAT IRRITATE POTENTIAL BUMP SKIERS

One of the biggest problems that intermediate and advanced skiers face in moguls is the abundance of advice available from other skiers on how to tackle the bumps. There are as many ways to ski bumps, if you listen to your buddies, as there are bumps on the slope: turn your skis on the top of the bump, follow the troughs, absorb the bumps like a human shock-absorber, plant your poles harder, keep your feet tight together. These suggestions may all be valid tactics you can use in the bumps, but they fail to provide you with a comprehensive method that will always work—no matter what. Most bump advice comes in the form of quick tips that may help you do one specialized thing, but these tips rarely give a struggling bump skier the kind of fundamental help he desperately needs.

The second largest problem facing potential bump skiers is the fact that these mounds of snow on an otherwise perfectly good slope provide enough of an obstacle so you can't necessarily turn when and where you want to. Basically, the bumps call the shots on turn size, shape, and timing. For some skiers this presents a major problem. Many skiers, without knowing it, will tend to make only one kind of turn—regardless of where they are skiing. Many skiers also tend to turn in places where making a turn will be easy: after a small hump that helps them unweight their skis or simply when they feel like it. In bumps, these skiers are suddenly forced to make a small-radius turn and make it as often as the bumps appear before them. The size of the turn, and where it occurs, is suddenly nonnegotiable—and the skiers described above are hating life.

Another big issue for struggling bump skiers is fear. Now, any advanced skier worth his salt will never admit to being frightened by a few little bumps. But advanced skiers are often intimidated enough that they begin making ineffective movements. Because bumps cause a lot of skiers problems, many skiers approach a bump run with an unconscious (or maybe conscious) expectation to fall or lose control. When skiers expect to fall or are intimidated by the terrain, they exhibit a familiar pattern: they try to go where it's safe.

On a foreboding slope, a skier may think the safest place to be is toward the hill. If an intimidated skier has his skis pointing straight down the hill, he may tend to lean on the tails of his skis to escape the bump-ridden abyss below. If he is completing a turn or traversing across the slope, he may lean on his inside ski toward the hill. He might even rotate his face to the hill to turn his back on his deepest fears. The methods I will discuss should help intimidated skiers approach bumps without the fear factor.

If you consider the profile of a typical mogul, fear in the bumps is understandable. They are like mini-mountains all across the slope, and they produce a pitch that varies greatly. On the top of a bump the slope may be nonexistent; on the bump's front side the slope may actually go in the opposite direction; on the back side of the bump the pitch may drop steeply. This pitch configuration is problematic for skiers unable to negotiate bumps in a way that avoids the stop-start rhythm of an abrupt collision with a bump's face, followed by a death-defying acceleration down its back side.

In addition to the pitch profile of a mogul, the snow often varies considerably within the space of a single bump. The front face of the bump holds softer snow, while its back side has been scraped away to ice by fearful skiers who sideslip down it. Sometimes the troughs are filled with wind-blown snow or powdery shavings from the back sides of the bumps above. This can prove tricky for skiers who slide sideways into the fluff, expecting firm snow.

Skiers who have trouble in bumps tend to display a few common patterns. Some gain speed with each new turn until they reach a critical speed, at which time they take drastic action or crash. The action often is a last-minute hockey stop or a high-speed traverse for safety toward the side of the run. Other skiers may hang on, even after this maximum speed has been surpassed, until they reach the bottom of the run. This technique is marked by a lot of deflection off the tops of moguls, like small jumps, all the way down. Other skiers may be unable to start a

Leaning back in bumps may initially be caused by fear, but this can develop into a bad habit.

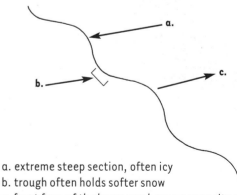

a. extreme steep section, often icy
b. trough often holds softer snow
c. front face of the bump can have an opposite slope

The anatomy of a bump.

turn when they want to or need extra time to finish their turns and end up skiing a Z-shaped path of linked traverses. Still others utilize an overly slow and halting style of creeping to the top of each bump and side-slipping down its back side. All these skiers make it down the hill—but the trip down is not a whole bunch of fun.

## SOLVING THE PROBLEMS OF THE BEAT-UP BUMP SKIER

Let's begin with the undeniable facts of bump skiing. In order to ski bumps, you must be able to start a small turn when and where the bump dictates, then finish that turn to control speed and prepare to begin another turn. In short, you must be able to start and finish a small turn.

I always work with aspiring bump skiers on groomed snow first, since the fundamentals of making small-radius turns on groomed snow are pretty much the same in bumps—except bumps make the job easier once you have the three basic tools you need. You must be able to apply pressure to your ski while on edge to engage it in a turn; this provides direction change and controls speed. You must be able to release your edges to make your skis flat so you can steer them. Finally, you must be able to steer both skis into a new turn when they are flat and easily steered. These three factors sound like an abbreviation of the basic carved turn, which is exactly what they are.

You must do all of the above before you get to the next bump. This is an important point: bumps put a time constraint on each turn. You do not have to do anything differently, just more quickly. This is the key to making effective small-radius turns. Perform the essential movements of a carved turn, but do it in less time: apply pressure to your skis, flatten your skis, steer your skis. Repeat this a hundred times and you can ace a continuous line through the bumps.

Since the smaller turn is a serious tool in bumps, it will help to break the turn down and

analyze exactly what's happening at each point in the sequence on groomed snow.

To apply enough pressure to your skis to engage their edges and make them bend a little bit in order to change direction and control speed, you must get them on edge and give them a push. The main method of getting your skis on edge is to drop your hips toward the center of the turn. When you make a turn, you produce some force that will engage the skis' edges and begin to bend your skis for you. To get the job done correctly, you increase the pressure on your skis with leg flexion and extension. The combined movements of hip angulation and leg flexion I call *settlement*. This is a crucial yet subtle movement in a small carved turn (short swing), both on firm snow and in the bumps.

You complete your turn to reduce your speed. In bumps this means getting your skis across the fall line. This can be accomplished with the settling move described above. Most skiers will implement some steering as well to help skid their skis across the fall line and reduce their speed. With practice, you will learn to carve a small-radius turn (methods for improving these turns are covered in the final section, Getting Techno). In bump skiing, however, it's not necessary to carve your skis through the entire small turn. There can be a lot of skidding going on in the bumps, so you should feel free to skid your skis across the fall line if that's what it takes to control your speed.

Once your turn has been completed and your speed is under control, you should focus on enhancing what your skis should be doing naturally: flattening. This has to happen for the next turn to start, but many skiers have trouble with this in the bumps and find themselves doing a traverse instead of making another turn. Releasing your edges is easy if you let it happen. Every turn you make produces a certain amount of valuable force. You are always working against the force that is pushing you toward the outside of the turn. If your speed has been controlled, then this force helps you release your edges. Simply go with the flow and return to a tall, cen-

After you have completed a small turn to control your speed and have fully released your edges, you are ready to steer both skis into the next turn. You are now at your most elongated body position, or in the stretch mode of a settle-then-stretch cycle. It is easiest to steer your legs when they are relatively straight. Your edges are also getting flat at this point; this aids steering because your edges are not catching in the snow. You have just elongated your body in concert with your skis' rebound from finishing the turn, and this vertical energy has conveniently unweighted your skis a little bit, making them even easier to steer. All you have to do is maintain a balanced stance and steer your feet and legs to guide your skis across the fall line and into another turn.

## Intermediate Approach

Let's look at how this turn's three parts—settle, release, and steer—function at an intermediate level in a bumpy environment. Settling, or the flexion of the legs and movement of the hips toward the inside of the turn, is your means of speed control. The skis are being edged, bent, and steered through the turn, which slows you down. Settlement can be considered the brakes of the small-radius turn.

In bumps, it's important that settlement happen at the base of a mogul's front side. The bump's front face is like a cushion you can use to slow yourself down. At the base of the bump's front side there usually is softer snow that has been shaved from the bump above. You must be able to control your speed by completing a turn at this location. As you settle into the cushion of the bump's front side, you plant your pole firmly on the same bump a little farther down the hill from your skis. At first, try to plant your pole at about the same time as you set your edges against the bump. This coordination of your skis positioned across the fall line and your pole plant will help you check your speed and prepare for the next turn.

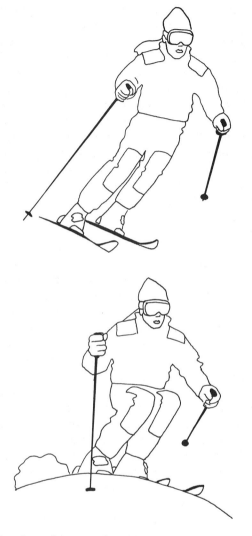

**Top:** Enter the turn with an elongated stance and an upright torso.
**Bottom:** Engage the skis in a small-radius turn by flexing the lower body, keeping the torso upright, and settling against the skis.

tered stance to let your skis roll onto the other set of edges in preparation for the next turn (see illustration, next page). You must allow your center of mass to move across your skis, and this means leaning away from the hill and toward the bottom of the run.

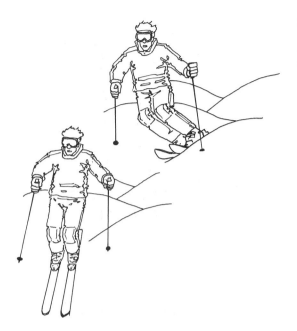

After checking speed against the front side of the bump, shift your hips forward and across your skis; this drives the ski tips down the trough and simultaneously releases their edges.

Some fundamentals of small-radius turns actually become easier to perform on bumps than on groomed snow. One such element is edging. In moguls, you can control your speed with less edge angle. The cushion effect of the front side of the bump and the soft snow at its base reduce the need for extreme edge engagement. In fact, it's often helpful to allow your skis to skid sideways into the bump's face, which also slows them down. Less edge engagement means edge release will be easier to accomplish too. This often means bump skiing doesn't require major hip angulation for edging movements. Edging in the bumps is not a major priority, because the moguls themselves do the work. At higher levels of performance, this allows you to maintain a slightly taller stance.

Releasing your edges after controlling your speed is easy in the bumps—if you are confident you can control your speed again. Releasing your edges requires you to move your center of

mass across your skis and toward the bottom of the hill, which results in a buildup of speed. This plunge down the steeper back side of the bump troubles most struggling bump skiers. But if you know you can steer, pressure your skis into a small turn, and settle into the front side of the next bump, you'll feel better about releasing your edges and taking that plunge.

As you release your edges, you begin steering both skis into the fall line and toward the next bump. Essentially, the intermediate skier steers around the bump after he's slowed down and released his edges. But it's at this point of releasing and steering that many skiers encounter a major problem.

The problem is the topography of the bump. If you were releasing and steering on groomed snow, your skis would easily maintain contact with the snow. As you release your edges and steer your skis into the fall line in bumps, the snow falls away from you in the valley between two bumps. Your ski tips and shovels can lose contact with the snow, and thus you can lose control.

As you release and steer, you must exert pressure against your shins and on the balls of your feet in order to drive your ski tips back down onto the snow where they can be controlled. It is impossible to pressure the fronts of your skis

When settling against the front side of a bump, guide your skis as they skid sideways and brace yourself with a firm pole plant.

from a backseat stance, so the key to releasing and steering toward the next turn is to keep driving your hips downhill and maintain a centered stance. From this position, you can pressure the fronts of your skis.

Initially, you must learn to settle into the face of a bump and then elongate as you release your edges and steer your skis toward the next mogul. It is important that you learn to return to a tall stance as you release and steer your skis. This *reloads* you for your next slow-down phase, when you settle on the next bump's front side. If you don't return to a tall stance in each turn, you may be compressed smaller and smaller each time you settle against a bump. Being in an overly compressed stance will prevent you from making functional movements.

The key to beginning your mastery of moguls is to be able to perform this simple turn in the bumps: control your speed, release your edges, steer toward the next bump, and slow down again. This tactic sets you up for the next turn, since skiing bumps well is all about getting ready for the next mogul. Proper use of the

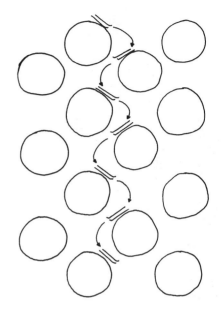

Speed control on the front side of every bump is followed by good edge release and steering to get to the next bump.

After controlling your speed in bumps, you must maintain ski-to-snow contact. Drive the skis' tips onto the snow by moving your hips down the hill and toward the next bump, which will help you press your shins against your boot tongues. Extend your legs to fill the trough between the bumps.

bump for basic speed control is the first step toward becoming a bump expert. This allows you to ski a continuous line, even if it is at a slow speed. This approach to bump skiing places an emphasis on speed control—the foundation for high performance in the bumps.

## Advanced Approach

Advanced skiers will need to alter the settle, release, and steer system for bump bashing. As you improve in the bumps, you'll be looking for higher speed and more continuous flow down the hill. The method described above works well for skiers who are beginning to get serious about bumps, but it tends to produce a stop-start rhythm that an advanced skier will want to progress beyond. However, the principles of more advanced mogul skiing are the same as those discussed above.

The primary differences in skiing the bumps at a more advanced level are speed and continuity of flow. But these elements are a product of something simple: the line you take through the bumps. You've already learned how to ski a continuous line without traverses or complete stops. Now you can make more advanced turns using the same principles on the *same* bumps. This is a helpful factor to note: the bumps you turn on when you're learning don't have to change as you improve. Use the same bumps, but ski them at a faster pace with an altered line and slightly different foot and leg work. The best way to start understanding how to make this leap to higher performance is to look at it.

In the right illustration on page 179, note the degree to which the intermediate bump skier turns his skis across the fall line. In effect, he is making a partial hockey stop at the base of the bump. This reduction in speed gives him the confidence and ability to make another turn without losing control. Notice that the skis of the advanced skier do not turn quite as far across the fall line. He takes a more direct route downhill even though he chooses the same bumps to turn on. Also notice that the advanced skier does not check his speed in the center of the bump the way the intermediate skier does. The advanced skier utilizes the inside half of the bump.

By not turning his skis across the fall line, the advanced skier is going to go faster. I will discuss ways to manage this speed to maintain control, but there is no getting around the fact that an advanced bump skier will be traveling at a greater velocity—and that is simply part of the performance bump-skiing game. By cutting over the inside half of the bump—instead of slowing down at the front side of the bump and steering around each bump—the advanced skier also encounters an even more three-dimensional, bumpy path. The advanced skier must deal with a continually rolling surface, which creates a need for shock absorption.

Exerting pressure on the shovels of your skis when entering a new turn—in order to keep

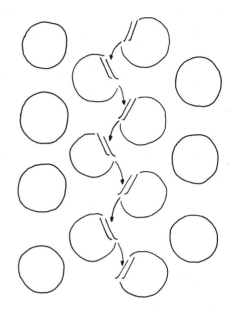

Speed increases with a more direct line through the bumps. The same line is taken straighter through the bumps, skiing over the inside half of each mogul rather than checking speed on the front face of each bump and steering around it.

your skis in contact with the snow—remains one of the golden rules of bump skiing. But this move requires more effort in advanced bump skiing, requiring piston action from the legs.

To understand how to use your legs like shock absorbers, imagine skiing on a snow-covered conveyor belt that tilts downhill but runs uphill fast enough so you stay in one place. Imagine that a constant series of humps travel up that conveyor belt toward you. You can't avoid them, but you need to maintain contact between your skis and the snow. You must deal with them by flexing and extending your legs.

Begin thinking about how you will encounter moguls at higher speeds, and think of the mogul in two parts: the bump and the trough. Your legs must retract to suck the bump up as it passes beneath you, and your legs must extend to fill up the trough. Sucking and filling, or retracting and extending, are the legs' bread-and-butter movements of high-performance bump skiing because they allow your skis to maintain contact with the snow, even at higher speeds. You haven't abandoned the basic pattern of settle, release, and steer. You have simply sped up the process and placed its components on different parts of the bump.

Instead of using the intermediate movement of settlement to edge and bend his skis into a finished turn on the soft front side of the bump, the advanced skier extends his legs into the trough and drives his skis into the valley be-

Elongate the lower body to prepare to absorb another bump, essentially filling the trough by extending the legs. Get ready to suck up the next bump, and repeat.

tween bumps where they can bend into a carved turn. In the same way that an intermediate skier initially settles into the soft snow at the bump's base, the advanced skier will drive his skis through that softer snow and use it to help control his speed. The advanced skier plants his pole on the bump he is slowing down on, just as the intermediate skier did. But, because of his greater speed, the advanced skier will use a lighter touch and aim a little farther downhill on the bump (see illustration, next page).

While the intermediate skier has time to elongate and release his edges and then steer toward the next turn, the advanced skier doesn't have that much time. In high-performance mogul skiing, you must release your edges and steer your skis toward the next turn in less than a second— before you fill the next trough with your legs. This means that the advanced skier releases, steers, and begins to engage the new set of edges while he's absorbing the approaching bump. This is easier than it sounds. When you retract your skis to absorb a bump, you naturally unweight them, making the skis easier to manage (see photo, page 183).

Because the advanced mogul skier is not turning his skis across the fall line as much as the intermediate skier, he must use other means to control his speed. Aside from the basic turn and the impact of striking the bump and the soft snow at the base, the advanced mogul skier's brakes are the shovels of his skis and the flex of his boots. By driving his skis down into the trough aggressively, the skier can guide the tips of his skis into the bump on a slight angle across the fall line. By maintaining firm pressure on the balls of his feet and shins, the skier can force the skis and boots to flex. The bending of the skis at their shovels and the flex of the skier's boots absorbs energy that would otherwise translate to increased speed. This is part of the reason why good mogul skiers will look for a specialized boot and ski that are designed to play the role of shock absorber. (I will cover gear-related issues in the troubleshooting section of this chapter.)

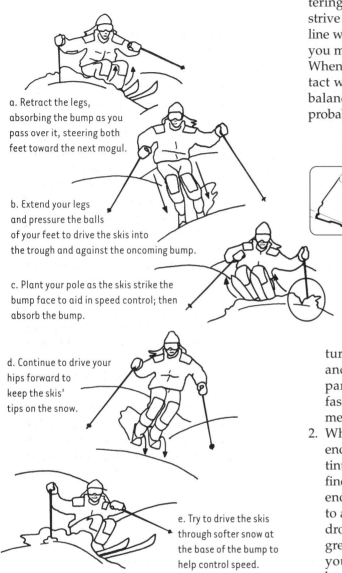

a. Retract the legs, absorbing the bump as you pass over it, steering both feet toward the next mogul.

b. Extend your legs and pressure the balls of your feet to drive the skis into the trough and against the oncoming bump.

c. Plant your pole as the skis strike the bump face to aid in speed control; then absorb the bump.

d. Continue to drive your hips forward to keep the skis' tips on the snow.

e. Try to drive the skis through softer snow at the base of the bump to help control speed.

Everything happens a little faster with a more advanced line through the bumps.

There is a vast difference between intermediate and expert bump skiing. Where the intermediate turns his skis completely across the fall line to ensure good speed control, the expert hardly deviates from the fall line. This is the key to mas-tering expert-level performance in the bumps: strive to turn your skis a little less across the fall line while remaining in control. Remember that you must heed your personal speed threshold. When you are unable to keep your skis in con-tact with the snow and you fail to maintain a balanced stance and a quiet upper body, you probably are going faster than you should.

### *You can feel* WHEN YOU'RE MASTERING MOGULS

1. One of the first things you may feel when you begin to master bumps is the sensation of having fast feet but slow downhill speed. In order to ski bumps like an expert, you must be able to start and finish small-radius turns quickly. This takes precise footwork, and it can result in control. Try to find this paradox in your skiing: things happening fast with your feet and skis but slow movement down the hill.

2. When you learn to control your speed enough with each turn so you can ski a continuous line through a mogul field, you may find that the sensation is like skiing down an enormous staircase where you nearly come to a complete stop on each large step before dropping off onto the next one. Focus on progressively softening this complete stop until you maintain some movement from one bump to the next.

3. Skiing bumps well will make you feel tall. Because the bumps do much of the work of turning for you, and also help slow you down, there is less need for major edging in the bumps. This results in a more upright, less angulated stance. Try to achieve the feeling that the bumps alone are responsible for altering this upright stance. You may settle into the bump or absorb it momentarily, but

After absorbing a bump, drive the hips forward to push the skis back down onto the snow where they can be controlled. Note how the hand pushes forward after planting the pole. CHRIS SMITH ON CANYON, MT. BACHELOR

then your body returns to its normal, taller stance. This stay-tall attitude will help keep your skis on the snow and allow for quicker movements.

4. Skiing bumps like an expert will feel like an athletic game of connect the dots, because a good bump skier is always looking downslope for her next destination. Think of each turn as simply a way to get to that soft spot on the front side of the next bump. This is where you will use your skis to control the speed you just gained after leaving the previous bump. If you know you can check your speed on the next bump's softer front side, then you'll always feel confident—no matter how steep the run. So connect the dots by looking downslope for your next place to slow down.

*You can see*
## WHEN YOU'RE
## MASTERING MOGULS

1. As you start each new turn after controlling your speed on the front side of a bump, you will have to release your edges and begin steering your skis toward the bump below. It is crucial to keep your skis in contact with the snow by pressuring the shins and balls of your feet enough so your skis' shovels dive down the back side of each bump and into the trough leading to the next bump. You can see whether you're successfully driving your skis down into the troughs: if your ski shovels move more than a few inches off the snow, you may not be pressuring the fronts of your skis enough.

2. Successful bump skiers see their line in bumps as a zigzag row of targets arranged downslope, like a zipper. Look for this perfect line in a field of bumps and use it. The more symmetrical a line you find, the easier your job will be.

3. Poling plays a major role in expert bump skiing, but you rarely notice your poles—unless you're doing something wrong with them. The keys to pole use here are: quick, light, and forward. You should be able to see your

Look at your line through a field of bumps as a series of targets running downslope.

hands at all times. After planting your pole on the top of the bump, break your wrist over as if you were tapping a nail with a hammer. This allows the pole to tip over forward, keeping your hand driving ahead in front of you rather than being dragged back toward your hip as you ski by. Letting your hand fall behind you after planting your pole will tend to pull your center of mass backward, making it impossible to keep the fronts of your skis on the snow. Keep your hands in sight.

4.  As you begin to take a more direct line through the bumps, using the flex of your skis and boots as well as retraction and extension to manage your speed, you may notice that the impact with which you strike the front side of each bump sends snow flying into the air. When you are aggressively driving your shovels into the front side of a mogul, a brief explosion of snow chunks will fly into your face. Watch for this as you approach higher levels of performance.

## OTHER DRILLS

These drills will help you master bump skiing.

### Ski the Line

This drill will help you simulate the need to stay in a continuous line in the bumps by linking small-radius turns. Find a line in the snow left by a grooming machine or have a partner draw a line down the run using the tip of his ski pole. Link short-radius turns down this line and concentrate on steering your skis completely across this line to fully control your speed. Increase the difficulty of the drill by asking your partner to ski the line at a very slow pace, then follow, making short turns without overtaking him. This slower-than-usual speed will simulate the need for extra speed control in the bumps.

### Ski the Hump

This drill will help take your ability to make small-radius turns on groomed snow to the next level and ease your transition into the bumps. Find a ridge or hump in the snow left by a groomer or at the edge of a run. This hump should run downhill like the line in the last drill. The presence of the ridge or hump adds a three-dimensional feature to your small-radius turns in the same way that a mogul makes skiing more challenging. Perform the previous drill along the hump, focusing again on speed control at the finish of each turn. Also concentrate on keeping the shovels of your skis in contact with the snow throughout each turn by keeping pressure on the balls of your feet and against your shins.

### Linked-Bump Hockey Stops

To reinforce how easy it is to ski one continuous line through bumps without crashes, unwanted speed, or safety traverses, break things down to their most basic level and link some hockey stops through the bumps. Stand with your skis across the fall line at the base of a bump's front side, give yourself a push, and steer your way around the bump. Aim for the soft front side of the bump below and perform a hockey stop at that point. After coming to a complete stop, repeat the maneuver to the bump below. The only difference between this and skiing a more dynamic line through the bumps is the presence of a complete stop.

### Soften the Hips' Ride

Because most skiing takes place from the hips down, think of skiing moguls as taking your hips for a ride down through the bumps. In the hockey stop drill above, the hips come to a somewhat abrupt halt at the front side of each bump before moving on to the next bump. To progress to a higher bump-skiing level, soften the ride for your hips by letting them glide through that speed-control phase rather than coming to a stop. Before slowing too much, drive your hips downhill toward the trough between the bump you're on and the one you're heading for. This downslope movement of your hips smoothes out the turn's finish and helps you push your ski tips down the back side of the bump.

### Backpedal Bumps

As you become more proficient in the bumps, you will move beyond settling into the bump's front side for speed control: you will want to keep moving at a faster pace. To do this, you will absorb each bump as you encounter it. The basic movements used in absorption come from below your hips. Lengthen your legs to fill the trough; then retract your legs to suck the bump up. A good way to visualize this movement pattern is to pretend you are riding a bike with only one pedal so that you must place both feet on it, side by side, and pedal the bike backward. Backpedaling with both feet simultaneously mimics the leg movements used in bumps. Your feet meet the bump first and begin absorbing it, your hips pass over the bump, and then your feet drive down the back side to fill the trough.

### Explodo-Bumps

As an advanced skier takes a more direct line through the bumps, she encounters more speed and less time to deal with that speed during each turn. The primary speed-control method used by expert bump skiers is to make some kind of turn across the front side of the bump. However, expert skiers are also utilizing ski and boot flexion to absorb energy that would otherwise be converted into unwanted speed. This requires applying pressure and driving the skis almost directly into the inside half of the bump's front side. To experiment with this advanced technique, stand at the top of a bump and pick a bump just below. Ski into the bump below at a slight angle and try to apply pressure to the front of your skis enough so they flex and conform to the shape of the bump as they strike it. As you pass over the bump, absorb the rebound of the bump and skis by retracting your legs, then escape to the side in a traverse. Perform the same maneuver angled in the other direction. Then attempt it on two bumps consecutively. Try to explode the bumps rather than let them explode you.

## TROUBLESHOOTING BUMP SKIING

The biggest problem intermediate skiers have with bumps is lack of preparation of the skills they need to do the job correctly. You must be able to perform solid, small-radius turns on groomed snow before you can enjoy skiing bumps. Many skiers are able to make small turns on groomed snow, but they do so with a skills blend that works only on groomed snow. For example, a skier who initiates new turns by stepping onto the new ski may make snappy turns on smooth snow but will be unable to smoothly release his edges and steer both skis into the trough toward the next bump in a mogul field. Often this skier is seen lifting up his inside ski as a last-ditch means of making a turn, which throws him off balance and causes him to gain speed.

Proper technique in making small-radius turns is all it takes to gain entry into the bumps, but mastering the basics will take work for many skiers. The tools required are described in the Creating a Toolbox section. For the skier who wants to master moguls but hasn't been able to link five turns together in the bumps, these tools are worth reviewing. Skiers who tend to have the most trouble in bumps are those who use their edging and pressuring tools most heavily. They have a harder time letting their skis skid, which is what you must do to steer your skis across the fall line to control your speed. These skiers should spend time reviewing the edge release and steering segments in Creating a Toolbox.

There are other problems skiers have with bumps that have nothing to do with short-radius turns—and some of them have nothing to do with a skier's natural ability at all. One of the most common reasons that skiers cannot become experts in the bumps is that their skis and boots are simply not suited for use in a mogul-ridden environment. Stiff skis will not do you any favors in the bumps because they will not flex enough to ease you onto and around the bump. A stiff ski rides like a car with very stiff suspension: speed bumps send groceries flying in a car, and stiff skis will knock you around on your skis. A stiff ski, especially one with a stiff

shovel, commonly sends you backward on your skis, which makes it difficult to keep the skis in contact with the snow. Stiff skis also pack a serious punch when it comes to rebound. If you do manage to get a stiff ski to bend, whether on purpose or by accident, the ski snaps back with enough energy to launch you into the air.

Shaped skis don't necessarily make the best bump skis. In fact, competitive bumpers are the only folks who regularly use fairly traditional ski designs anymore. The problem with shaped skis in the bumps is that they like to engage a carved turn; they can tend to *lock into* a carved radius and are not as easily broken loose to skid, the way a straight ski will. Being able to skid is a good thing in moguls. So, if you're a bump fan who's looking for a good all-mountain ski that

Find a clean "zipper line" in the bumps and you'll make your life easier. CHRIS SMITH ON
LITTLE CANYON, MT. BACHELOR

goes everywhere, look for softer flexing shaped skis with less radical sidecut profiles. Also note that fat skis aren't the best in bumps simply because their girth makes them a little more sluggish from edge to edge—and big, wide tips can be bounced around a bit in moguls.

A stiff boot reacts similarly to the stiff ski in bumps. But a stiff boot can make matters worse in combination with a stiff ski, because the boot is the link between you and the snow. What the snow does to the ski, the boot does to you, and vice versa. The boot transfers your physical commands to your ski, and a stiff boot shows no mercy when you send it flawed messages. Stiff boots and stiff skis offer you little margin for error in the bumps. While many expert skiers will tell you that they do just fine on their stiff racing gear in moguls, remember that they aren't the ones with problems in the bumps. You are. If skiing well in bumps is your goal, do yourself a favor and demo some different skis and boots. It is also easy to have the flex in your boots softened at a good ski shop.

Sometimes the way your skis are tuned can have a negative effect on your performance in the bumps—specifically, if the tune prevents your skis from being flattened out and steered. Skis with edge-high bases will ski as if they have sled-like runners attached to them. Edge-high skis tend to go in straight lines very well, because their edges dig too deeply into the snow.

Skiers who carve most of their turns on firm snow may not know that their edges need filing, because they're spending most of their time laying their skis on edge and bending them. These skis will hamper your ability to flatten your skis between bumps, steer your skis across the fall line, and control your speed. Skidding and steering are big parts of learning how to shred the bumps, and if your skis don't want to do either of those things, you are at a major disadvantage. If this situation sounds familiar, you might have edge-high skis. Review the information on ski tuning in the chapter on skis.

Fear causes too many skiers to give up on bump skiing. Most skiers who fear bumps had bad experiences in moguls at the start, and they no doubt had little guidance and scant knowledge about how to make skiing bumps an enjoyable experience. Most of these skiers still fear the possibility of uncontrolled speed and the pain of crashing. Both these outcomes are easily avoided by following the basic steps outlined in this chapter. If you know you can slow down at will, then speed becomes tolerable. If you know you can make a turn where you need to, then fear of crashing becomes a thing of the past. Bump skiing is about taking control and maintaining control—all the way down the run. If you've been afraid to dive into moguls before, stop worrying and start dominating the bumps.

# 18

# Steeps

Steepness can be a subjective matter, but we can also establish an objective standard of what qualifies as steep for the purposes of learning. In this chapter I will be discussing slopes approaching and exceeding 45 degrees. Most expert runs at developed ski areas rarely exceed a 35- to 40-degree pitch. With some exceptions, few ski areas have entire runs tilted at 45 degrees, but many have runs with brief drops that may exceed a 45-degree pitch.

I will deal here with tactics to be used in snow that is not very deep. Deep powder on steep runs often provides enough friction so you can simply ski it with solid powder technique. You should begin implementing the tools in this chapter only when a powder run becomes so steep that excessive speed buildup is a problem.

The beauty of truly steep runs is that fewer skiers use them. The snow remains softer longer, and rarely do you find moguls on really steep pitches. These runs are often steep enough that new snow sloughs off them regularly, leaving small amounts of well-bonded snow rather than deep accumulations of fluff. As skiers ski steep terrain, much of the snow they push around cascades downslope to fill in ruts below. Steeps offer a different sort of playground than any of the other advanced skiing situations we've explored—because of the quality of the snow and the different sensation that skiing the steeps provides.

Some of the steepest slopes a skier can manage are pitched at around 60 degrees, so when

For a real adrenaline rush, there's no substitute for the steeps. BRIAN ELLING IN TREE CHUTE, MONTANA SNOWBOWL

you begin to descend slopes of 45- and 50-degree pitches, you are treading on really challenging terrain. Beyond 50 degrees, a slope feels near-vertical and falls can result in cartwheeling disasters and injury, or even death. In this near-vertical environment, the skiing experience changes dramatically. Instead of focusing on the nuances of dealing with problematic snow conditions, or concentrating on blending pressure between the right and left skis, you begin to harness a series of controlled free falls down the slope. Between turns in steep terrain, you fall through the air with little or no real contact with the snow beneath you until you meet the slope again. The steeper the terrain, the more time you will spend losing vertical footage without firmly touching the snow. Because you spend less time in firm contact with the snow, moments of ski-to-snow contact become crucial: they are tenuous moments that will decide the fate of your next three seconds of existence. This is the game of the steep slope. It is one of committing yourself to the fall line inextricably at the risk of serious falls. But in exchange, you will feel the sensation of cascading downhill in gravity-stricken plunges that bring out the best skier in each of us.

## THE IDEAL GOAL

The goal in steep terrain is to make each turn a successful one—because falling on the steeps or blowing a turn and accelerating are not very attractive options. Not only do you want to make a successful turn, you want to stick *each one* to control your speed and set yourself up aggressively for your next turn. True steeps are not the place for skiers who question their ability to make turns when, where, and how they want. Skiing the steeps successfully requires the intense and focused mind-set that allows you to ski offensively on this challenging terrain.

Because steep terrain prevents you from letting your skis run in the fall line for more than a second or two without a tremendous buildup of speed, we can break down ideal steep skiing technique into two primary phases. Of primary importance is speed control, or the edge-set phase of a turn. This phase is like the hockey stop that beginning bump skiers might use on each bump, except there are no helpful bumps to stop against on really steep slopes. The edge-set is what keeps you safe and in control every time you turn on steep terrain. But you also need to be able to get to the next edge-set, and this intermediary phase between edge-sets is called the *transition*. Part of the fun of skiing steep terrain is the skill blending of edge-set and transition, because this combined technique generates an enjoyable rhythm of give and take. In each edge-set, you take control back from the mountain and from gravity. In each transition *between* edge-sets, you give momentary control back to the hill and let gravity rule (see illustrations next page).

Ideally, you will reach a balance between how much control you need for speed reduction and how much you're willing to give in to gravity and remain in the fall line. The skier who spends more time setting her edges and slowing down will fail to find the natural rhythm that comes with allowing the skis to accelerate during each turn. However, the skier who has no qualms about giving in to gravity's pull and fails to keep her speed in check will find that her ability to recover from mistakes is hampered.

## COMMON PROBLEMS THAT PREVENT SUCCESS ON THE STEEPS

Fear. It's an undeniable fact that many skiers get scared on extremely steep terrain. Fear keeps them, first, from skiing it well and, second, from enjoying it. Fear of steep slopes is understandable. They are almost vertical, sometimes icy, and often peppered with hazards such as rocks and trees. For many skiers, steep terrain, and the falls that can result, hold the recipe for pain—a recipe that reasonable adults will avoid. I hear the refusal to ski steep slopes often: "That? No way are you getting me up there!" Yet I know

a. At the edge-set phase on steep terrain, keep the outside leg extended to maintain solid contact with the snow. Here, the pole is planted firmly below for stability and speed control.

b. and c. To begin the transition phase between turns, drive your hips across your skis and downhill (here, by pushing off of the uphill ski to tip the skier over) and elongate your body frame. This releases your edges, up-unweights your skis, and enables airborne guidance of them. Note here the aggressive head and hip positioning.

d. Foot and leg steering are keys in guiding the skis through the transition to the next edge-set. Note the continued upper body positioning, which keeps shoulders facing downhill through entire sequence.

e. Look downslope for a target area where you will engage your edges. Note how this skier begins extending his legs and reaching for the next point of edge-set.

that the skier who is avoiding the steeps has the skills to perform there expertly with a little training. She could be enjoying this part of the mountain.

We all know why steeps are scary, but many skiers don't realize what their fears do to otherwise effective movements. Addressing the physical result of intimidation is the first step in conquering this advanced skiing situation.

Simply standing still on steep terrain with your skis perpendicular to the fall line can be difficult. To generate enough edge angle, you need to shift your hips and move them toward the hill. Major edge adjustment using your hips requires good balance and an understanding of how to hip angulate, which I will discuss later. Failure to understand how to use your edges to stand still on steep terrain can lead to ineffective movements during turns. Skiers often stand leaning back toward the hill and rotate their upper bodies to face uphill. This stance gives them a false sense of security since they are as close to the hill as possible and assume their chances of falling to the bottom are diminished. But they are wrong.

This pseudo-safe body position is fundamentally flawed on any slope—but especially on steep terrain. The skier who rotates her body to face the side of the run is visually disadvantaged because her focus is not downhill, where her body movements need to be directed to make a successful turn. Over-rotation has other negative outcomes. Rotating the body away from the direction of the next turn is wasted movement, and you will need to correct this stance before initiating a turn. On a more technical level, failure to open your hips (face them downhill) on steeps prevents you from moving your hips toward the center of the turn and therefore puts your edge-set in jeopardy. Rotating your hips away from the fall line prevents you from hip angulating, which is central to making a solid edge-set on steep terrain. The skier who tends to lean her entire body mass toward the hill inhibits her ability to make the movement across her skis to start a new turn.

I have described how intimidated skiers stand still on steep terrain because it reflects the way they attempt to make turns on it. Fearful skiers assume that over-rotated position, which they equate with safety, in each turn. But this stance leads to the things the intimidated skier dreads most: It prevents you from initiating turns quickly, so you spend more time accelerating in the fall line; it prohibits you from making reliable edging movements, so you cannot slow yourself down and prepare for another turn.

## SOLVING THE PROBLEMS OF THE STEEPS-FEARING SKIER

The easiest way to master steep terrain is to understand that it is a dance with two main steps: the edge-set phase and the transition phase that links edge-sets together. Approaching steeps this two-step way is just a start. It will be more helpful to break down these steps into their basic elements.

The edge-set should be solid. Edging on steep terrain is simply a more extreme version of how you use your edges on other terrain. Your hips are the primary agents of major edging movements. Because the edge-set on steep terrain necessitates aggressive edge angles, the hips play an important role in speed control on the steeps.

Creating aggressive edge angles using hip angulation requires you to make some specialized movements that were not so crucial in other skiing situations. In order to move your hips far enough to the inside of the turn so your skis achieve an extreme edge angle, your hips must face downhill a bit. This opening of the hips is called *counter-rotation*, because your hips are rotated in a direction other than the one your skis are traveling in. Without hip counter-rotation, the angle you need for good edging cannot be created. Your body simply won't bend that way.

This opening of the hips to face downhill may be one of the biggest hurdles to overcome, since it contradicts everything your body wants to do. For skiers who find this difficult, first try to

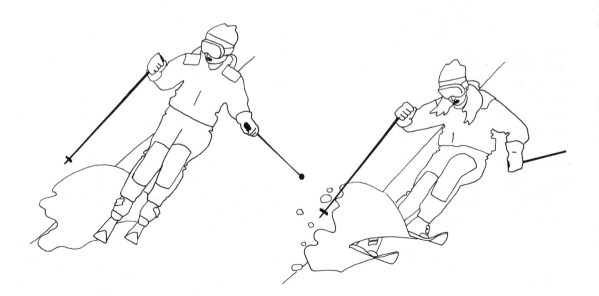

An over-rotated, banked-turn finish on steep terrain causes problems. Maintain open hips and upper body, as well as a hip-angulated body position.

Skiing steep terrain well requires you to take control—then give it up for a bit.

BRIAN ELLING ON RED BUD RIDGE, MONTANA SNOWBOWL

increase the amount of tip-lead you have by sliding your uphill ski farther forward. This helps the hips to face downhill. The hip counter-rotation you achieve by increasing your uphill ski's tip-lead allows you to begin dropping your hips toward the hill rather than leaning your entire body into the hill. Hip angulation with counter-rotation is a major goal, because this move places you in a position unlike the one a frightened skier assumes. Instead of rotating away from the next turn and leaning toward the hill, you now hold your hips and upper body in a fashion that anticipates the next turn and ensures positive edge grip.

This hip position translates to the rest of your upper body so your torso is twisted and helps align your shoulders perpendicular to the fall line. This twisting of the torso will eventually help you initiate your next turn, and it also lets you make an aggressive pole plant directly below your boots at the time of edge-set to powerfully check your downward momentum.

Skiing steeps is about give and take. I have covered the "take" part of the equation: taking

The pole plant coincides with the edge-set on steep terrain. Note the parallel alignment of feet, knees, and shoulders. This is one sign of solid edge-set body positioning.

For aggressive edge engagement, the hip must make a large shift laterally, back toward the hill, while the upper body remains upright and opened to face the fall line. It doesn't take much, but the hip must rotate to face in the direction of the fall line rather than in the direction the skis are traveling in.

control of the momentum and speed that build in a turn on steep terrain. The next step is to understand how to give in to the forces that want to suck you downhill. Understanding why you need to do this will help you accomplish this step.

At the point of edge-set, you are dealing with a lot of stored energy. This is because you slowed your speed by getting your skis across the fall line and setting your edges. This energy must go somewhere, so it is stored in your body and your skis. By slowing down so aggressively on the steeps, you in effect create three springs: your severely bent skis, your compressed and angulated body position, and your twisted torso. You are now *loaded up*. Like a balloon that's about to burst, you must do something with this energy.

What you do is give in to the force you previously resisted. You can do this now because you have slowed to a reasonable speed and you know you will be able to slow down again as needed. In giving in to the force of the steeps, you allow these three springs to release their energy. Your skis begin to snap back or rebound. As they do, they propel you up and slightly off the snow. You return to a taller stance. This enhances your upward and downhill movement, which relieves the friction between your skis and the snow and makes the steering movements of turn initiation easier. The release of the third spring, the muscular tension in your torso, starts the turn for you. Because your torso is slightly twisted and your shoulders are facing downhill while your skis point across the fall line, your skis will begin to steer downhill when their edges are released. This automatically completes the first half of the turn, usually the most difficult half, and all you need to do is continue to steer your skis across the fall line and finish the turn that your body started for you.

As with all turns, it is of utmost importance for you to move your center of mass, your hips, across your skis and toward the next turn. In steep terrain, this crossover involves shifting your mass straight downhill, because at edge-set your skis have been brought completely across the fall line. Body mass movement across the skis and down the hill on very steep terrain is often intimidating, and many skiers resist

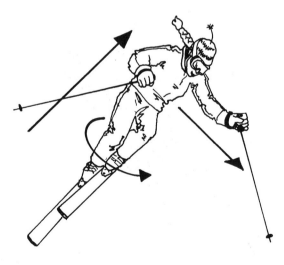

Keeping the upper body facing downhill as the body elongates and moves across the skis will enhance steering movements of the lower body.

making this movement—even though it ensures successful turn initiation.

There are two main ways to improve your body mass movement at the start of a new turn. One is to transfer weight to the new outside ski just after finishing a turn. This weight transfer essentially tips you across your skis and into the next turn. Another way is to stop resisting the force that tries to drag you downhill. By relaxing the outside leg just as a turn is finished, you will find yourself tipping over that downhill leg and into the next turn.

*You can feel*
**YOUR SUCCESS ON STEEP TERRAIN**

1. There are some common kinesthetic cues skiers feel when making powerful edge-sets on steep terrain. Because your outside ski plays such an important role on steeps, you may often notice that your head remains balanced over your outside ski while your center of mass has dropped toward the hill. You may also feel that your hip socket above your inside leg is cocked, or elevated and advanced in front of the other side because of the way your hips must be rotated to face downhill.

2. Setting your edges on steep terrain is not an entirely defensive maneuver, because a ski's edge will only hold so much. If you jam a ski on edge and stand against it stiffly, it will fail to hold you solidly and will tend to skid. You must load your ski with a *resilient* leg—one that progressively weights the ski and just as smoothly releases it. In doing so, your legs may feel bouncy rather than stiff. Your muscles must be ready to react firmly against your skis' contact with the snow but should not be held rigidly.

3. Giving in to the force of a turn and allowing your body's center of mass to cross over your

skis toward the next turn will always create a feeling of falling toward the bottom of the hill on steep terrain. If you do this properly, you will feel as if your head and hips are leading the charge toward the abyss. The amount of time you spend dropping downhill toward your next edge-set is determined by how steep the terrain is and how aggressively you unweighted out of your previous edge-set.

4. In terms of balance, it's important to remain centered while skiing steeps. The portion of your ski that makes contact with the snow at the start of your edge-set is a good indicator of this balance. Try to engage the shovels of your skis a fraction of a second ahead of your skis' waists (unless the snow is deep). This will help you keep your hips moving forward during the turn. After edge-set, as you elongate and unweight your skis, try to prevent your shovels from leaving the snow first. If you lift the entire ski off the snow at once, you will keep yourself from sliding into a backseat stance.

*You can see*
**YOUR SUCCESS ON STEEP TERRAIN**

1. Because of the need for both solid edge engagement and aggressive body mass movement across your skis in order to successfully initiate turns, your head is always "hanging out" in front of the rest of your body. This gives you an unobstructed view of the slope directly below you. You will not see much of your skis or much of the slope to either side. If much of your body is readily visible out of your peripheral vision, you may not be properly angulated at the edge-set phase, or you may be leaning toward the hill at the turn initiation phase rather than aggressively diving down the hill to start the turn.

2. You are checking your speed properly when you look down at your skis at the point of edge-set and see your hips facing almost directly downhill and your skis pointing

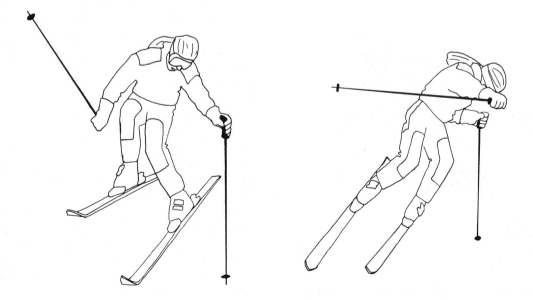

Note the head's position at edge-set initiation and during transition. Avoid letting your head and upper body lean back toward the hill.

toward the side of the run. Your forearm should also point directly downhill when you plant your pole to make a near-right angle with your outside ski.

3. Snow often gets pushed downhill at the time of edge-set, and this snow usually continues to cascade down the hill for a few seconds. If you find yourself free falling toward another turn amid a small avalanche of tumbling snow, it is a good visual sign that you are maintaining good flow of movement down the hill and using the energy generated from your edge-set to help start the next turn. Keep turning as the snow continues to roll downhill; trying to keep up with the loose snow's descent is a good way to think about continuing to move your hips across the skis to start each new turn.

4. Because skiing the steeps involves using a lot of edging to control your speed, you will encounter a fair amount of ski rebound as you enter a new turn. This often results in an airborne entry into the next turn. By varying the amount of leg retraction and extension you use, you can control how much time your skis spend off the snow. Letting down or holding up your landing gear (your legs) enables you to look downslope for the best snow to set your edges on and control your speed.

## OTHER DRILLS

The following drills will help you rip up the steeps.

### Tip-Lead Railroad Turns

To understand how hip angulation and counter-rotation coexist when skiing the steeps, try using maximum hip counter-rotation on a smooth, flat road. While skiing straight down a road, which usually has some degree of cross fall line (or side-hill), progressively increase the amount of tip-lead between your skis. To do this, slide

your uphill ski forward, ahead of the other ski. First push it ahead 6 inches, then 1 foot, then 1½ feet. It is important to let your hips rotate as you slide your ski forward. As you increase your tip-lead and hip counter-rotation, notice that your skis will want to roll on their edges. The more you counter-rotate, the more they tend to roll over. Relax your body while you perform this drill to feel how your hips and head will fall into position, with your hips slightly toward the uphill side of the road and your head balanced toward the downhill side of the road.

### Heavy Tips Hoppers

During the transition phase between edge-sets on steep terrain, you must deal with the rebound of your skis, body mass movement across your skis, and body mass movement down the hill. To simplify these combined movements, perform hop turns on steep, groomed snow but maintain contact between your ski tips and the snow—as if your tips were extremely heavy. To perform this drill, you must maintain a balanced stance so you can apply extra pressure against your ski tips; this may require you to shift your center of mass forward slightly. Utilize smooth bouncing movements to generate enough of a hop to initiate each hop turn and try to move from one hop turn into the next to reproduce the flow of energy from turn to turn when skiing steeps.

### Linked Hockey Stops, One-Way

Begin this drill by entering a slope with an extremely brief straight run; then come to an almost complete edge-set, or hockey stop. After you set your edges, you will feel a release of energy from your skis as they return to a less-bent state and from your body as it elongates. Use this energy to begin initiating a turn, but don't worry about crossing the fall line. Think about returning to a taller stance momentarily, briefly allowing your skis to seek the fall line, and exert pressure on the balls of your feet by shifting your body mass forward. Then drop back into an edge-set traveling in the same direction you started in and repeat the drill. Continue this staircase pattern until you reach the side of the run. Then travel back toward the other side performing the same drill.

### Slow Feet Drop-Ins

Because the start of each new turn on steep terrain feels as if you are tipping over your skis, some skiers call starting a run on the steeps *dropping in*. To work on the skills needed to start a new turn after controlling your speed in an edge-set, perform Slow Feet Drop-Ins. As you begin each new turn on the steeps, pretend that your feet move a half-second behind all your other body parts. Focus on leaving your feet behind you as you start a new turn, as if you had glue underfoot. Imaginary slow feet will force you to use your center of mass properly to get the turn started.

## TROUBLESHOOTING STEEPS

The primary problem skiers tend to have with steep terrain is gaining excessive speed after turn initiation. With practice of the drills described here and an understanding of the movements of edge-set, this problem should disappear. However, if you've put yourself in a really sketchy spot, there's a chance that what you really need in order to control your speed is an entirely different method for tackling the steeps.

Some slopes are simply too steep for the edge-set and transition mode of descent. The method described above focuses on how to take control by checking your speed with an aggressive edge-set, but this also involves a committed body mass movement across your skis and down the hill into a controlled free fall. This downhill plunge makes a smooth, reliable turn initiation possible on steep slopes. However, in runs that are really steep, this tactic leaves you in the fall line too long.

On slopes that are so steep that you need to reduce your amount of downhill travel at turn initiation, you will need to alter your body mass movement. Rather than direct your center of mass across your skis and down the hill, you must move it vertically, up and off the snow. It's crucial on steep terrain to ensure that the start of each turn is successful, and freeing your edges from their grip on the snow is the key. But on extreme steeps, you must do this by moving more vertically than laterally, since too much downhill movement will result in uncontrollable speed. The technique for turn initiation on extreme slopes is called a pedal turn. Developed in Europe by alpinists descending slopes with a 55- to 60-degree pitch, this move is also effective any time you wish to avoid spending too much time in the fall line on steep terrain.

To perform a pedal turn, you must first adequately control your speed with the same kind of edge-set already discussed. At the point of edge-set, you will find yourself in a position commonly referred to as *long leg, short leg*. Your outside leg is almost fully extended, reaching downhill for positive edge hold and pressuring your outside ski. Your inside leg is bent to allow the inside ski to maintain firm contact with the snow without altering your angulated and counter-rotated stance. From this position, you are ready to forcefully stand up on the inside ski and use it as a launching pad to pop vertically off the snow and guide your airborne skis into the next turn. Instead of allowing gravity's pull and the forces generated by the edge-set to propel you downhill, you artificially clear your skis from the snow by vaulting off the inside ski vertically. This method is called a pedal turn because the inside leg presses off the inside ski in the way that a bicyclist moves through a pedal stroke.

While the pedal turn is an effective means for getting turns started on survival-style pitches, it's rarely the ticket for the less extreme slopes we are usually skiing. But in either case, the

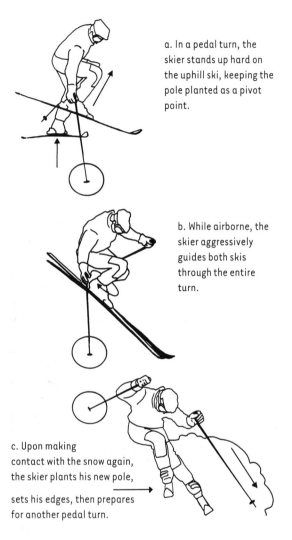

a. In a pedal turn, the skier stands up hard on the uphill ski, keeping the pole planted as a pivot point.

b. While airborne, the skier aggressively guides both skis through the entire turn.

c. Upon making contact with the snow again, the skier plants his new pole,

sets his edges, then prepares for another pedal turn.

most common problem is the same: excessive speed during turn initiation.

This excessive speed may be caused by spending too much time in the fall line, or by not using your time there effectively. Remember that the goal of the transition phase is to get to the next edge-set as quickly as the steepness level necessitates. The key to being fast and effective in the transitions between edge-sets is steering. Steering your skis with your feet and legs while they are free from firm contact with the snow is imperative. They need to be worked

simultaneously so both skis reengage the snow at the same time and in a parallel fashion. Reviewing the basic skills of steering in Creating a Toolbox may be just what you need. Here's another important hint: a counter-rotated torso will help generate additional steering torque.

The other major problem skiers face on the steeps is skidding at the edge-set phase. This wreaks havoc with your skiing potential in steep terrain, because that secure feeling of dependable speed control is gone. Without this security, it's hard to start another turn with confidence. You may display a symmetrical skid, where both skis fail to bite solidly into the snow, or your outside ski may blow out, lose its edge grip, slip away from you, and place you on your inside ski. These are common results of leaning toward the hill rather than tipping your head out over the outside ski in a sound position of hip angulation. Once you lean your head back toward the hill on steep terrain, precious weight is transferred from the outside ski to the inside ski and neither will hold effectively. If you lean inside too far or too abruptly, your outside ski will lose pressure and blow out.

When controlling your speed through edge-setting, you may notice that your outside ski's tail breaks loose from its hold on the snow. This is commonly caused by a slight reduction of edge angle at the turn's finish, which allows the portion of your ski under the most stress to wash out. Generally, your tail skids away for a few inches and regains its hold when it has reached a point where an adequate edge angle is reproduced. This slight reduction in edge angle is caused by your hips: If you allow your hips to stop counter-rotating and let them twist to face in the same direction as your skis at the finish of a turn, your skis will flatten slightly—just enough so the tails will wash out. To solve the problem, maintain your inside ski's tip-lead at the finish of your turn and resist the urge to swing your outside pole completely through the turn, as this will tend to twist your hips in the wrong direction. Of course, having sharp edges will minimize skidding, too.

# 19

# Trees

Some expert skiers tend to have the most fun and excitement in one favorite type of snow. Others gravitate toward a particular terrain to enjoy a challenge. But there is a select group of skiers who head with cultlike fervor to a favorite spot that is characterized by both snow type and terrain: they head to the trees.

Skiers either love ripping down tree-filled slopes, or they hate it. This advanced skiing situation can reward you with untracked lines through wild and magical spots, but it can scare your socks off. The only way to become one of the followers of tree skiing is to learn how to ski in the trees and enjoy the experience without risking serious injury with every third turn. This is something that any skier who has come this far can do. But before I begin to discuss how to ski the trees like an expert, there are a few unwritten ground rules that are important to know.

First, ski in the trees with a buddy. We have all come up with excuses why this rule can be broken: it's just a short run; the trees are just off the side of the run; my buddies aren't around, and I'm fine by myself. None of these reasons to ski alone will do you any good if you're upside down and suffocating in a tree well, or if you knock yourself unconscious on a tree branch and die of hypothermia overnight. Skiing with a buddy will mean you have help nearby—or at the very least, someone who can tell the ski patrol which trees he last saw you in.

The second rule is to keep track of your group. Whether you stop to regroup or signal

to each other, you should know where your friends are. There usually are good spots to stop on any tree run: at a point where you will make a major direction change; on flat benches; on ridges that could divide the group. If you can, select a commonly known spot as a meeting point. It may also be a good idea to simply regroup by giving a whistle or hoot that your partner can return, signaling, "Everything's cool!" It's no fun to reach the bottom of a tree run and have no clue whether your buddy is up ahead of you, just behind you, or having trouble somewhere. And it's nobody's fault but your own for not knowing. I hate to say it but those annoying, little two-way radios are great for keeping track of your bros (or bro-ettes) when you're ripping it in the woods.

Rule three is to know where you are going and where you will meet. This is simple common sense. If you don't know where the tree run ends up, you don't belong there. Most skiers who become lost off-area get that way by skiing through trees without knowing exactly where they lead. Someone in the group should know the area and take the time to orient other skiers about the route of descent, major landmarks, and where they'll be stopping. Have a specified meeting place for after the run that everyone in the group is aware of, and have a general plan for what the group will do if not everybody returns. This can be as casual as, "If you're not at the chair, I'll wait ten minutes. Then I'm skiing our same line again. I'll leave you a message on the board." Even though it sounds extreme, know where you'll meet at the very end of the day in case your group gets split up—at least then you'll know whether to get the patrol involved in a search.

Rule four: Goggles. Wear 'em. You can lose an eye even when you're wearing sunglasses. And consider wearing a helmet. If you don't want to wear one, fine; but be willing to accept the consequences of taking a stout tree stob in the melon.

My final rule is that the last run of the day is not done in the trees. Some skiers may feel that this is overly protective, but most ski areas post this as one of their inbounds skiing policies, and I think it's a good one. Most injuries come at the end of the day when skiers are tired and the light is fading. If someone were to have trouble in the trees, it's helpful to have the time to ski that run again and have time to involve the ski patrol within their hours of operation. There aren't many patrollers who want to search through the trees in the dark for some gaper.

## THE IDEAL GOAL

Tree skiing is probably the most variable of all advanced skiing situations. Not only can the slope vary from mellow cruisers to ultrasteep drops, but the snow quality can range from light powder, to heavy mung, to fast corn. Because of the shade that trees provide, snow conditions below them can vary from turn to turn depending on how you intersect with shaded or sunbaked areas. Snow will also hang in the trees and melt after a storm, then drip onto the snow below and become icy. Add to all of this the trees themselves: Trees don't move, even when you hit one—and they aren't soft.

Ideally, skiing the trees requires you to have mastered all the advanced skiing situations covered up to this point and have the ability to apply one or all of them, depending on the snow and the run's pitch. And you must do this without braining yourself on a tree.

This, believe it or not, is a lot of fun. If you can perform as outlined above, you will be able to enjoy some of the last and best powder on the mountain, get away from the crowds, ski the forest the way it was meant to be skied, and generally have a great time. Half the fun of skiing in the trees is finding a line through them. As you get better in the trees, you'll try finding longer, less interrupted lines through the woods.

Tree skiing can be as technical or as mellow as you want to make it. There are tight trees on steep slopes and there are open glades on mellow pitches. The ideal of tree skiing is that there is no ideal; it's pretty much freestyle. An accomplished tree skier can go where he wants at whatever speed works for him and just enjoy skiing.

## COMMON PROBLEMS THAT PREVENT SKIERS FROM ENJOYING THE TREES

There is one basic requirement for skiing in the trees: control. If you aren't comfortable making a turn when and where you want or need to in variable snow conditions, you don't belong in the trees. The skier who lacks the ability to avoid obstacles, control his speed, and come to a complete stop at will needs to work on the skills covered previously in this book.

However, there are many skiers who have the skills for tree skiing but who are intimidated. The problem is both psychological and tactical. Most skiers who don't enjoy skiing on tree-filled slopes usually can't see the forest for the trees. This skier becomes so focused on his fear of hitting a tree that he fails to see all the open space around that tree (and around every other tree). There is infinitely more space occupied by unobstructed snow than by trees. Look at it mathematically: if you placed odds on whether a small object falling from the sky into a field of stumps would land on dirt or on a stump, you'd have to place better odds on the dirt. There is plenty of room to ski around the trees. But any skier

Some of the deepest and steepest lines are hidden in the Land of Oz: the trees.
RICK "OZ" OSWALD AT MOUNT BAILEY SNOWCAT SKIING

knows that if he gets out of control, he will no doubt find one of those trees and hit it.

This is where it could pay to be less intelligent. If you couldn't think ahead to what might happen if you screw up, you wouldn't worry so much—and you'd probably tear it up through the trees like an expert. But skiers are intelligent, and so they must learn to deal with the rational fear of getting out of control and hitting a tree. Dealing with this fear is easy if you master a few tactical tricks for successfully navigating the trees.

Trees themselves put a limit on how and where you must make turns. This factor is not imagined. Skiing trees is similar to skiing bumps or running gates in a race course, except there is more freedom in the trees. Here, you can still go wherever you want; you just can't turn where there's a tree. This restriction can be enough to throw a kink into your skiing style, especially if you're the type who tends to make only small turns or only large ones. But this complication is easily cured. Read on.

## SOLVING THE PROBLEMS OF THE TREE SKIER

To begin shredding the foliage, you must learn to find a line through the trees. Rather than focusing on the obstacle—the tree itself—you should look for the spaces around the tree and neighboring trees where you can ski. For a reader, white space is as important as the words on the page; white space gives your eyes a rest. It is the same when skiing trees. The white spaces between trees give you a way of finding a line through the bark: you can tie a run together by linking consecutive chunks of white space.

In trees, there seems to be a patchwork pattern of open trees and tight trees. Usually, as you descend through the trees a wider opening will appear. You of course gravitate toward that open space—because that is where you can let your skis run and enjoy the snow. But this open glade comes to an end all too soon, and the trees begin to tighten again. It's important to find the best possible escape route from the rapidly ending glade. Rather than look directly at the trees at the end of the glade, peer beyond them into the trees far below and to the sides, scanning for the most white space. Where you see the most snow, you will have the most room to turn, and that is where you should go. Once you have a downslope destination in mind, you can then look for a specific gap at the bottom of the glade that will get you there.

The trick of focusing on white space to find a line through the trees is that you usually are dealing with powder or some variation of it. Powder requires you to maintain a minimum speed for good flotation on the snow, but trees and speed don't always mix well. If you continue on at a speed adequate for effective powder skiing, your margin for error in finding a line through the trees becomes narrower. If you slow to below the minimum speed for solid powder technique, your ability to turn predictably is affected. Neither option is ideal in the trees. Advanced tree skiers can travel quite fast through the trees because they have become adept at picking a line as quickly as you are reading the words on this page. This "speed reading" takes time to learn.

A safety traverse can be an option in the trees. Rather than come to a complete stop when a line runs out, make a left or right into a slightly downhill traverse. This allows you to maintain adequate speed for flotation in powder so you don't lose your good momentum, but it eliminates the need to make turn after turn. On a traverse, you can look ahead for slots in the trees so you can continue traversing. Usually this comes down to a simple choice of going either left or right around the tree directly in front of you. When a more open slot appears below, drop down into the fall line and continue downhill in the original white space mode. It generally doesn't take much of a traverse to find another great line, so you don't have to lose much vertical headway going sideways. If you need to stay

Scan the trees for open lines or slots, where you can make unobstructed turns.
JAY "GOOD EXAMPLE" GARRICK AT MOUNT BAILEY SNOWCAT SKIING

within a particular corridor of trees in order to stay on course with your group's meeting place, first traverse right to hunt for a line, then later traverse back left to stay on target.

There are times when even expert tree skiers run out of room. Sometimes there's time to hang left or right into a traverse and find a new line. Sometimes there isn't enough time, and the skier must stop quickly. Often the only thing that keeps a tree skier from eating bark is being able to throw down an emergency hockey stop.

There's a certain amount of skill involved in performing one.

The trick is to retract both skis and suck them up toward you in order to unweight them and free them from the snow. As you retract both skis, steer them across the fall line. Once you've guided your skis completely across the fall line, drive them down into the snow and set your hips aggressively back toward the hill. Because of the deeper snow in the trees there is a tendency to get pitched over the handlebars when hockey stopping. Allowing your hips to settle deep to the inside of the turn will prevent this; sitting down is a better option than meeting a tree with your head.

In addition to these tactics for dealing with line selection, there are many times in the trees where the ability to vary turn size and shape comes in handy. Because there are great and not-so-great places to turn, you may need to let your skis run straight through less desirable sections of snow in order to arrive at an open, softer patch of snow. This means accepting the buildup of speed that comes with taking a straight line through a tight slot. Slow down by making round, finished turns where you can—and keep your eyes open for those spots, because you'll need them.

### *You can feel* WHEN YOU'RE THREADING THE TREES

1. Strive to feel as though you are moving in slow motion in comparison to the trees whizzing by. Rushed movements in the trees make for blown turns and trouble. Because of the nature of snow in the trees, you must make predictable, smooth movements to negotiate powder and crud. Feeling slow while going fast is the key.
2. You can pretend you are a B-52 bomber pilot on a strafing run through the trees. The bombs you drop are your turns. You can try to settle into each turn, bending your skis at precise locations—your targets. While you ski, you should be identifying your next two or three target areas. Sound effects work great for this one.
3. If you feel like a wild animal being chased by a predator or like a crazed guerrilla mercenary as you rip down through the trees, taking branches across your face, good. You're successfully skiing the trees.

### *You can see* WHEN YOU'RE SKIING TREES LIKE AN EXPERT

1. The key to tree skiing is being able to see your line through the jungle. You should see paths of snow meandering downslope rather than an impassable wall. Begin noticing low-hanging branches you can duck under, small flexible shrubs you can plow over, and tunnel-like slots through thickets. The fun of tree skiing is to be creative with your line selection, keeping safety as your primary concern.
2. Good tree skiers look ahead, downhill along their prospective line. I find myself looking two turns ahead, focusing on the white path that I want to follow. But looking too far ahead, or looking ahead without knowing how close you are to trees immediately beside you, can lead to trouble. The closest trees will reach out and smack you if you forget about them.
3. Always look for escape routes to the left and to the right. You may be able to tell that the right is particularly tight, which means your escape route is stage left. Pay attention to a wide swath of forest but select a single path through it. Try not to get tunnel vision.

## OTHER DRILLS

The following are drills that will help you enjoy the woody way.

### Tree Traverse to Start

Since most skiers will encounter powder conditions in the trees, be sure to utilize smart powder skiing tools. For example, the best way to begin any run in powder is with a small straight run to get up to planing speed. In the trees, perform this straight run as a traverse while you look for a line to drop in on. You can't force turns in powder, especially in trees. Maintain good floating velocity and make smooth movements.

## Tree Garlands

This drill is an adaptation of the Tree Traverse. Begin by traversing and then drop into the fall line when room permits. Remain in the fall line for only a second or two, without making a complete turn and then pull out in the original direction. Continue making half-turns to create a staircase track down through the trees; then head back the other way performing the same drill.

## Conifer Slalom

Take creative line selection out of the picture and focus on turning around the trees as if they were a slalom or GS race course. Begin by turning left around a tree, then prohibit yourself from making a right turn until you can do it around a tree. Try to do this with as little traversing as possible.

## Follow the Leader

The best way to introduce yourself to expert line selection in the trees is to follow an expert. Find a friend who shreds through the forest and let him know you're following him (he may take pity on you and begin with easy lines). Try to match his line without getting hung up in his tracks.

## TROUBLESHOOTING TREE SKIING

Problems in the trees have less to do with the plant matter and more to do with your ability to ski whatever kind of snow happens to be there. Review the material on powder, crud, steeps, or whatever kind of advanced skiing situation is giving you trouble in the trees. Tree skiing is a stage where you apply other expert skiing tools rather than a call for a special technique. Trees are tactical, not technical. Strive to relax and address whatever snow you find in the forest, and then utilize some of the strategies I have discussed up to this point.

If you don't like this solution, then go and get yourself some fat skis. I used to be an old-school holdout when it came to fats, and I had some crude jokes that went along with that mind-set. But now I'm a changed man. It's not that I'm getting old (yeah, right). It's that the fat skis have gotten better. They have appropriate shape and they are stiff enough to handle some serious speed and junky snow. And fats are, well, fat. They've got huge surface area.

The fatties do one thing that's magic for tree skiing: they let you slow down and still make great turns in deep snow. A skier who has been unable to ski the trees because he could not reach appropriate speeds without endangering himself will be able to ski those lines on fat skis. Fat skis also let more advanced skiers thread super-tight lines in the trees for the same reason: slower speed. Fatties are fun in the forest.

However, many accomplished tree skiers may not like fat skis in the trees (in the lengths they'll be apt to try) because of their extreme surface area. Fat skis can't be driven as deeply down into the powder as narrower skis. Many good tree skiers use this depth-charge method of driving the skis deeply to control their speed. A fat ski in longer lengths will tend to stay up on top of powder and surf along the surface. This can get pretty fast. Many skiers who want to use a fat ski in moderately and tightly spaced trees are using a little shorter ski—one that still has plenty of surface area but not so much that it can't be pushed down into the snow for speed control.

There are two other major concerns in the trees: covered obstacles and tree wells. Depending on the depth of the snowpack, downed trees can become a major problem for tree skiers. There's nothing scarier and potentially more hazardous than having your skis dive beneath a log or buried branch. Sometimes there is no warning and nothing you can do to prevent this from happening. Your only clue is that fallen logs and branches can appear as soft mounds or humps in the powder. Lumps and humps may be balls of snow that fell from tree branches and are covered with more snow—or they may be something else. Avoid skiing through such irregularities in the snow. If you have to, try to get your ski tips up and over the object. It's easy to ski up and over partially buried logs and branches if you can clear the tips of your skis. It feels like smacking a very firm mogul, but it probably won't kill you.

Tree wells are produced by the branches of conifers, which shelter the trunk of the tree from snowfall. Thick, layered boughs can basically create a kind of roof that keeps snow from packing in around the tree. This produces a hollow space around the tree's central axis that is often camouflaged by branches and a little snow. These holes can be deadly because snow tends to cascade down on top of a skier who falls in one, potentially suffocating him. If you manage to go in headfirst and are not able to get out, and your friends don't see this happening, you could be toast.

So don't be careless about where and how you fall in the trees. Be aware that tree wells will virtually suck you in, and be ready to arrest your descent if you happen to drop into one. Do not allow yourself to continue deep into the well: grab branches, spread your legs, whatever it takes. Start shouting immediately. You may feel stupid yelling for help. But if you go in deep and can't get out, you'll be thankful one of your buddies heard you.

# PART V
# Getting Techno

The biggest drawback of being a professional ski instructor is no matter how well you ski, some other wiser and more enlightened instructor is always picking on your skiing. There are few skiers who enjoy having their skiing criticized— even when it's done by their closest friends. But the nit-picking and the microcritical analysis my skiing has received over the years has actually helped me. It was always rough on the ego, but it improved my skiing in the long run.

This section is a brief compilation of the kind of technical advice I've found especially useful.

For those fanatics out there, this section's for you.

KYLE EDGREN IN THE PARKING LOT GLADE, MT. BACHELOR

There are some ideas for technical gear manipulation as well.

A trick that has worked for me is to rethink advice I receive in terms I can understand and then find a way to use the new information to improve my skiing in the kinds of advanced skiing situations I've covered in this book. To that end, I have provided this advanced technical information in a readily available fashion with a slant toward practical application. These techno goodies are brief, concentrated shots of juice intended for the true fanatic.

This section is not for everybody. If you don't care if your skis are waxed and can't tell when your edges are dull, then the information in this section won't matter much to you. However, if the nuances of technique and equipment give you a thrill, then read on.

## UPPER BODY COUNTER-ROTATION (ANTICIPATION)

The term *counter-rotation* describes the hips and upper body in relation to the skis. In counter-rotation, which is also called anticipation, these body parts are rotated *counter* to the direction the skis are traveling in. The hips and upper body usually work in concert to produce functional countering movements that enhance both turn initiation and edge control in all kinds of skiing. But it's easier to understand how and why skiers counter-rotate if we discuss the upper body and hips as separate entities.

The upper body—abdomen, ribcage, shoulders—can twist right or left even if the hips are kept still. This twisting movement requires that you stretch your muscles a bit, primarily the abdominals, thoracics, and latissimi. Sit in a chair and, without letting your rear end slide around, twist your upper body as far as you can to the right and left. Feel the stress this places on your body. When you're skiing, this movement of upper body counter-rotation has no direct effect on your skis, but it places you in an aggressive

Counter-rotating the upper body independently of the hips is awkward, but it can be done. Usually, muscular counter-rotation of the torso (anticipation) is used in conjunction with hip counter.

body position in which you'll face downhill at the finish of a turn.

Facing, or "anticipating," the fall line, you can see where you want to turn, and you'll have committed your upper body to that goal by facing in that direction. This position of anticipation of the next turn is invaluable in skiing steeps, where a visual focus toward the side of the run or back toward the hill can make starting the next turn difficult. This muscular twist of the upper body toward the fall line at the end of a turn also prepares you for easier entry into the next turn. Twisting the upper body is like twisting a rubber band on a toy airplane: let go of the propeller and it spins. When you release your edges and move toward the next turn, your skis will turn in the same fashion as that propeller and automatically steer into the fall line.

## HIP COUNTER-ROTATION (STRONG INSIDE HALF)

While upper body counter-rotation (aka anticipation) relies on twisting and stretching muscles, hip counter-rotation requires the shifting of joints. Specifically, this occurs where the femur meets the pelvis. The hips can shift to point (imagine pointing with the zipper on your pants) in a different direction than your skis if you shuffle your feet. Similarly, when you walk you slide one leg forward and the hip socket on that side also travels forward. On a step forward with your right leg, your hips end up pointing to the left; on a step with the left leg, the hips shift to point right. The bigger the step, the more the hips must shift.

In making a turn, notice how the inside ski runs slightly ahead of the outside ski, as if it had taken a step forward, pointing the hips toward the outside of the turn (downhill, in most situations). This shifting of the hips in counter-rotation pushes the inside ski ahead. The hips must shift to point toward the outside ski; without such movement it becomes difficult to edge the skis. To test this, try edging without allowing the hips to shift: it's tough. To create the big edge angles required for aggressive carving and edge-setting on steep terrain, you need to move your hips to the inside of the turn.

Hip counter-rotation must include a tip-lead of the inside ski and leads to a body position that has a strong inside half.

Instructors these days are referring to hip counter and the subsequent advanced tip of the inside ski (and inside shoulder and hand) and upper body anticipation as simply a *strong inside half*, meaning the whole half of the body toward the inside of the turn is slightly advanced to facilitate sound edging and smooth movements from turn to turn. This is a good simplification of how the torso and the hips both twist to *open*, or face outside the turn and typically downhill.

## HIP ANGULATION

Hip angulation is the angle created at the hips by your upper and lower body when you tip your skis on edge. I've discussed hip angulation as the preferred way to drop your center of mass toward the inside of a turn, because it allows your upper body to remain upright with your head balanced over the outside ski. This produces a versatile stance for dynamic balancing during turns on variable terrain by not committing the upper body toward the inside of the turn, where it's harder to recover from mistakes. Hip angulation comes naturally to skiers who master movements of hip counter-rotation, since such hip shifting actually enables you to hip angulate.

There are a few tricks that can help you polish your hip angulation skills. From a position of proper hip angulation, with your balance over the outside ski, you can apply extra pressure to the inside ski if necessary. To test this, you should be able to lift the inside ski off the snow at any point during a turn and resist tipping toward the inside of the turn. If you commonly fall off balance toward the inside, strive to place your head farther out over the outside ski, thus increasing the angle produced at the hip.

Your hands can also serve as an indicator of good hip angulation. Proper angulation places the hands so that an imaginary line drawn between them parallels the slope of the snow. A skier who leans into the turn, failing to hip

Add some edging via hip angulation and maintain both hip counter-rotation and muscular torso counter-rotation (anticipation) and you've got a strong inside half.

## LATERAL CROSSOVER

Lateral crossover describes how your body mass moves from the end of one turn to the start of the next. Rather than confuse things by thinking of body mass movement at turn initiation as *downhill* movement (since body mass is not always moving downhill to start a turn), the concept of lateral crossover helps us understand that shifting the hips from one side of the skis to the other is required to exit one turn and enter the next. While this may seem like a difference of semantics, the assumption that you move downhill to start turns can lead to a bad habit of overfinishing turns and steering the skis farther across the fall line than necessary to make that precious movement downhill to start the next turn. A turn is finished when speed is controlled, or when you say it is, *regardless* of where the skis are pointing. At that moment you need to cross over laterally into the next turn.

This is easy, though there is no magical body mass muscle and you cannot simply will your body to cross over into a new turn. Body mass movement is about a balance of power and how you manipulate that balance to get the job done. Simply put, you can change your center of balance and allow your mass to shift laterally by standing more or less on one ski than the other. For example, if during a turn your balance is completely on your outside ski, you will tip over into the new turn if you begin pressuring your inside ski. Another way to use lateral crossover to exit a turn and enter another is simply to not resist the turn's centrifugal force. Letting your legs go a little limp at the end of a turn allows the turn's force to "suck" you over your skis into the next turn.

## DIAGONAL CROSSOVER

After mastering lateral body mass movements, expert skiers need to know how moving diagonally in the lateral plane will advance their skiing in all kinds of situations, especially when

angulate, will notice that her inside hand drops much closer to the snow than the outside hand.

Another simple way to ensure functional movements of the hips is to adopt a slightly wider stance, which helps free the hips to counter-rotate more easily and enhances movements of hip angulation.

It's possible to have too much of a good thing. Too much hip angulation can put you in a contrived body position that's hard to move out of toward a new turn. I was (and still am, from time to time) afflicted with a tendency to overdo my hip angulation. Aside from looking like the incredible folding man, I was limiting my movements of smooth flow from one turn to the next. I found myself "parking" my hips to the inside of the turn and remaining there, static, for far too long. This created a kind of dead spot in my turns, where I stopped continual steering and pressure changes. Skis with increased sidecut can increase your propensity for getting into this bad habit, so be careful. All you need is enough hip angulation to generate adequate edge angle and avoid banking too far to the inside of the turn where your balance is fouled.

carving on hardpack. As you move laterally from turn to turn, you will have a tendency—especially if you are an aggressive skier—to end up on your heels at the turn's finish. During a carved turn, you often will work the tail of your ski at the turn's finish to ensure good edge grip all the way through the turn—even if it's just a little bit. This places your center of mass a little behind center. If you then move laterally to start the next turn, you will be entering the turn on your heels.

It's important to enter a turn *centered* on your skis. Starting a turn on your heels results in a lack of pressure on the skis' shovels, allowing the skis to wander off in undesired tangents. In fact, most expert skiers enter turns with a little extra pressure on the balls of the feet, especially on firm snow. This encourages the skis' shovels to respond more predictably and "hook up" earlier in the turn. Even though modern shaped skis don't require you to *drive* the shovel of the ski, slightly more pressure on the front of the foot at the start of the turn still helps a ski en-

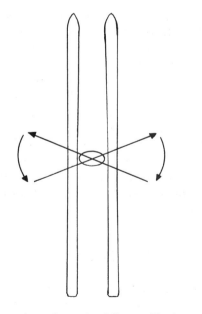

A bird's-eye view schematic of diagonal body mass movement.

gage cleanly. If you finish your aggressively carved turn a tad on your heels and you want to start the next turn just a bit on the balls of your feet, what should you do? Cross over diagonally.

You achieve this by adding a forward-driving (or *linear*) component to lateral crossover. You merely shift your hips an inch or two forward at the same time you're moving laterally. The muscle you use to make this move, the anterior tibialis, is located along the outsides of the shins. As you pull your toes toward the top of your boot, your body mass tips forward. From turn to turn on a hypothetical overhead schematic view, diagonal crossover would produce a sideways figure eight.

## FORE-AFT ALIGNMENT: TWEAKING IT

I've stressed how important it is to stay centered on your skis, and now I've covered how experts might deviate from center, moving forward or aft slightly to enhance their skis' turn initiation or finish capabilities. Minor changes in how your weight is distributed fore and aft on the ski can effect major changes in how the ski performs. One of the most common complaints I hear from skiers who struggle to break into expert-level performance is they often feel unable to *get centered.* Usually skiers will feel as though they are behind the center of the ski, or in the *backseat.*

What I've discovered after much experimentation (and some mentoring from the gear gurus at the Green Mountain Orthotic Lab at Stratton Mountain, Vermont) is that nine times out of ten, it's not the skier: the skier's gear is to blame for poor fore-aft alignment.

It's not that there's anything wrong with the skier's gear, but rather that the gear (meaning the boot and binding) was designed for somebody who is perfectly centered—and that just doesn't happen to be you! Good skiers can feel small amounts of change in their fore-aft alignment; so it isn't a surprise that if your gear is just a little bit off, you can feel like a total hack. Below I'll discuss a couple ways to play with fore-aft alignment.

## Binding Placement

Just about the time shaped skis were hitting the slopes, ski manufacturers began experimenting with moving the ski's center of effort forward of a traditionally located center mark. The idea was to help skiers engage the front of the ski for carving applications. This was often done without considering how the ski would perform in soft snow; and not surprisingly, many of these skis' tips would dive in deep powder. I played around quite a bit with mounting my bindings behind the suggested ski center mark and met with some success.

But times and designs have changed, and when ski manufacturers move the sidecut profile and ski center mark forward on an all-mountain ski, they are also widening the tip dimension enough so the extra surface area in the shovel will still buoy the tips—even with the more forward mount. I have experimented with mounting some shaped skis a little back of center (4–5 mm) for the sake of powder performance, but I've tended to find that small amount will make the ski feel overly long on groomed slopes.

There are bindings out there that offer fore-aft adjustability (see page 111). If you are a skier who wants to be able to play with binding placement, get them. You will appreciate the fact that you can move the binding back to center when you feel you need to—because at some point you will. Many women feel they need to move their boots forward of the recommended mounting point on their skis. These kinds of bindings are perfect for them.

## Fore-Aft Alignment: Project Delta

A season ago, I changed my skis and bindings and noticed that I was skiing differently than I had on previous models. In the powder, my tips

seemed to dive and the shovel tended to feel very "hooky" during the turn. On groomed slopes I realized that my legs always felt bent: I had a squatty stance. In the powder, I discovered that the skis performed better if I stood hard on my heels. In all skiing conditions I felt like my quadriceps were always burning a little more than usual.

I tried remounting the bindings just a bit farther back (for the heck of it), and the skis performed better in powder snow, but my legs felt just the same: overly bent and burning. I felt as if I had too much forward lean in my boot—which had been shifting my weight forward onto the front of the ski— making the ski hook or dive in the powder and putting me into an overly squatty stance. I was at a loss until I remembered some experiments the gang at the Green Mountain Orthotic Lab (GMOL) were doing. They were reducing the amount of ramp in the binding itself. This is a trick that's not new to World Cup race room technicians, for elite racers have been playing with this for years.

Every binding has a certain amount of *high heel*, or ramp angle, built into it. The level at which the boot's toe rides on the AFD (antifriction device) is lower than the level at which the boot's heel rides on the heel plate of the binding. The difference between these two *stand heights* is an amount that corresponds to the binding's ramp angle. The higher the difference, the greater the ramp. The GMOL guys were calling the binding's degree of ramp *delta*, as a way to differentiate it from the ramp built into the boot itself.

The idea behind manipulating delta is to raise the toepiece of the binding just a bit by using a shim, or to lower the heelpiece of the binding by grinding the plastic plate the heelpiece sits on. This essentially *flattens* the amount of ramp in the binding and makes your boot feel more upright when it's in the binding.

I went ahead and tried it. I shimmed my toepiece by ⅛ of an inch and discovered that, not only did the concept work, it worked too well! This adjustment by ⅛ of an inch was huge! While skiing, I felt overly tall and leaned-back,

An alignment technician takes an accurate stand height measurement to figure out a binding's ramp angle, or *delta*. PAT SULLIVAN AT MT. BACHELOR SKI AND SPORT

and my short shaped skis felt like 223 cm downhill boards. The change was pretty striking. I replaced those shims with ⅟₁₆-inch shims and felt very balanced. I stood tall and could relax into the tongue of my boot, letting my quadriceps take it easy for a change. But better yet, my skis floated better in the powder and ceased hooking—even after I moved the bindings back into the forward set of holes.

Since then, I've experimented a bit and have found exactly how much ramp works with my boots. You can discern a difference in stand height changes of as little as 0.5 millimeter (about 0.02 inch). I found it pretty easy to find the happy medium between too bent a stance and too tall a stance. The too-squatty stance made for tired legs and diving tips, but the too-tall stance put me in

the backseat and my skis did not carve as well on hard snow and in short turns.

Some bindings have more ramp than others. Some boots are more upright than others. Many people don't have an issue with this, and they have no idea why anybody would start shimming or grinding a perfectly good binding. So get ready to catch some flack if you start playing with this like I do, but it is 100 percent worth the time—and worth the ribbing from your friends. Do your best to find a bootfitting and alignment specialist who is accustomed to working with this issue if you need help.

Check out www.skiguru.org (see the appendix) for sources of microthin shimming materials if you want to hide in your basement and do this yourself (probably a good idea).

*Attention Skiers with Limited Ankle Dorsiflexion*

Skiers who discover that many of their boot-fitting problems stem from not being able to flex their ankles as far as their ski boots require may need to manipulate their bindings' ramp angle. Many skiers have to use heel lifts in their boots to take care of a particular bootfitting problem. Adding heel lift increases ramp angle and tips a skier farther forward in the boots. Skiers with too much heel lift for sound fore-aft balance will experience the same problems as any other skier with too much forward lean in a boot, too much binding ramp, or both.

Often, the only way a skier who uses heel lifts for another problem can find proper fore-aft balance is by reducing ramp angle (delta) in the binding. If you add heel lifts and discover that your feet feel better but your skiing stance suffers, try reducing your binding's ramp angle, as discussed above.

## ARC LOCUS

One of the final hurdles for advanced and expert skiers is learning *where* in a turn you should do the most work. Arc locus (or the *location* of your turn) addresses the timing, or placement, of a turn's control phase in relation to the skier and the space around him. Most skiers can benefit from doing most of the work of turning early in the turn, bending the skis when they're out to the skier's side. As beginners and intermediates, most skiers typically struggle to start turns and often have more speed than they'd like toward the end of the turn. This tendency leads many skiers to focus attention on turn *finish* to make sure their speed is under control. The result is an advanced skier who coasts for the majority of a turn and uses aggressive edging, pressure, and steering too late in the turn phase to complete the turn and control speed.

Waiting until late in the turn to control speed causes several problems. As you guide your skis

Heel lifts can be one cause of too much ramp angle and forward tilt in the lower leg. Here, the leg is bent but the back is straight and the balance board shows a backseat stance.

Sometimes reducing too much ramp angle by raising the toes straightens the lower leg and brings the lower legs and the spine into a more parallel relationship. The balance board shows good fore-aft balance.

farther and farther across the fall line, you might be forced out of your correct, hip counter-rotated (strong inside half) body position at the end of the turn. Essentially, you've steered the skis so far that your femurs simply can't rotate any farther in the hip sockets, and the skis' turning force takes your hips with them. When your hips suddenly become "square" at the finish of a turn or rotate to point in the same direction as the skis' tips, the skis' edge angles are decreased. This can cause skidding at turn finish, especially at the skis' tails.

You can avoid this simply by doing more work earlier in the turn. Rather than coasting after entering a turn, begin to edge, pressure, and steer right off the bat. This will produce a turn that occurs more to your side, toward the side of the run, rather than below you with skis completely across the fall line. Now your hips can function effectively to promote powerful edging throughout the turn.

## PELVIC TILT AND THE HOLLOW BACK

A properly tilted pelvis puts your rear end in a slightly tucked-in position and lets your back curl forward naturally. An incorrectly tilted pelvis can cause your butt to stick out and your back to become *hollow,* or overly arched, which reduces the hips' rotational movement and thus limits hip counter-rotation. This forces you to ski with your hips squared to your skis and can cause you to bank your turns and steer with your entire body. It ends up fouling edging movements at turn finish.

A problem with pelvic tilt is easy to see in other skiers if you look for dinosaur arms—arms that are pulled back so they appear shrunken in relation to the body. In this stance, the back is arched and the shoulder blades are pinched close together.

In a single movement, you can rectify the problem by rolling your shoulder blades forward, bringing the arms forward with them, and doing a basic Elvis pelvic thrust to properly

This skier exhibits a hollow back.

This skier prevents a hollow back by tucking his pelvis and rolling his shoulders forward.

tuck in your rear. Skiing in this position should properly align the pelvis, back, and shoulders and free the hips for functional rotation. If this doesn't work, here's another tip: some skiers have said that pretending they had to clench a coin between their buns while skiing helped move their hips into a more sound position.

## SPINAL CRUNCH

If you've ever skied a few hundred too many bumps in a single day, you may know what spinal crunch feels like—an achy back. As you become more aggressive on skis, especially in moguls and on steep terrain, you will begin dealing with a greater buildup of force during turns. Impacting moguls at speed and setting your edges hard and deep on steep terrain are notorious for generating a lot of force in a short time. It can be difficult to deal with this pressure underfoot.

Ideally, a skier maintains an erect upper body and absorbs shock and increased pressure with the legs, flexing at the ankles and knees and allowing the legs to retract. In bumps, this might mean that both knees could hit the skier's chest, but the upper body remains tall. On steeps, the inside knee could be pushed almost into the skier's armpit, but the back and shoulders would be unaffected. In less-than-ideal technique, a skier lets his back curl forward or fold over at the waist. Using either of these movements to absorb shock and pressure puts your back at risk. Here's a simple rule to follow: If you can't avoid using the spine to absorb shock and increased pressure, back off and find some user-friendly terrain.

# Appendix

## Additional Resources

There are many sources of information and equipment you can tap to fuel your athletic improvement. Most of them are found on the Web. Here are a few Web sites that I have found helpful.

### www.BlackDiamondEquipment.com

This Web site has information on alpine touring (AT) bindings and other equipment you can use for getting into the backcountry. You can also call 801-278-5544.

### www.bootfitters.com

Head here for a nationwide directory of ski shops that have sent their staff to bootfitting seminars at Masterfit University, one of the few organizations that provides a quality, standardized curriculum.

### www.gmolfoot.com

This is the Web site of the Green Mountain Orthotic Lab at Stratton Mountain, Vermont, and contains information on bootfitting, footbed, and alignment services on the East Coast.

### www.masterfituniversity.com

This site has information on attending one of the Masterfit University bootfitting seminars (for you or your local shop technician).

Additional inquiries can be directed to:
Masterfit Enterprises
11 Magnolia Rd.
Briarcliff Manor NY 10510
914-944-9038; 914-944-0377 (fax)

### www.mtbachelor.com

This is the site of the Mt. Bachelor Ski Resort, or call 800-829-2442.

### www.rossignol.com

Head to this site for information on Rossignol skiing equipment.

### www.skiguru.org

Check this Web site out for additional consumer information on ski equipment beyond the scope of the traditional magazines' buyer's guides. The site also has information on personal guided alignment and skills training and is a source for specialty bootfitting and alignment products.

### www.tognar.com

For ski tuning tools and supplies, as well as some do-it-yourself bootfitting materials, head to the Tognar (pronounced "tone-ar") Toolworks' online catalog.

Additional inquiries can be directed to:
Tognar Toolworks
P.O. Box 212
Mount Shasta CA 96067

Wait, there's more. ETHAN DEVOLL ON UPPER AVALANCHE, MT. BACHELOR

In memory of Derek Dahl, a true all-mountain skier.

# Index